Spoon measurements

in level spoonfuls

LIQUID

Metric	Imperial	American
5 ml	1 teaspoon	
10 ml	2 teaspoons	
15 ml	1 tablespoon	
30 ml	1 fl oz	⅛ cup
60 ml	2 fl oz	¼ cup
75 ml	3 fl oz	⅜ cup
125 ml	4 fl oz	½ cup
150 ml	5 fl oz	⅝ cup
175 ml	6 fl oz	¾ cup
200 ml	7 fl oz	⅞ cup
225 ml	8 fl oz	1 cup
300 ml	10 fl oz	1¼ cups
350 ml	12 fl oz	1½ cups
375 ml	13 fl oz	1⅝ cups
400 ml	14 fl oz	1¾ cups
500 ml	17 fl oz	2 cups
600 ml	21 fl oz	2½ cups
700 ml	24 fl oz	3 cups
800 ml	28 fl oz	3½ cups
1 l	1¾ pints	4¼ cups
1.25 l	2¼ pints	5¼ cups
1.5 l	2¾ pints	6½ cups
2 l	3½ pints	8½ cups
2.5 l	4¼ pints	11 cups

	TABLE-SPOON	TEA-SPOON
Liquid	15 ml	5 ml
Almonds, ground	5 g	1.5 g
Baking powder	13 g	4 g
Black tea	5 g	1.5 g
Breadcrumbs, dried	7 g	2.5 g
Cheese, grated	8 g	3 g
Cinnamon, ground	7 g	2.5 g
Cocoa powder	5 g	1.5 g
Coffee, ground	5 g	1.5 g
Coffee, instant	3 g	1 g
Condensed milk	13 g	4 g
Cooking oil	13 g	4 g
Cornflour (cornstarch)	9 g	3 g
Crème fraîche	14 g	3.5 g
Flour, plain (all purpose)	6 g	2 g
Gelatine, powdered	13 g	4 g
Hazelnuts, ground	5 g	1.5 g
Honey	20 g	7 g
Icing sugar	8 g	3 g
Margarine	13 g	4 g
Mayonnaise	13 g	4 g
Mustard	15 g	5 g
Oat flakes	10 g	3 g
Paprika powder	7 g	2.5 g
Rice	13 g	4 g
Salt	15 g	5 g
Semolina	10 g	3.5 g
Sour cream (10 % fat)	12 g	4 g
Sugar	12 g	4 g
Tomato ketchup	15 g	5 g
Tomato puree	15 g	5 g
Whipping cream (30 % fat)	14 g	5 g

ABBREVIATIONS

kg	kilogram	C	carbohydrate
g	gram	F	fat
l	litre	P	protein
ml	millilitre	CU	carbohydrate unit
kJ	kilojoule		
kcal	kilocalorie		

DR. OETKER

GERMAN
BAKING
TODAY

THE ORIGINAL

DR. OETKER

GERMAN BAKING TODAY

THE ORIGINAL

Dr. Oetker Verlag

You take a look in the oven: is the cake done?
A beautiful golden colour as you expect it to be? Yes, and even a little better:
the texture is fluffy, the smell is delicious and the appearance is irresistible!
It's just waiting to be eaten! A delight for all the senses …

German Baking Today is the standard work for everyone who loves baking and for those who
want to learn. It will make it easy for you to create masterpieces with simple ingredients.
Whether you want to make mole cake, buttermilk cake or classics such as apple strudel and
marble cake, the recipes in this book never fail!

Dr. Oetker's Test Kitchen has carefully checked that every dish
is easy to prepare – even for beginners – and that it will also taste delicious.
Step-by-step instructions and detailed photographs ensure that the result will be successful.
The many new recipes will inspire you to try out and bake many of them.

Every day more people are discovering the art of baking and you too can enjoy home-made
Schnecken ("snail" buns), a cream torte you have decorated yourself, your own fragrant
rye bread or delicious crispy rolls. You will be stirring, mixing, kneading,
rolling and lovingly decorating your cakes and pastries as you enjoy:

German Baking Today!

We wish you a lot of pleasure in your baking experiments and much success.
Now, enjoy yourself!

General advice about the book

To ensure that the cakes, pastries and puddings you make taste as delicious and look as irresistibly mouthwatering as you imagine them, here are a few tips before you start cooking:

Tip 1 – Preparation
Read the recipe through carefully before you start your preparations – better still, do this even before you go shopping. Many things will become much clearer when you understand the links between the various steps. Gather together all the ingredients, the appropriate tin or mould and the kitchen and baking utensils that you will need before you begin.

Tip 2 – Conversions and equivalents
The conversions and equivalents (weights, volumes and spoonfuls) listed on the inside pages of the cover will help you measure the correct quantities for your ingredients.

Tip 3 – Preparation time
The preparation time indicated in the recipe is only given as a guideline; it is a rough estimate and will depend on your baking experience. The preparation time only refers to the actual time needed to prepare the ingredients for baking. Cooling times and the time dough takes to rise are only included in the preparation time if they take place at the same time as other preparation activities. The baking time is indicated separately.

Tip 4 – Baking tins and moulds
All the recipes in this book use the baking tins or moulds listed below, which are all available in the shops (photograph 1):
» Baking sheet (40 x 30 cm/ 16 x 12 in), also with a high rim
» Muffin mould for 12 muffins
» Tart tin (diameter 26-28 cm/ 10¼-11 in)
» Bundt pan or kugelhopf mould (diameter 22 cm/9 in)
» Ring mould (diameter 22 cm/9 in)
» Rectangular cake tin (25 x 11 cm/ 10 x 4½ in)
» Bread tin (30 x 11 cm/12 x 4½ in)
» Fruit flan mould (diameter 28 cm/ 11 in)
» Springform tin (diameter 26 cm/ 10¼ in) with interchangeable flat bases and a base with a tube in the middle for making a ring cake.
Baking tins and moulds are available in various materials.
Tin moulds are good for gas ovens but are not acid-resistant. Therefore

it is advisable to line the inside of a springform mould with baking parchment paper if it is used as a pie ring for fruit pies.
Black moulds are very traditional and particularly good for use in electric and fan ovens. These moulds have excellent non-stick properties and heat conductivity; they are also resistant to fruit acids and easy to clean.
Both tin moulds and black moulds are also available with a non-stick coating which makes it much easier to remove the cake from the mould.
Enamel baking tins have an enamel finish which also acts as a scratch-resistant non-stick coating. They are very long-lasting and resistant to fruit acids. They give the cake an intense, even brown colour.

In addition, tins and moulds are also made of aluminium, ceramic, glass and silicon, all of which are suitable for use in any type of oven.

Tip 5 – Baking temperature and baking times

The baking temperatures and baking times indicated in the recipes are given as a guide and they may be increased or reduced depending on the heating performance of the oven being used. We recommend that you always preheat the oven fully and only put the cake in the oven when it has reached the temperature indicated in the recipe.

To make sure that the cake is done, use the checking test when the baking time indicated has elapsed.

Tip 6 – Checking if it is done

Sponge and all-in-one sponge: At the end of the baking time indicated in the recipe, stick a wooden skewer deep into the thickest part of the cake, then remove it again. If the skewer comes out dry, without any sponge sticking to it, the cake is done (photographs 1 and 2).

Fatless sponge: This is done when it is no longer moist to the touch but feels soft, and when no impression is left on the surface by a finger pressing it lightly.

Biscuits: These are done when they look golden yellow or golden brown.

Yeast dough and quark & oil dough: Lift up a corner of the pastry or cake with a wide-bladed knife (photograph 3). If the underside is lightly brown and dry, it is done.

Tip 7 – Nutritional values

These values have been rounded and refer to a single piece or the total amount, as indicated in the recipe.

Tip 8 – Information

At the beginning of most chapters dealing with the various kinds of sponge, dough and pastry, you will find an information section with general explanations, helpful tips and advice about the preparations of the recipes.

You will also find general information about a wide range of subjects related to baking: ovens, height of the oven shelves, kitchen utensils and baking accessories, baking ingredients, garnishing and decorating, as well as glossary of baking terms.

In addition, after each recipe you will find numerous tips as well as suggested recipe variations, modifications and explanations

Tip 9 – Level of difficulty

For each recipe the level of difficulty is indicated, making it easier for you to match the recipe to your experience.

 FOR BEGINNERS

 FOR EXPERIENCED BAKERS

 FOR ADVANCED BAKERS

Sponge

With its moist, light texture, sponge pastry is not only very versatile but it can also be refined or varied by the addition of flavouring, cocoa powder, cornflour (cornstarch), pieces of chocolate, raisins etc. And another important plus: it is incredibly easy to make because the ingredients are just stirred in one after the other. The basic ingredients for this type of pastry are butter or margarine, sugar, eggs, flour and baking powder.

This is how you make a sponge

Step 1: Prepare the baking sheet
Using a pastry brush, grease the baking tin generously and evenly with spreadable margarine or butter. In the case of a springform mould, you should only grease the base and not the sides so that the sponge does not slide down along the sides. To make it easier to remove the cake from the tin, sprinkle some flour, breadcrumbs, ground almonds or other ground nuts after greasing the tin or mould and distribute them evenly by tipping and tapping it (photographs 1 and 2).
A rectangular tin can also be lined with baking parchment after

greasing – this will make it easier to remove the cake from the tin. To ensure that the baking parchment fits the tin properly, place the base of the tin on the baking parchment and draw round it, then tip the tin on each side – one side after the other – and draw lines round them too. Finally cut out the corners, fold the lines along the bottom – and you have the liner for your tin!

Step 2: Mix the butter or margarine
Whether you are using butter or margarine it must spreadable, which means that it must be neither too liquid nor too hard. It is therefore important to take the butter or margarine out of the refrigerator in good time. Using a hand-mixer with a whisk attachment, mix the butter or margarine at the highest setting until it is soft.

Step 3: Add the sugar
Now mix together the sugar and vanilla sugar and little by little stir it into the butter or margarine until the mixture is smooth and even. In this case castor (superfine) sugar is preferable to granulated sugar because it dissolves more easily.

Step 4: Add the flavouring
Flavouring will give the cake a kick – provided that it is added in the right amount. In the case of flavour essence, it is essential to follow the manufacturer's instructions shown on the bottle.

Step 5: Add the eggs
Add the eggs to the softened butter/margarine-sugar mixture one after the other. Whisk each egg into the mixture on the highest setting for about ½ minute before whisking in the next egg. If the eggs are too cold, the butter or margarine may curdle and the sponge may look grainy – but don't worry, it will not influence the result.

Step 6: Mix together the flour and baking powder
The flour and baking powder must be mixed together well before being added to the egg-sugar-butter mixture. If you are also adding cornflour (cornstarch) or cocoa powder, these should be mixed with the flour now too, except in the case of marble cake where the cocoa powder is only added to one part of the sponge.

Step 7: Whisk in the flour

Using the medium setting, whisk in about half the flour, alternating briefly with any liquid (milk), then the other half of the flour. Only add enough liquid so that the sponge mixture slips heavily from a wooden spoon (photograph 3) – this is the right texture. If you add too much liquid the cake will not only be soggy but solid ingredients such as raisins will sink to the bottom because the sponge is too soft. There is one exception, namely when the sponge contains a lot of butter and eggs and little or no liquid. This mixture can be runny because the eggs will firm up the sponge while baking.

Baking powder begins to work as soon as it comes into contact with liquid. This is why it is first mixed with the flour and is only stirred in towards the end of the preparation process. This will ensure that the texture of the cake remains light and fluffy and prevent air holes from forming.

Step 8: Add the other ingredients

When you have added all the ingredients and the mixture is ready, you can begin adding the raisins or fruit as indicated in the recipe. Tinned fruit or fruit preserved in jars should be drained thoroughly to prevent too much liquid getting into the mixture. After draining, put them on a piece of kitchen paper so that any remaining juice is absorbed. Then fold the fruit or other solid ingredients into the sponge, using a pastry scraper. You can also stir them in with a hand-mixer on the medium setting – briefly! Be careful not to squash the fruit, since this would also colour the sponge in a rather unsightly manner. Cherries or other heavy ingredients will not sink to the bottom if you sprinkle them with a little flour before stirring them into the sponge (photograph 4).

Step 9: Put the sponge in the mould

Now transfer the sponge mixture into the prepared mould or tin and smooth the surface; it is best to do this with a spatula or a pastry scraper. The mould or tin should be about two-thirds full.

Step 10 – Bake the sponge

The sponge mixture must be baked as indicated in the recipe immediately after it has been made. Before removing it from the oven at the time given in the recipe, check whether it is done. Insert a wooden skewer in the highest part of the cake: if it comes out dry and is not sticky with sponge mixture, the cake is ready.

Leave the cake in its tin on a cake rack for about 10 minutes after taking it out of the oven, then turn it out and leave it to cool on the rack (photograph 5). Bases baked in a fruit flan mould can be removed from the mould immediately.

Storing cakes correctly

Wrapped in aluminium and stored in a cold place, a cake will remain fresh for several days. If the cake has been frozen it should be allowed to defrost at room temperature while still wrapped.

Cakes with whipped cream or quark should be kept in the refrigerator or freezer. If frozen, defrost them in the refrigerator.

3

4

5

Loaf cake
Basic sponge recipe

Preparation time:
about 20 minutes,
excluding cooling time
Baking time: about 60 minutes

For the tin (25 x 11 cm/10 x 4½ in):
a little fat
some flour

For the sponge:
250 g/9 oz (1¼ cups) soft
margarine or butter
150 g/5 oz (¾ cup) sugar
1 sachet vanilla sugar
1 pinch salt
4 eggs (medium)
300 g/10 oz (3 cups) plain
(all purpose) flour
4 level teaspoons
baking powder
2 tablespoons milk

Per slice:
P: 4 g, F: 16 g, C: 25 g,
kJ: 1104, kcal: 264, CU: 2.0

1 Grease and flour the cake tin. Preheat the oven:
Top/bottom heat:
about 180 °C/350 °F (Gas mark 4)
Fan oven:
about 160 °C/325 °F (Gas mark 3)

2 To make the sponge: whisk the margarine or butter in a mixing bowl using a hand-mixer with whisk attachment until soft. Gradually add the sugar, vanilla sugar and salt, stirring all the time, until you obtain a smooth, even mixture. Add the eggs, one after the other, whisking each for about ½ minute on the highest setting.

3 Mix together the flour and baking powder and whisk into the egg mixture in two instalments, alternating with the milk, on the medium setting.

4 Pour the sponge mixture into the tin and smooth the surface to make it even. Put the tin on a shelf in the bottom third of the preheated oven. **Bake for about 60 minutes.** After it has baked for about 15 minutes, make a lengthways incision about 1 cm/⅜ in deep in the middle of the cake, using a sharp knife.

5 After 60 minutes, remove the cake from the oven and leave in the tin for about 10 minutes, then take it out of the tin and place on a cake rack. Leave to cool.

Variation: You can give the cake a more sophisticated touch by adding 100 g/3½ oz (⅞ cup) chopped nuts, chocolate (¾ cup) (at the back in the photograph) or praline (½ cup) to the sponge mixture.

PROBLEMS

» Sogginess in the cake: sogginess is almost always caused by too much milk being added to the mixture. Therefore make sure you only add enough milk to ensure that the mixture remains quite firm. Never add so much milk that the mixture becomes runny. This is why the milk should only be added little by little.
» Air holes in the cake: air holes can occur in your sponge cake if the sponge mixture is whisked too vigorously while or after the flour and baking powder is stirred into the egg mixture. They can be avoided by whisking the mixture in two instalments and only very briefly.

Plain waffles

FOR CHILDREN (ABOUT 8 WAFFLES)

Preparation time:
about 30 minutes

For the waffle iron:
a little cooking oil,
e.g. sunflower oil

For the batter:
175 g/6 oz (⅞ cup) soft butter
or margarine
175 g/6 oz (⅞ cup) sugar
1 pinch salt
4 eggs (medium)
200 g/7 oz (2 cups) plain
(all purpose) flour
40 g/1½ oz (5 tablespoons)
custard powder (vanilla
pudding mix)
1 level teaspoon baking
powder
100 ml/3½ fl oz (½ cup) milk
or water

Per piece:
P: 6 g, F: 22 g, C: 49 g,
kJ: 1771, kcal: 423, CU: 4.0

1 Preheat the waffle iron on the highest setting. (Be sure to follow the maker's instructions.)

2 Whisk the margarine or butter in a mixing bowl using a hand-mixer with whisk attachment until soft. Gradually add the sugar and salt, stirring all the time, until the mixture is smooth and even. Add the eggs, one after the other, and whisk each one into the mixture for ½ minute.

3 Mix the flour, custard powder and baking powder and briefly whisk in two instalments, alternating with the milk, on the medium setting.

4 Reduce the temperature to the medium setting and grease the mould with a pastry brush.

5 Spoon about 2 tablespoons of batter onto the waffle iron for each waffle, smooth flat with the spoon and cook until they are golden brown. Remove the waffles from the waffle iron and put them side by side on a cake rack. Serve lukewarm.

TIPS » Sprinkle the waffles with icing (confectioners') sugar and serve with crème fraîche or lightly whipped whipping cream.

Waffles with an apple filling

FRUITY (ABOUT 8 PORTIONS)

1 Preheat the waffle iron on the highest setting. (Be sure to follow the maker's instructions.)

2 For the waffle batter, peel the apples, cut them into quarters, then core and grate them. Pour lemon juice over the grated apples, mix in the sugar and put to one side.

3 Whisk the margarine or butter in a mixing bowl using a hand-mixer with whisk attachment until soft. Add the sugar, vanilla sugar and cinnamon until the mixture is smooth and even, stirring all the time.

4 Add the eggs one after other and whisk each for about ½ minute on the highest setting. Mix the flour and baking powder and whisk briefly in two instalments on the medium setting, alternating with

the crème fraîche. Finally add the grated apple.

5 Reduce the temperature of the waffle iron to the medium setting and grease the mould with a pastry brush (photograph 1). Spoon about 2 tablespoons of batter onto the waffle iron for each waffle and smooth the batter down slightly (photograph 2).

6 Cook the waffles until golden brown, remove from the waffle iron and place on a cake rack to cool.

TIP » If you like you can also stir 50-75 g/2-3 oz (⅓-½ cup) raisins or currants to the batter.

SERVING TIP » You can also serve the waffles with the remaining crème fraîche.

Preparation time:
about 45 minutes

For the waffle iron:
a little cooking oil

For the batter:
275 g/10 oz sharp apples
2–3 tablespoons lemon juice
1 tablespoon sugar
100 g/3½ oz (½ cup) soft margarine or butter
125 g/4½ oz (⅝ cup) sugar
1 sachet vanilla sugar
½ level teaspoon ground cinnamon
3 eggs (medium)
200 g/7 oz (2 cups) plain (all purpose) flour
½ level teaspoon baking powder
75 g/3 oz (⅜ cup) crème fraîche

Per piece: P: 5 g, F: 16 g, C: 40 g, kJ: 1390, kcal: 333, CU: 3.5

Amerikaner cookies

FOR CHILDREN (12 PIECES/2 BAKING SHEETS)

Preparation time:
about 30 minutes,
excluding cooling time
Baking time: about 20 minutes
per baking sheet

For the baking sheet:
baking parchment

For the sponge:
75 g/2½ oz (⅜ cup) soft
margarine or butter
100 g/3½ oz (½ cup) sugar
1 sachet vanilla sugar
a few drops Dr. Oetker Natural
Vanilla Extract
1 pinch salt
2 eggs (medium)
250 g/9 oz (2½ cups) plain
(all purpose) flour
3 level teaspoons baking powder
100 ml/3½ fl oz (½ cup) milk

For brushing:
about 2 tablespoons milk

For the icing:
200 g/7 oz (1 cup) icing
(confectioners') sugar
about 3 tablespoons lemon
juice or water
150 g/5 oz dark chocolate
1 tablespoon cooking oil,
e.g. sunflower oil
peeled chopped almonds
chopped pistachio kernels
granulated sugar
grated coconut

Per piece:
P: 5 g, F: 14 g, C: 48 g,
kJ: 1452, kcal: 347, CU: 4.0

1 Line the baking sheet with baking parchment. Preheat the oven:
Top/bottom heat:
about 180 °C/350 °F (Gas mark 4)
Fan oven:
about 160 °C/325 °F (Gas mark 3)

2 For the sponge, whisk the margarine or butter in a mixing bowl using a hand-mixer with whisk attachment until soft. Add the sugar, vanilla sugar, vanilla extract and salt and whisk until the mixture is smooth and even. Then add the eggs, one after the other, whisking each egg for about ½ minute on the highest setting.

3 Mix together the flour and baking powder and whisk briefly in two instalments on the medium setting, alternating with the milk. Divide the sponge mixture into 2 portions and, using 2 tablespoons, from one portion into 6 little heaps on the baking sheet, not too close to each other. Using a moistened knife, smooth down the little heaps. Put the first baking sheet on the middle shelf of the preheated oven. **Bake for about 20 minutes; after about 15 minutes in the oven, brush the surfaces with a little milk.**

4 Use the remaining sponge mixture to make 6 more little heaps on another sheet of baking parchment. Slide the finished cakes together with the baking parchment onto a cake rack. Now slide the little heaps of sponge mixture on the second sheet of baking parchment onto the baking sheet and bake as above. Leave to cool.

5 To make the icing, sift the icing (confectioners') sugar and stir in the lemon juice or water to make a syrupy glaze. Coarsely chop the chocolate and melt it with the cooking oil in a bain-marie over low heat, stirring all the time. Coat the undersides of the cooled cakes with the icing. If you like, you can also sprinkle them with some almonds, pistachios, coarse sugar and grated coconut (photograph 1).

Recipe variation: To make 24 mint-flavoured cookies (photograph 2), reduce the amount of sugar in the sponge mixture to 50 g/2 oz (¼ cup) and the milk to 50 ml/ 1½ fl oz (3 tablespoons). Heat up the milk and dissolve 75 g/3 oz of finely chopped peppermint fondant (white/pink) in it. Add to the sponge mixture and continue as instructed in the recipe. Bake the mint cookies for about 15 minutes. For the glaze: chop up finely 150 g/ 5 oz peppermint fondant and heat in a small pan with about 2 tablespoons water until it has melted. But do not let it boil! Leave the fondant to cool until it thickens, then coat the underside of the mint cookies with this fondant glaze, using a pastry brush. Or you can make a glaze with 200 g/7 oz (1½ cups) icing (confectioners') sugar and 2-3 tablespoons mint liqueur and colour the glaze with food colouring.

Pound cake

TRADITIONAL (ABOUT 15 SLICES)

Preparation time:
about 30 minutes,
excluding cooling time
Baking time: 75–80 minutes

For the tin (25 x 11 cm/10 x 4½ in):
a little fat, flour

For the sponge:
250 g/9 oz (1¼ cups) soft
margarine or butter
225 g/8 oz (1⅛ cups) sugar
1 sachet vanilla sugar
1 pinch salt
a few drops Dr. Oetker Natural
Lemon Extract
4 eggs (medium)
125 g/4½ oz (1¼ cups) plain (all
purpose) flour
125 g/1 oz (3 tablespoons) cornflour (cornstarch)
1 level teaspoon baking powder

For the glaze:
150 g/5 oz dark chocolate
1 tablespoon cooking oil

Per slice:
P: 3 g, F: 20 g, C: 33 g,
kJ: 1371, kcal: 328, CU: 3.0

1 Grease and flour the cake tin. Preheat the oven:
Top/bottom heat:
about 200 °C/400 °F (Gas mark 6)
Fan oven:
about 180 °C/350 °F (Gas mark 4)

2 Whisk the margarine or butter in a mixing bowl using a hand-mixer with whisk attachment until soft. Add the sugar, vanilla sugar, salt and flavouring, stirring all the time until you obtain a smooth, even mixture.

3 Add the eggs, one after the other, whisking each egg for about ½ minute on the highest setting. Mix together the flour, baking powder and cornflour (cornstarch) and whisk briefly in two instalments on the medium setting. Transfer the sponge into the cake tin, smooth the surface and put it on a shelf in the bottom third of the preheated oven.

4 **Bake the cake for 15-20 minutes.** Then make a lengthways cut about 1 cm/⅜ in deep in the middle of the cake with a sharp knife. Put the cake back in the oven and **reduce the oven temperature to top/bottom heat: about 180 °C/350 °F (Gas mark 4), fan oven: 160 °C/325 °F (Gas mark 3). Bake the cake for a further 60 minutes.**

5 Remove the cake from the oven and leave in the tin for about 10 minutes. Then take it out and leave to cool on a rack.

6 For the glaze, break the chocolate into chunks and melt with the oil in a bain-marie over low heat, stirring all the time. Coat the cooled cake with this glaze (small photograph on the left). Leave the glaze to set.

Preparation time:
about 20 minutes
Baking time: 55–60 minutes

For the tin (25 x 11 cm/10 x 4½ in):
a little fat, flour

For the sponge:
200 g/7 oz (1 cup) soft
margarine or butter
100 g/3½ oz (½ cup) sugar
1 sachet vanilla sugar
1 tablespoon rum
1 pinch salt
3 eggs (medium)
200 g/7 oz (2 cups) plain
(all purpose) flour
2 level teaspoons cocoa powder
1 level teaspoon ground
cinnamon
2 ½ level teaspoons baking
powder
100 g/3½ oz (1 cup) grated
chocolate
50 g/2 oz (⅜ cup) peeled
chopped almonds
100 ml/3½ fl oz (½ cup) red
wine

Per slice:
P: 4 g, F: 16 g, C: 21 g,
kJ: 1056, kcal: 252, CU: 2.0

Red wine cake

EASY (ABOUT 15 SLICES)

1 Grease and flour the cake tin
(small photograph on the right).
Preheat the oven:
Top/bottom heat:
about 180 °C/350 °F (Gas mark 4)
Fan oven:
about 160 °C/325 °F (Gas mark 3)

2 Whisk the margarine or butter in a
mixing bowl using a hand-mixer
with whisk attachment until soft.
Add the sugar, vanilla sugar, rum
and salt little by little, stirring
all the time, until you obtain a
smooth, even mixture. Whisk in
the eggs, one after the other, for
about ½ minute each on the highest setting.

3 Mix the flour with the cocoa, cinnamon and baking powder. Then
quickly whisk in, one after the other,
the grated chocolate, almonds and
red wine using the medium setting.

4 Transfer the mixture into the cake
tin and put on a shelf in the bottom
third of the preheated oven. **Bake
the cake for 15-20 minutes**. Then
make a lengthways cut about 1 cm/
⅜ in deep in the middle of the cake
using a sharp knife. **Bake the cake
for another 40 minutes**.

5 Leave the cake in the tin for about
10 minutes, then take it out and
leave to cool on a rack.

Hazelnut cake

WITH ALCOHOL (ABOUT 15 SLICES)

Preparation time:
about 30 minutes,
excluding cooling time
Baking time: about 60 minutes

For the tin (25 x 11 cm/
10 x 4½ in):
a little fat, flour

For the sponge:
100 g/3½ oz (⅝ cup) ground
hazelnuts
100 g/3½ oz (⅝ cup) chopped
hazelnuts
200 g/7 oz (1 cup) soft
margarine or butter
150 g/5 oz (¾ cup) sugar
1 sachet vanilla sugar
1 pinch salt
1 tablespoon rum
3 eggs (medium)
150 g/5 oz (1½ cups) plain
(all purpose) flour
2 level teaspoons baking
powder

For the glaze:
150 g/5 oz milk chocolate
1 tablespoon cooking oil,
e.g. sunflower oil

For sprinkling:
50 g/2 oz (⅓ cup) chopped
hazelnuts

Per slice:
P: 5 g, F: 27 g, C: 25 g,
kJ: 1522, kcal: 364, CU: 2.0

1 To make the sponge, roast the hazelnuts lightly in a pan without fat (photograph 1), stirring all the time, then leave to cool on a plate. Grease and flour the cake tin. Preheat the oven:
Top/bottom heat:
about 180 °C/350 °F (Gas mark 4)
Fan oven:
about 160 °C/325 °F (Gas mark 3)

2 Whisk the margarine or butter in a mixing bowl using a hand-mixer with whisk attachment until soft. Add the sugar, vanilla sugar, salt and rum little by little, whisking all the time until you obtain a smooth mixture. Whisk in the eggs, one after the other, for about ½ minute each on the highest setting.

3 Mix together the flour and baking powder, stir in the roasted hazelnuts and whisk briefly in two instalments on the medium setting. Spoon the cake mixture into the cake tin (photograph 2) and put the tin on a shelf in the bottom third of the preheated oven. **Bake for about 60 minutes** and, if you like, cover the cake with baking parchment towards the end of the baking time.

4 Leave the cake in the tin for about 10 minutes, then take it out and transfer onto a cake rack to cool.

5 To make the glaze, coarsely chop the chocolate and melt with the oil in a bain-marie over low heat while stirring all the time. Coat the cooled cake with the chocolate glaze, using a knife or pastry brush, then sprinkle chopped hazelnuts on top (photograph 3).

TIPS » You can also make this cake in a kugelhopf mould (diameter 22 cm/9 in).
» It is best to use a non-stick pan to roast the hazelnuts.

Recipe variation: To make a chocolate-hazelnut cake, add 100 g/3½ oz (1 cup) grated chocolate to the sponge mixture.

Marble cake

TRADITIONAL (ABOUT 20 SLICES)

Preparation time:
about 30 minutes
Baking time: about 55 minutes

For the Bundt pan or kugelhopf
mould (diameter 22 cm/9 in):
a little fat

For the sponge:
225 g/8 oz (1⅛ cups) soft
margarine or butter
200 g/7 oz (1 cup) sugar
1 sachet vanilla sugar
1 pinch salt
4 eggs (medium)
275 g/9½ oz (2¾ cups) plain
(all purpose) flour
3 level teaspoons baking
powder
about 2 tablespoons milk
15 g/½ oz (2½ tablespoons)
cocoa powder
15 g/½ oz (1 tablespoon) sugar
about 2 tablespoons milk

For dusting:
a little icing (confectioners')
sugar

Per slice:
P: 3 g, F: 11 g, C: 22 g,
kJ: 849, kcal: 203, CU: 2.0

1 Grease the Bundt pan or kugelhopf mould. Preheat the oven:
Top/bottom heat:
about 180 °C/350 °F (Gas mark 4)
Fan oven:
about 160 °C/325 °F (Gas mark 3)

2 To make the sponge mixture, whisk the margarine or butter in a mixing bowl using a hand-mixer with whisk attachment until soft. Add the sugar, vanilla sugar and salt little by little, whisking all the time until you obtain a smooth mixture. Whisk in the eggs, one after the other, for about ½ minute each on the highest setting.

3 Mix together the flour and baking powder and whisk briefly in two instalments on the medium setting, alternating with the milk.

4 Put two-thirds of the sponge mixture in the mould. Sift the cocoa powder and stir into the rest of the sponge together with the sugar and milk. Spoon the chocolate sponge on top of the light-coloured sponge and, using a fork, draw swirls through the two layers to create a marble pattern. Put the mould on a shelf in the bottom third of the preheated oven. **Bake for about 55 minutes.**

5 Leave the cake in the mould for about 10 minutes, then take it out and leave to cool on a cake rack.

6 Sprinkle the cake with icing (confectioner's) sugar.

TIP » Add a touch of sophistication by stirring about a tablespoon of rum into the sponge mixture.

Recipe variation: To make a "tricolour" marble cake, remove 3 x 2 tablespoons sponge mixture from the main sponge mixture and "colour" them as follows. Stir 30 g/1 oz (¼ cup) ground pistachio nuts into 2 tablespoons of sponge mixture, stir 1 teaspoon cocoa powder into 2 tablespoons of sponge mixture and stir 50 g/ 2 oz (⅜ cup) finely chopped glacé cherries into 2 tablespoons of sponge mixture. Put the rest of the sponge mixture in the prepared mould, then spoon in the three coloured mixtures, each covering one-third of the plain sponge (photograph 1).
Draw a spiral pattern through each third of plain and coloured sponge, using a fork.
Bake the cake at the same temperature for about 50 minutes.
Then make the icing. Mix together 200 g/7 oz (1½ cups) icing (confectioners') sugar to make a semi-liquid glaze. Divide it into three portions, then add the food colouring and cocoa to obtain red, green and brown icing. Sprinkle or coat the cake with it when cool (photographs 2 and 3).

2

3

Frankfurt crown

TRADITIONAL (ABOUT 16 SLICES)

Preparation time:
about 60 minutes,
excluding cooling time
Baking time: about 40 minutes

**For the ring mould
(diameter 22 cm/9 in):**
some fat, aluminum foil

For the sponge:
100 g/3½ oz (½ cup) soft
margarine or butter
150 g/5 oz (¾ cup) sugar
1 sachet vanilla sugar
a few drops Dr. Oetker
Natural Lemon Extract
1 pinch salt, 3 eggs (medium)
150 g/5 oz (1½ cups) plain
(all purpose) flour
50 g/2 oz (6 tablespoons)
cornflour (cornstarch)
2 level teaspoons baking powder

For the almond praline:
10 g/⅓ oz (2 teaspoons) butter
60 g/2 oz (¼ cup) sugar
125 g/4½ oz (1½ cups) peeled
chopped almonds

For the butter cream:
40 g/1½ oz (5 tablespoons)
custard powder (vanilla
pudding mix)
100 g/3½ oz (½ cup) sugar
500 ml/17 fl oz (2¼ cups) milk
250 g/9 oz (1¼ cups) soft butter

3 tablespoons red currant jelly
glacé cherries

Per slice:
P: 5 g, F: 26 g, C: 38 g,
kJ: 1705, kcal: 408, CU: 3.0

1 Grease the ring mould. Preheat the oven:
Top/bottom heat:
about 180 °C/350 °F (Gas mark 4)
Fan oven:
about 160 °C/325 °F (Gas mark 3)

2 To make the sponge, whisk the margarine or butter in a mixing bowl using a hand-mixer with whisk attachment until soft. Add the sugar, vanilla sugar, lemon extract and salt little by little, whisking until you have a smooth mixture. Whisk in the eggs, one after the other, for about ½ minute each on the highest setting.

3 Mix together the flour, cornflour (cornstarch) and baking powder and whisk into the egg and sugar mixture on the medium setting. Spoon the sponge into the ring mould and smooth the surface. Put the mould on a shelf in the bottom third of the preheated oven. **Bake for about 40 minutes.**

4 Remove from the oven and leave the cake in the mould for about 10 minutes. Then take it out (photograph 1) and put on a cake rack to cool.

5 For the praline, heat the butter, sugar and almond in a pan until the mixture has turned brown. Pour onto piece of foil and leave to cool.

6 For the butter cream, make custard following the instructions on the packet but with 100 g/3½ oz (½ cup) sugar and with milk. Leave the custard to cool (but do not refrigerate), stirring occasionally.

7 Whisk the butter using a hand-held mixer with whisk attachment until soft. Then stir in the cooled custard, spoonful by spoonful, having made sure that the butter and custard are at room temperature (the butter cream might curdle otherwise).

8 Cut the ring horizontally twice to make three layers (photograph 2). Stir the jelly until smooth with a whisk or rub the jam through a sieve and spread on the bottom layer. Now spread half the butter cream on the bottom two layers. Then put all the layers back on top of each other to reconstruct the ring.

9 Coat the entire ring inside and out with the rest of the butter cream (having first put 1-2 tablespoons aside) and sprinkle with the praline (photograph 3). Put the reserved butter cream in a piping bag fitted with a star-shaped nozzle and decorate the top of the ring with it, then garnish with glacé cherries. Put the cake in the refrigerator for about 2 hours.

Variation: Bake the Frankfurt crown in a larger ring mould (diameter 26 cm/10¼ in).Then make a sponge mixture with 200 g/7 oz (1 cup) soft margarine or butter, 300 g/10 oz (1½ cups) sugar, 2 packets vanilla sugar, 1½ teaspoons rum, 1 pinch salt, 6 eggs (medium), 300 g/10 oz (1½ cups) plain (all purpose) flour, 100 g/3½ oz (1 cup) cornflour (cornstarch) and 4 level teaspoons baking powder, following the instructions in the recipe. Bake at the temperature indicated for about 45 minutes. Make the praline with 25 g/1 oz (2 tablespoons) butter, 125 g/4½ oz (⅝ cup) sugar and 200 g/7 oz (2½ cups) chopped almonds. For the butter cream, use 80 g/3 oz (½ cup) vanilla-flavoured custard powder, 200 g/7 oz (1 cup) sugar, 1 litre/1¾ pints (4¼ cups) milk and 500 g/18 oz (2½ cups) butter. Cut the cake horizontally three times to make four layers and fill. In addition, you will need 150 g/5 oz (⅝ cup) red currant jelly or jam and a few glacé cherries.

Sachertorte

Preparation time:
about 45 minutes,
excluding cooling time
Baking time: about 50 minutes

For the springform mould
(diameter 26 cm/10¼ in):
a little fat
baking parchment

For the sponge:
150 g/5 oz dark chocolate
6 egg whites (medium)
160 g/5½ oz (⅞ cup) soft
margarine or butter
160 g/5½ oz (⅞ cup) sugar
1 sachet vanilla sugar
6 egg yolks (medium)
100 g/3½ oz (1 cup)
breadcrumbs

For the filling:
125 g/4½ oz (½ cup) apricot
jam

For the glaze:
60 g/2 oz (¼ cup) sugar
7 tablespoons water
200 g/7 oz dark chocolate

For decoration:
50 g/2 oz dark chocolate

Per piece:
P: 7 g, F: 25 g, C: 47 g,
kJ: 1855, kcal: 443, CU: 4.0

1 To make the sponge, first break the chocolate into pieces, melt over low heat in a bain-marie, stirring all the time, then leave to cool. Grease the base of the springform mould, then line with baking parchment. Preheat the oven:
Top/bottom heat:
about 180 °C/350 °F (Gas mark 4)
Fan oven:
about 160 °C/325 °F (Gas mark 3)

2 Beat the egg white until stiff. Whisk the margarine or butter in a mixing bowl using a hand-mixer with whisk attachment until soft. Add the sugar and vanilla sugar little by little, whisking all the time until you obtain a smooth mixture.

3 Whisk in the egg yolks one after the other with the hand-mixer on the highest setting. Stir in the melted chocolate and breadcrumbs with the mixer on the highest setting. Very gently fold in the stiffly beaten egg whites. Now spoon the sponge mixture into the springform mould. Put the mould on a shelf in the bottom third of the preheated oven. **Bake for about 50 minutes.**

4 Remove the cake from the tin and place on a cake rack lined with baking parchment. Leave to cool. Then remove the baking parchment and cut the cake horizontally once to make two layers. Place the bottom layer on a cake platter.

5 For the filling, spread the jam on the bottom layer, then put the top layer on top of it.

6 To make the glaze, add the sugar to the water in a pan and boil until it is completely dissolved. Remove the pan from the heat. Break the chocolate into pieces and stir in gradually; continue stirring until the chocolate has completely melted and the mixture is shiny.

7 Pour the glaze onto the middle of the cake (photograph 1) and spread it evenly all over the cake by slightly "moving and tipping" it on the platter (photographs 2 and 3). If necessary, spread the glaze along the sides with a knife. To ensure that the glaze spreads evenly over the cake, lift the platter about 2 cm/ ¾ in and "tap" it on a wooden surface once or twice.

8 Loosen the bottom of the cake from the cake platter by sliding a long knife under it; then slide the cake onto a cake stand by slightly tipping the cake platter and guiding the cake with the knife. Leave the icing to set.

9 To decorate the cake, melt the chocolate in a bain-marie while stirring. Cut the cake into 12 slices. Pour the melted chocolate into a paper icing bag or a small freezer bag, cut off a small corner and write the word "Sacher" on each slice. Keep the cake in a cool place until serving.

Apple cake, very delicate
GOOD TO PREPARE IN ADVANCE (ABOUT 12 PIECES)

Preparation time:
about 30 minutes
Baking time: about 45 minutes

For the springform mould
(diameter 26 cm/10¼ in):
a little fat

For the topping:
25 g/1 oz (2 tablespoons)
butter
750 g/1½ lb apples, e.g. Elstar

For the sponge:
125 g/4½ oz (⅝ cup) soft
margarine or butter
125 g/4½ oz (⅝ cup) sugar
1 sachet vanilla sugar
1 pinch salt
a few drops Dr. Oetker
Natural Lemon Extract
3 eggs (medium)
200 g/7 oz (2 cups) plain (all
purpose) flour
2 level teaspoons baking
powder
1–2 tablespoons milk

For the apricot glaze:
2 tablespoons apricot jam
1 tablespoon water

Per piece:
P: 4 g, F: 13 g, C: 32 g,
kJ: 1084, kcal: 259, CU: 2.5

1 Grease the bottom of the spring-form mould. Preheat the oven:
Top/bottom heat:
about 180 °C/350 °F (Gas mark 4)
Fan oven:
about 160 °C/325 °F (Gas mark 3)

2 To make the topping, melt the butter in a small pan. Peel the apples, cut into quarters, remove the cores and make several lengthways incisions.

3 For the sponge, whisk the margarine or butter in a mixing bowl using a hand-mixer with whisk attachment until soft. Add the sugar, vanilla sugar, salt and lemon extract little by little, whisking all the time until you obtain a smooth mixture.

4 Whisk in the eggs, one after the other, for about ½ minute each on the highest setting. Mix together the flour and baking powder and whisk briefly in two instalments on the medium setting, alternating with the milk. Transfer the mixture into the springform mould and smooth to make it even. Arrange the apple quarters in two concentric circles on the sponge mixture and pour the melted butter over the apples. Put the springform mould on a shelf in the bottom third of the oven. **Bake for about 45 minutes.**

5 Rub the apricot jam through a sieve and bring to the boil in a small pan with a little water, stirring all the time. Pour on the cake immediately after taking it out of the oven. Release, then remove the ring part of the springform mould. Loosen the cake away from the bottom of the springform mould, then leave to cool on cake rack.

TIPS » Before baking sprinkle 40 g/1½ oz (¼ cup) raisins over the apples.
» You can prepare the cake 1-2 days before it will be eaten.
» This cake is also suitable for freezing.

Recipe variation 1: To make **apple crumble cake** (photograph 1), whisk together with a hand-mixer 100 g/3½ oz (1 cup) plain (all purpose) flour, 50 g/2 oz (¼ cup) sugar, 1 sachet vanilla sugar, 1 pinch of ground cinnamon and 80 g/2½ oz (⅜ cup) softened butter in a mixing bowl until the mixture has acquired a "crumbly" consistency. Spread the crumble over the apples, then bake as instructed above. But in this case do not coat with apricot glaze.

Recipe variation 2: To make a **very delicious cherry cake** (photograph 2), instead of the apples, use 600 g/1¼ lb fresh morello cherries (rinse, stone and drain well) or 1 jar of drained morello cherries (drained weight 350 g/12 oz).

Mole cake

POPULAR (ABOUT 16 PIECES)

Preparation time:
about 30 minutes,
excluding cooling time
Baking time: about 30 minutes

For the springform mould
(diameter 26 cm/10¼ in):
a little fat

For the sponge:
4 egg whites (medium)
125 g/4½ oz (⅝ cup) soft
margarine or butter
125 g/4½ oz (⅝ cup) sugar
1 sachet vanilla sugar
4 egg yolks (medium)
50 g/2 oz (½ cup) plain
(all purpose) flour
10 g/⅓ oz (1½ tablespoons)
cocoa powder
4 level teaspoons baking
powder
75 g/3 oz (¾ cup) ground
hazelnuts
100 g/3½ oz (½ cup) grated
dark chocolate

For the filling:
1 jar morello cherries
(drained weight 350 g/12 oz)
2 medium bananas
(about 250 g/9 oz)
2 tablespoons lemon juice
600 g/20 oz (2½ cups) chilled
whipping cream (min. 30 % fat)
25 g/1 oz (2 tablespoons) sugar
1 sachet vanilla sugar

Per piece:
P: 4 g, F: 25 g, C: 26 g,
kJ: 1449, kcal: 346, CU: 2.0

1 Grease the bottom of the spring-form mould. Preheat the oven:
Top/bottom heat:
about 180 °C/350 °F (Gas mark 4)
Fan oven:
about 160 °C/325 °F (Gas mark 3)

2 To make the sponge mixture, beat the egg so stiff that when an incision is made with a knife, the cut remains visible. Whisk the margarine or butter in a mixing bowl using a hand-mixer with whisk attachment until soft. Stir in the sugar and vanilla sugar until thoroughly incorporated. Whisk in the egg yolks one by one on the highest setting.

3 Mix together the flour, cocoa powder and baking powder, stir in the hazelnuts and grated chocolate and whisk in two instalments on the medium setting. Then carefully fold in the beaten egg whites and whisk briefly with the hand-mixer on the medium setting.

4 Transfer the sponge mixture into the springform mould and smooth flat. Place the mould on a shelf in the bottom third of the preheated oven. **Bake for about 30 minutes.**

5 Leave the cake in the springform mould for about 10 minutes, then take it out and leave to cool on a cake rack.

6 Make a circular incision on the surface with knife to leave an edge 1-2 cm/⅜-¾ in wide all round. Then, using a tablespoon, hollow out the cooled cake within the circle to a depth of about 1 cm/⅜ in (photograph 1). Crumble the cake remains you have just hollowed out into a bowl (photograph 2).

7 To make the filling, drain the cherries thoroughly, then put them on a kitchen paper. Peel the bananas, cut in half lengthways, sprinkle with lemon juice and arrange in the hollowed-out cake. Distribute the cherries in between the bananas (photograph 3).

8 Whip the cream with the sugar and vanilla sugar until stiff; spoon over the fruit to form a dome and sprinkle the crumbled remains of the cake on top (if necessary, press the crumbs slightly into the cream). Put the cake in the refrigerator for about 1 hour.

Variation: Instead of morello cherries you can use 2 tins of mandarin oranges (drained weight 175 g/6 oz each).

Lemon-quark-cream torte

POPULAR (ABOUT 16 PIECES)

Preparation time:
about 35 minutes,
excluding cooling time
Baking time: about 25 minutes

**For the springform mould
(diameter 26 cm/10¼ in):**
a little fat, baking parchment

For the sponge:
150 g/5 oz (¾ cup) soft margarine or butter
150 g/5 oz (¾ cup) sugar
1 sachet vanilla sugar
1 pinch salt
3 eggs (medium)
125 g/4½ oz (1¼ cups) plain
(all purpose) flour
25 g/1 oz (3 tablespoons)
cornflour (cornstarch)
1 level teaspoon baking powder

For the filling:
10 sheets clear gelatine
400 g/14 oz (1¾ cups) chilled
whipping cream
1 teaspoon grated lemon zest
100 ml/3½ fl oz (½ cup)
lemon juice
150 g/5 oz (¾ cup) sugar
1 sachet vanilla sugar
500 g/18 oz (2 cups) low fat
quark
250 g/9 oz (1 cup) full fat
quark (40 % fat dry weight)

20 g/¾ oz (2½ tablespoons)
icing (confectioners') sugar

Per piece:
P: 9 g, F: 19 g, C: 30 g,
kJ: 1398, kcal: 334, CU: 2.5

1 Grease the bottom of the springform mould. Preheat the oven:
Top/bottom heat:
about 180 °C/350 °F (Gas mark 4)
Fan oven:
about 160 °C/325 °F (Gas mark 3)

2 For the sponge mixture, whisk the
margarine or butter in a mixing
bowl using a hand-mixer with
whisk attachment until soft. Add
the sugar, vanilla sugar and salt
little by little, whisking all the time
until you obtain a smooth mixture.

3 Whisk in the eggs, one after the
other, for about ½ minute each on
the highest setting. Mix together
the flour, cornflour (cornstarch)
and baking powder and then whisk
briefly in two portions on the medium setting. Spoon the sponge
mixture into the springform mould
and smooth flat. Put the springform mould on middle shelf in
the preheated oven. **Bake for about
25 minutes**.

4 Remove the cake base from the
springform mould and leave to cool
on a kitchen rack, then cut once
horizontally to make two layers.
Put the bottom layer on a cake
platter.

5 For the filling, soften the gelatine
according to the instructions on
the packet. Meanwhile, beat the
cream until stiff. Stir together the
lemon peel with lemon juice,
sugar, vanilla sugar and quark.
Squeeze the gelatine and dissolve

it in a small saucepan over low heat
while stirring.

6 Stir the gelatine into 4 tablespoons
of the quark mixture, then stir this
into the rest of the quark mixture.
Next immediately fold the cream
into the quark mixture. Now line
the springform mould ring or a
cake setting ring with baking parchment and place it round the bottom
layer of the torte. Fill it with the
quark and cream mixture, then
smooth flat.

7 Cut the top layer of the torte into
16 slices and place over the filling.
Refrigerate the torte for at least
3 hours.

8 Before serving, loosen the springform mould ring or cake setting
ring with a knife and remove
completely. Sprinkle the torte with
icing (confectioners') sugar.

Variation: The torte will taste
even fruitier if you add 1 tin of
mandarin oranges (drained weight
175 g/6 oz), drained thoroughly in
a sieve and then folded into the
quark mixture with a dough scraper.

Recipe variation: To make an
Orange-quark-cream torte, replace
the 100 ml/3½ fl oz (½ cup) lemon
juice with the same amount of
orange juice plus 1 tablespoon lemon juice and replace the lemon
zest with orange zest.

Gooseberry meringue
QUITE LAVISH (ABOUT 16 PIECES)

Preparation time:
about 40 minutes,
excluding cooling time
Baking time: about 20 minutes
per baking sheet

For the springform mould
(diameter 26 cm/10¼ in):
a little fat

For the meringue:
3 egg whites (medium)
150 g/5 oz (¾ cup) caster
(superfine) sugar

For the sponge:
75 g/2½ oz (⅜ cup) soft
margarine or butter
75 g/2½ oz (⅜ cup) sugar
1 sachet vanilla sugar
1 pinch salt
3 egg yolks (medium)
100 g/3½ oz (1 cup) plain
(all purpose) flour
½ level teaspoon baking powder

For sprinkling:
75 g/3 oz (⅝ cup) slivered
almonds

For the filling:
1 jar gooseberry jam
(drained weight 390 g/14 oz)
250 ml/8 fl oz (1 cup)
gooseberry juice (from the jar)
1 sachet clear cake glaze
2 tablespoons sugar
400 g/14 oz (1¾ cups) chilled
whipping cream (min. 30 % fat)
2 teaspoons sugar

For sprinkling:
icing (confectioners') sugar

1 Grease the bottom of the spring-form mould. Preheat the oven:
Top/bottom heat:
about 180 °C/350 °F (Gas mark 4)
Fan oven:
about 160 °C/325 °F (Gas mark 3)

2 For the meringue, beat the egg whites so stiff that when an incision is made with a knife, the cut remains visible. Gradually fold in the sugar.

3 Whisk the margarine or butter in a mixing bowl using a hand-mixer with whisk attachment until soft. Add the sugar, vanilla sugar and salt little by little, whisking all the time until you obtain a smooth mixture.

4 Whisk in the egg yolks one after the other on the highest setting. Mix together the flour and baking powder and whisk briefly in two instalments on the medium setting.

5 To make the first of the two layers, spread half the sponge on the bottom of the springform mould. Spread half the stiffly beaten egg whites on top (photograph 1) and then sprinkle over half the almonds. Fit the springform ring round the base and put the whole mould on the middle shelf in the preheated oven. **Bake for about 20 minutes.** After baking remove the springform ring, slide the layer off the bottom of the springform mould and leave to cool on a cake rack.

6 Make the second layer in the same way, using the remaining sponge, beaten eggs and almonds. When baked, remove the layer and leave it to cool on a cake rack.

7 To make the filling, drain the gooseberries thoroughly in a sieve and reserve the juice. Measure 250 ml/8 fl oz (1 cup) of the juice, topping up with water if necessary. Prepare the glaze with 2 table-spoons sugar, the juice and glaze powder, following the instructions on the packet. Stir in the goose-berries and leave the mixture to cool.

8 Whip the cream stiff with the sugar. Spread one cake layer first with the gooseberry mixture, then cover with the cream mixture. Cut the other layer into 16 slices (photo-graph 2) and place on top of the cream mixture (photograph 3). Keep the torte in the refrigerator for at least 1 hour before serving, then sprinkle with icing (confec-tioners') sugar.

TIP » Use morello cherries or yel-low plums (mirabelles) from 1 jar (drained weight 350 g/12 oz each). If you use cherries you should use red glaze.

Per piece: P: 4 g, F: 16 g, C: 30 g, kJ: 1183, kcal: 283, CU: 2.5

Lemon cake

FOR CHILDREN (ABOUT 20 SLICES)

Preparation time:
about 35 minutes
Baking time: about 25 minutes

For the baking sheet
(40 x 30 cm/16 x 12 in):
a little fat, aluminium foil

For the sponge:
350 g/12 oz (1¾ cups) soft
margarine or butter
350 g/12 oz (1¾ cups) sugar
2 teaspoons grated lemon zest
5 eggs (medium)
275 g/9½ oz (2¾ cups) plain
(all purpose) flour
120 g/4 oz (1 cup) cornflour
(cornstarch)
2 level teaspoons baking
powder

For the icing:
250 g/9 oz (2 cups) icing
(confectioners') sugar
about 7 tablespoons lemon
juice

1 Grease the baking sheet. Preheat the oven:
Top/bottom heat:
about 180 °C/350 °F (Gas mark 4)
Fan oven:
about 160 °C/325 °F (Gas mark 3)

2 Whisk the margarine or butter in a mixing bowl using a hand-mixer with whisk attachment until soft. Gradually whisk in the sugar and lemon rind until you have a smooth, even mixture. Add each egg, whisking for about ½ minute on the highest setting.

3 Mix the flour, cornflour (cornstarch) and baking powder and whisk in briefly in two instalments on the medium setting. Spread the sponge mixture on the baking sheet (photographs 1 and 2). Fold a length of aluminium foil several times into a long, narrow strip and place it round the mixture. Put the baking sheet on the middle shelf of the preheated oven. **Bake for about 25 minutes**.

4 For the icing, sift the icing (confectioners') sugar and stir in enough lemon juice to make a thick glaze. Place the baking sheet on a cake rack and pour the icing on the cake while it is still hot (photograph 3): the hotter the cake the better the glaze will be absorbed. Leave on the baking sheet to cool on the cake rack.

TIPS ›› You can also put a pastry frame the same size of the baking sheet on the baking sheet and

spread the sponge mixture in it.
›› Or bake the cake in a roasting tin, then you will not need any aluminium foil.

Recipe variation: For a drenched orange cake (small photograph left), grease and flour a rectangular cake tin (25 x 11 cm/10 x 4½ in). Prepare the sponge mixture as indicated in the recipe with 250 g/9 oz (1¼ cups) soft margarine or butter, 200 g/7 oz (1 cup) sugar, 1 packet vanilla sugar, 1 teaspoon each grated orange zest and lemon zest, 1 pinch of salt, 4 eggs (medium), 250 g/9 oz (2½ cups) plain (all purpose) flour, 30 g/1 oz (3 tablespoons) cornflour (cornstarch) and 2 level teaspoons baking powder. Transfer the sponge mixture into the cake tin and put on a shelf in the bottom third of the oven. After about 15 minutes, take the cake out of the oven and make a lengthways incision about 1 cm/⅜ in deep in the middle of the cake, using a sharp knife. Put the cake back in the oven and bake for another 40 minutes. Leave in the tin for about 10 minutes, then turn out onto a cake rack, turn it over again and make several holes with a wooden skewer. For the soaking, pass 125 ml/4 fl oz (½ cup) orange juice with 2 tablespoons lemon juice through a sieve, stir in 30 g/1 oz (3 tablespoons) sugar and coat the cake while it is still hot with this mixture, using a pastry brush. Leave the cake to cool on a cake rack, then sprinkle with a little icing sugar.

Per slice: P: 3 g, F: 17 g, C: 46 g, kJ: 1458, kcal: 349, CU: 4.0

Layered cake
(Grilled cake)

WITH ALCOHOL (ABOUT 6 SECTIONS)

Preparation and baking time:
about 80 minutes

For the baking sheet:
baking parchment
square cake frame

For the sponge:
8 egg whites (medium)
400 g/14 oz (2 cups) soft
margarine or butter
400 g/14 oz (2 cups) sugar
2 sachets vanilla sugar
1 pinch salt
2 eggs (medium)
8 egg yolks (medium)
100 ml/3½ fl oz (½ cup) rum
250 g/9 oz (2½ cups) plain
(all purpose) flour
150 g/5 oz (1⅛ cups) cornflour
(cornstarch)
4 level teaspoons baking
powder

For the icing:
400 g/14 oz dark chocolate
3 tablespoons cooking oil,
e.g. sunflower oil

Per section:
P: 21 g, F: 93 g, C: 150 g,
kJ: 6547, kcal: 1564, CU: 12.5

1 Line a baking sheet with baking parchment and place a pastry frame (about 25 x 28 cm/10 x 11 in) on it. Then preheat the oven grill.

2 For the sponge mixture, beat the egg whites stiff. Whisk the margarine or butter in a mixing bowl using a hand-mixer with whisk attachment until soft. Add the sugar, vanilla sugar and salt little by little, whisking all the time until you have a smooth mixture. Whisk in the eggs, one after the other, for about ½ minute each on the highest setting. Now gradually stir in the egg yolks and rum. Mix together the flour, cornflour (cornstarch) and baking powder, then whisk briefly in two instalments on the medium setting. Carefully fold the beaten egg white into the sponge mixture.

3 Take 3 tablespoons of the sponge mixture and spread evenly on the baking sheet, using a wide pastry brush (photograph 1) or cake slice. Put the baking sheet in the oven so that the distance between the grill and layer of sponge is about 20 cm/ 8 in). Bake the sponge under the preheated grill for about 2 minutes (photograph 2).

4 Take the baking sheet out of the oven. Take another 3 tablespoons of the sponge mixture and spread it on top of the already cooked layer. Replace the baking sheet under the grill and bake for about 2 minutes. Repeat this process until all the sponge has been used up. If possible, move the shelf so that the

distance between the grill and the layer of sponge is kept at 20 cm/8 in.

5 After you have completed the baking, loosen the pastry frame with a knife, then remove completely. Remove the cake together with the baking parchment and place on a cake rack to cool. Then cut the cake into 6 rectangular pieces about 4 cm/1½ in wide.

6 For the chocolate icing, cut the chocolate into pieces, melt together with the oil in a bain-marie over low heat and coat the baked pieces with it (photograph 3). Leave the icing to set.

TIPS » Heat the grill to a temperature of about 260 °C/500 °F, being sure to follow the instructions of the oven manufacturer.
» Store the cake sections in aluminium foil to ensure that they remain moist; they can also be frozen.

Recipe variation: To make a layered cake in a cake tin (25 x 11 cm/ 10 x 4½ in), grease the tin and line with baking parchment. Prepare half the amount indicated in the recipe. Bake the cake in layers as described in the recipe but only use 1-2 tablespoons of sponge mixture per layer. Carefully loosen the finished cake from the sides of the tin using a sharp knife, turn out onto a cake rack, remove the baking parchment and leave the cake to cool.
To make the glaze, melt 150 g/5 oz plain chocolate with 3 teaspoons cooking oil as described in the recipe and pour over the cake.

Fried egg cakes

FOR CHILDREN (ABOUT 20 PIECES)

Preparation time:
about 30 minutes,
excluding cooling time
Baking time: about 35 minutes

For the baking sheet
(40 x 30 cm/16 x 12 in):
a little fat, baking frame

For the topping:
80 g/3 oz (½ cup) vanilla-
flavoured custard powder
80 g/3 oz (⅓ cup) sugar
750 ml/1¼ pints (3 cups) milk
1 can apricot halves
(drained weight 480 g/17 oz)
2 large containers
(250 g/9 oz each) crème fraîche

For the sponge mixture:
150 g/5 oz (⅔ cup) soft
margarine or butter
150 g/5 oz (¾ cup) sugar
1 sachet vanilla sugar
1 pinch salt
3 eggs (medium)
300 g/12 oz (2½ cups) plain (all
purpose) flour
2 level teaspoons baking powder
2 tablespoons milk

For the glaze:
500 ml/17 fl oz (2 cups)
apricot juice (from the can)
2 sachets clear cake glaze
50 g/2 oz (¼ cup) sugar

Per piece: P: 5 g, F: 16 g, C: 37 g,
kJ: 1352, kcal: 324, CU: 3,0

1 For the topping, make a custard with the custard powder, sugar and milk, following the instructions on the packet but using only 750 ml/ 1¼ pints (3 cups) milk. Leave the custard to cool a little, stirring occasionally. Grease the baking sheet and place a baking frame the same size as the baking sheet on top of it. Preheat the oven:
Top/bottom heat:
about 180 °C/350 °F (Gas mark 4)
Fan oven:
about 160 °C/325 °F (Gas mark 3)

2 Drain the apricots thoroughly in a sieve and reserve the juice. Stir the crème fraîche into the cooled custard.

3 For the sponge mixture, whisk the margarine or butter in a mixing bowl until soft, using a hand-held mixer on the highest setting. Add the sugar, vanilla sugar and salt little by little, whisking all the time until you obtain a smooth mixture.

4 Whisk in each egg for about ½ minute on the highest setting. Mix the flour and the baking powder together and in two stages whisk it and the milk into the mixture briefly on a medium setting. Spread the sponge mixture on the baking sheet.

5 Now spread the custard on the sponge mixture. Arrange the apricot halves evenly with the curved side upward, leaving a little space between each one. Then put the baking sheet on the middle shelf of the preheated oven. **Bake for about 35 minutes**.

6 Place the cake on the baking sheet on a cake rack and leave to cool.

7 To make the glaze, add water to the apricot juice to make it up to 500 ml/ 17 fl oz (2 cups). Prepare the cake glaze with sugar and juice, following the instructions on the sachet. Spread the glaze quickly over the topping and leave to set.

8 Carefully loosen the baking frame with a knife and then remove it.

VARIATION: For a low-fat cake: you can replace the crème fraîche with 250 g/9 oz low-fat quark and 250 g/9 oz yoghurt (3.5 % fat).

RECIPE VARIATION: **Apricot cake on a baking sheet (front cover recipe)**
Drain a tin of apricot halves (drained weight 480 g/19 oz) in a sieve. Prepare a sponge mixture as indicated in the recipe. Place the baking frame on the greased baking sheet and spread the sponge mixture inside it. Arrange the apricot halves on the sponge mixture with the curved side upward. Sprinkle 50 g/ 2 oz (scant ½ cup) slivered almonds on the sponge mixture. Bake the cake as indicated in the recipe for about 30 minutes, then immediately spread 50 g/ 2 oz (¼ cup) sieved apricot jam over the apricots. Loosen and remove the baking frame. Leave the cake to cool, then sprinkle icing (confectioners') sugar on top.

1

2

3

Donauwellen (Danube Waves cake)

TRADITIONAL (ABOUT 20 SLICES)

Preparation time:
about 45 minutes,
excluding cooling time
Baking time: about 40 minutes

**For the baking sheet (40 x 30 cm/
16 x 12 in) with high sides:**
a little fat, aluminium foil

For the sponge:
2 jars morello cherries (drained
weight 350 g/12 oz each)
250 g/9 oz (1¼ cups) soft
margarine or butter
200 g/7 oz (1 cup) sugar
1 sachet vanilla sugar
1 pinch salt
5 eggs (medium)
375 g/13 oz (3¾ cups) plain
(all purpose) flour
3 level teaspoons baking
powder
20 g/¾ oz (3½ tablespoons)
cocoa powder
1 tablespoon milk

For the butter cream:
40 g/1½ oz (5 tablespoons)
custard powder (vanilla
pudding mix)
100 g/3½ oz (½ cup) sugar
500 ml/17 fl oz (2¼ cups) milk
250 g/9 oz (1¼ cups) soft butter

For the icing:
200 g/7 oz dark chocolate
2 tablespoons cooking oil,
e.g. sunflower oil

Per slice:
P: 6 g, F: 28 g, C: 43 g,
kJ: 1898, kcal: 453, CU: 3.5

1 Grease the baking sheet. Preheat the oven:
Top/bottom heat:
about 180 °C/350 °F (Gas mark 4)
Fan oven:
about 160 °C/325 °F (Gas mark 3)

2 To make the sponge, drain the cherries thoroughly in a sieve. Whisk the margarine or butter in a mixing bowl using a hand-mixer with whisk attachment until soft. Add the sugar, vanilla sugar and salt little by little, whisking all the time until you obtain a smooth mixture. Whisk in the eggs, one after the other, for about ½ minute each on the highest setting.

3 Mix together the flour and baking powder and then whisk briefly in two instalments on the medium setting. Spread two-thirds of the sponge mixture on the baking sheet. Sift the cocoa powder and stir together with the milk into the rest of the sponge mixture, then spread over the light-coloured sponge mixture.

4 Place the drained cherries briefly on kitchen paper, then arrange the cherries over the chocolate sponge mixture and press lightly into the sponge with a spoon (photograph 1). Put the baking sheet on a shelf in the bottom third of the preheated oven. **Bake for about 40 minutes.**

5 Put the cake together with the baking sheet on a cake rack and leave to cool.

6 To make the butter cream, make a custard with the custard powder, 100 g/3½ oz (½ cup) sugar and milk, following the instructions on the packet. Leave the custard to cool but do not refrigerate, stirring occasionally.

7 Whisk the softened butter with a hand-mixer until smooth. Add the cooled custard to the butter, spoonful by spoonful. Be sure that the butter and custard are both room-temperature or the butter cream may curdle. Spread the butter cream evenly over the cooled cake (photograph 2). Now put the cake in the refrigerator for about 1 hour.

8 To make the chocolate icing, break the chocolate into pieces and melt with the oil in a bain-marie over low heat. Spread the chocolate icing over the set butter cream and decorate with a pastry comb (photograph 3).

TIPS » Put clingfilm (plastic wrap) directly on the top of the custard before leaving it to cool. This will prevent a skin from forming. Do not stir the custard any more.
» The cake is suitable for freezing.
» If you do not have a baking sheet with a high rim, you can use a pastry frame the same size as the baking sheet on a normal baking sheet and prepare the cake as instructed in the recipe.

Sophisticated chocolate slices

WITH ALCOHOL (ABOUT 20 SLICES)

Preparation time:
about 30 minutes,
excluding cooling time
Baking time: about 30 minutes

For the baking sheet
(40 x 30 cm/16 x 12 in):
a little fat

For the sponge:
300 g/10 oz dark chocolate
250 g/9 oz (1¼ cups)
margarine or butter
250 g/9 oz (1¼ cups) brown
sugar
1 sachet Bourbon vanilla
sugar
1 pinch salt
6 eggs (medium)
1 container (150 g/5 oz) crème
fraîche
300 g/10 oz (3 cups) plain (all
purpose) flour
50 g/2 oz (⅓ cup) cornflour
(cornstarch)
30 g/1 oz (5 tablespoons) cocoa
powder
3 level teaspoons baking
powder
100 ml/3½ fl oz (½ cup) rum

For sprinkling:
50 g/2 oz (scant ½ cup)
slivered almonds

For the icing:
200 g/7 oz dark chocolate
1–2 tablespoons cooking oil,
e.g. sunflower oil

1 Grease the baking sheet. Preheat the oven:

Top/bottom heat:
about 180 °C/350 °F (Gas mark 4)
Fan oven:
about 160 °C/325 °F (Gas mark 3)

2 To make the sponge, break the chocolate into pieces and melt with margarine or butter in a small pan, stirring all the time. Transfer this chocolate mixture into a mixing bowl and leave to cool a little. Add the sugar, vanilla sugar and salt little by little, whisking all the time until you obtain a smooth even mixture.

3 Whisk in the eggs, one after the other, for about ½ minute each on the highest setting. Stir in the crème fraîche. Mix together the flour, cornflour (cornstarch), cocoa powder and baking powder; add the rum and whisk briefly in two instalments on the medium setting.

4 Spread the sponge mixture on the baking sheet and smooth flat. Fold a piece of aluminium foil several times into a long strip and place it round the baking sheet. Put the baking sheet on the middle shelf in the preheated oven. **After baking for about 10 minutes** sprinkle the

almonds on the cake, put the cake back in the oven and **bake for a further 20 minutes**.

5 Put the cake together with the baking sheet on a cake rack and leave to cool.

6 To make the chocolate icing, break the chocolate into pieces and melt together with the cooking oil in a bain-marie over low heat, stirring all the time. Pour the icing over the cake and leave to set.

TIPS » Make an even more sophisticated icing by adding 1 tablespoon of orange zest to the chocolate.
» You place the folded strip of aluminium foil on the sloping sides of the baking sheet to prevent the sponge mixture "running away" which would make the sides of the cake uneven.

INGREDIENTS TIPS » Mixing cornflour (cornstarch) with the flour before baking makes the cake moister and lighter with a beautiful crumb.
» Rum is a spirit drink made from cane sugar which diffuses a delicate aroma during the baking process and at the same time acts as a baking agent.

Per slice: P: 6 g, F: 26 g, C: 37 g, kJ: 1751, kcal: 418, CU: 3.0

Rhubarb slices with crème fraîche topping

FRUITY (ABOUT 20 SLICES)

Preparation time:
about 40 minutes
Baking time: about 45 minutes

For the baking sheet
(40 x 30 cm/16 x 12 in):
a little fat
plain (all purpose) flour
square cake frame

For the filling:
750 g/1½ lb rhubarb

For the sponge:
250 g/9 oz (1¼ cups) soft
margarine or butter
250 g/9 oz (1¼ cups) sugar
1 sachet vanilla sugar
a few drops Dr. Oetker Natural
Vanilla Extract
4 eggs (medium)
250 g/9 oz (2½ cups) plain
(all purpose) flour
2 level teaspoons baking
powder

For the glaze:
80 g/3 oz (⅔ cup) custard
powder (vanilla pudding mix)
80 g/3 oz (⅜ cup) sugar
700 ml/24 fl oz (3 cups) milk
3 containers (150 g/5 oz each)
crème fraîche

Per slice:
P: 5 g, F: 20 g, C: 32 g,
kJ: 1395, kcal: 334, CU: 2.5

1 To make the rhubarb filling, wash but do not peel the rhubarb, leave to drain and cut into pieces about 2 cm/¾ in long.

2 Grease and flour the baking sheet, then place a pastry frame the same size as the baking sheet itself on top of it. Preheat the oven:
Top/bottom heat:
about 180 °C/350 °F (Gas mark 4)
Fan oven:
about 160 °C/325 °F (Gas mark 3)

3 To make the sponge, whisk the margarine or butter in a mixing bowl using a hand-mixer with whisk attachment until soft. Add the sugar, vanilla sugar and vanilla extract little by little, whisking all the time until you obtain a smooth mixture.

4 Whisk in the eggs, one after the other, for about ½ minute each on the highest setting. Mix together the flour and baking powder and whisk briefly in two instalments on the medium setting. Spread the sponge mixture on the baking sheet and smooth flat.

5 Distribute the pieces of rhubarb evenly across the sponge mixture. Put the baking sheet on the middle shelf in the preheated oven and **bake for about 30 minutes**.

6 To make glazed topping, first make a custard by mixing together the custard powder, sugar and milk, following the instructions on the packet but using only 700 ml/ 24 fl oz (3 cups) milk. Stir the crème fraîche into the custard while it is still hot and spread the mixture on the baked cake (photograph 1). Put the cake back into the oven and **bake for another 15 minutes**.

7 Put the cake together with the baking sheet on a cake rack and leave to cool.

8 Finally loosen and remove the pastry frame.

TIPS »To prevent it falling apart while baking, the rhubarb is not peeled.
» You can replace the crème fraîche by sour cream.

SERVING TIP » This is delicious served with whipped cream.

Variation: You can use 600 g/ 1¼ lb gooseberries instead of the rhubarb (photograph 2).

All-in-one sponge

» This kind of sponge is ideal for the baking novice. It is quick to make and uses the same ingredients as a sponge cake mixture. The only difference is that all the ingredients are mixed together at the same time instead of one after the other.

» All the ingredients are whisked together with a hand-mixer, first briefly on a low setting, then for 1–2 minutes on the highest setting until you have obtained a smooth, even mixture.

» Admittedly this kind of sponge has a less fluffy consistency than a sponge cake mixture but it is very suitable for cakes without heavy ingredients.

» The methods of preparing, baking and storing all-in-one sponge mixture are the same as those given in the Sponge Mixture Information section (pp. 8–9).

Fruit pie with strawberries

QUICK (ABOUT 12 PIECES)

Preparation time: about 30 minutes, excluding cooling time
Baking time: about 15 minutes

For the pie tin (diameter 28 cm/ 11 in) or springform mould (diameter 26 cm/10¼ in):
a little fat or baking parchment

For the all-in-one sponge:
125 g/4½ oz (1¼ cups) plain (all purpose) flour
2½ level teaspoons baking powder
100 g/3½ oz (½ cup) sugar
1 sachet vanilla sugar
4 eggs (medium)
3 tablespoons cooking oil
2 tablespoons vinegar, e.g. fruit vinegar

For the vanilla cream:
80 g/3 oz (½ cup) vanilla-flavoured custard powder
250 ml/8 fl oz (1 cup) milk
20 g/¾ oz (2 tablespoons) sugar

For the filling:
1 kg/2¼ lb strawberries
a little sugar if necessary

1 Grease the bottom of the pie tin or springform mould and line with baking parchment. Preheat the oven:
Top/bottom heat:
about 180 °C/350 °F (Gas mark 4)
Fan oven:
about 160 °C/325 °F (Gas mark 3)

2 To make the sponge, mix together the flour and baking powder in a mixing bowl. Add all the rest of the ingredients one after the other and whisk with a hand-mixer with whisk attachment, first briefly on the lowest setting, then on the highest setting for 1 minute until you have a smooth, even mixture.

3 Put the sponge mixture in the pie tin or springform mould and smooth flat. Put the tin or springform mould on a shelf in the bottom third of the preheated oven. **Bake for about 15 minutes.**

4 Turn out onto a cake rack lined with baking parchment and leave to cool.

5 To make the vanilla-flavoured crème pâtissière, make a custard with vanilla-flavoured custard powder using 250 ml/8 fl oz (1 cup) milk and 20 g/¾ oz (2 tablespoons) sugar, following the instructions on the packet. Leave to cool, stirring occasionally, then pour over the base (photograph 1).

6 For the topping, wash the strawberries, drain thoroughly, remove the stalks and cut the larger ones in half. Sprinkle the strawberries with sugar, leave to stand briefly and then arrange on the base (photograph 2).

7 Make the glaze with glaze powder, sugar and water, following the instructions on the packet. Then spoon over the strawberries (photograph 3). Leave the glaze to set and refrigerate until ready to serve.

TIPS » If you are using metal pie tins, you must grease and flour them first.

» You can also use 6 tartlet moulds (diameter 12 cm/4¾ in) and garnish with strawberries as indicated in the recipe.

» You can use different fresh fruits (such as bananas or grapes) or well-drained tinned fruit (such as peaches or pineapple; drained weight 500 g/18 oz). In this case prepare the glaze using the juice from the tin.

For the glaze:
1 sachet red cake glaze
2 tablespoons sugar
250 ml/8 fl oz (1 cup) water

Per piece:
P: 5 g, F: 6 g, C: 28 g,
kJ: 795, kcal: 190, CU: 2.5

Quick plum cake

FRUITY – SEASONAL (ABOUT 12 PIECES)

Preparation time:
about 35 minutes
Baking time: about 50 minutes

For the springform mould
(diameter 26 cm/10¼ in):
a little fat

For the topping:
800 g/1¾ lb plums

For the all-in-one sponge:
125 g/4½ oz (1¼ cups) plain
(all purpose) flour
1 level teaspoon baking
powder
125 g/4½ oz (⅝ cup) sugar
1 sachet vanilla sugar
1 teaspoon grated lemon zest
125 g/4½ oz (⅝ cup) soft
butter or margarine
2 eggs (medium)

For the crumble:
150 g/5 oz (1½ cups) plain
(all purpose) flour
100 g/3½ oz (½ cup) sugar
1 pinch ground cinnamon
100 g/3½ oz (½ cup) soft
butter

Per piece:
P: 4 g, F: 17 g, C: 41 g,
kJ: 1424, kcal: 341, CU: 3.5

1 To make the topping, wash the plums, pat dry, remove the stones and cut into slices or halves. Grease the bottom of the springform mould. Preheat the oven:
Top/bottom heat:
about 180 °C/350 °F (Gas mark 4)
Fan oven:
about 160 °C/325 °F (Gas mark 3)

2 To make the sponge mixture, mix together the flour and the baking powder in a mixing bowl. Add all the other ingredients, then mix using a hand-mixer with whisk attachment, first briefly on the lowest setting, then on the highest setting for about 2 minutes until the mixture is smooth and even.

3 Put the sponge mixture in the springform mould and smooth flat. Arrange the plums evenly on the sponge mixture (photograph 1).

4 To make the crumble, mix together the flour, sugar and cinnamon in a mixing bowl, than add the softened butter. Work into a crumble of the right texture using a hand-mixer with whisk attachment (photograph 2). Spread the crumble over the plums (photograph 3) and put

the plum cake on the middle shelf in the preheated oven. **Bake for about 50 minutes.**

5 Remove the cake from the springform mould and leave to cool on a cake rack.

Variations: You can also make this cake with apples. To do this, peel 800 g/1¾ lb apples such as Elstar or Jonagold, cut into quarters, remove the core and cut into slices. Alternatively you can make this cake with 1 tin drained peach slices (drained weight 500 g/18 oz). When arranging the peach slices on the sponge, leave about 1 cm/ ⅜ in free round the edge.

TIP » If you use a baking sheet (40 x 30 cm/16 x 12 in) instead of a springform mould, double all the quantities.

Buttermilk cake

QUICK (ABOUT 20 SLICES)

Preparation time:
about 20 minutes
Baking time: about 25 minutes

For the baking sheet
(40 x 30 cm/16 x 12 in):
a little fat

For the all-in-one sponge:
300 g/10 oz (3 cups) plain (all
purpose) flour
1 sachet baking powder
300 g/10 oz (1½ cups) sugar
1 sachet vanilla sugar
3 eggs (medium)
300 ml/10 fl oz (1¼ cups)
buttermilk

For the topping:
150 g/5 oz (¾ cup) butter
150 g/5 oz (¾ cup) sugar
200 g/7 oz (1⅔ cups)
slivered almonds
or chopped hazelnuts
or grated coconut

Per slice:
P: 4 g, F: 14 g, C: 35 g,
kJ: 1177, kcal: 281, CU: 3.0

1 Grease the baking sheet. Preheat the oven:
Top/bottom heat:
about 180 °C/350 °F (Gas mark 4)
Fan oven:
about 160 °C/325 °F (Gas mark 3)

2 To make the sponge mixture, mix together the flour and baking powder in a mixing bowl. Add all the other ingredients and mix everything with a hand-mixer with whisk attachment, first briefly on the lowest setting, then on the highest setting for about 2 minutes until you obtain a smooth, homogeneous mixture.

3 Spread the sponge mixture on the baking sheet and smooth flat. Put the baking sheet on the middle shelf in the preheated oven and **blind-bake for about 10 minutes.**

4 To make the topping, melt the butter with the sugar in a pan. Stir in the almonds, hazelnuts or coconut (photograph 1). Now pour this mixture onto the blind-baked sponge and spread it evenly over it (photograph 2). Put the baking sheet back in the preheated oven and **bake for another 15 minutes.**

5 Put the cake together with the baking sheet on a cake rack and leave to cool.

TIP » You can use whipping cream instead of buttermilk.

Recipe variation: To make a mandarin orange-buttermilk cake (photograph 3), thoroughly drain a 1 large tin of mandarin oranges (drained weight 480 g/19 oz) in a sieve. Make only half the amount of topping and then spread the mandarins and topping on the blind-baked sponge. Bake the cake for another 15 minutes as indicated in the recipe.

PROBLEM
» To prevent the mixing bowl from sliding about: if the mixing bowl does not have a rubber ring on its base, put a damp cloth under the bowl while mixing the ingredients. This will keep the mixing bowl steady.

Chocolate and cherry pound cake

POPULAR (ABOUT 16 SLICES)

Preparation time:
about 25 minutes,
excluding cooling time
Baking time: about 70 minutes

**For the Bundt pan or kugelhopf
mould (diameter 22 cm/9 in):**
a little fat, flour

For the all-in-one sponge:
1 jar morello cherries
(drained weight 350 g/12 oz)
200 g/7 oz (2 cups) plain
(all purpose) flour
80 g/3 oz (1 cup) custard
powder (chocolate pudding
mix)
1 sachet baking powder
125 g/4½ oz (⅝ cup) sugar
1 sachet Bourbon vanilla
sugar
5 eggs (medium)
150 ml/5 fl oz (⅝ cup) cooking
oil, e.g. sunflower oil
125 ml/4 fl oz (½ cup)
buttermilk
100 g/3½ oz (¾ cup) grated
chocolate

For the glaze:
100 g/3½ oz full milk or dark
chocolate
1 teaspoon cooking oil,
e.g. sunflower oil

Per slice:
P: 4 g, F: 13 g, C: 26 g,
kJ: 983, kcal: 235, CU: 2.0

1 Grease and flour the Bundt pan or kugelhopf mould. Preheat the oven:
Top/bottom heat:
about 180 °C/350 °F (Gas mark 4)
Fan oven:
about 160 °C/325 °F (Gas mark 3)

2 To make the sponge mixture, thoroughly drain the morello cherries in a sieve (photograph 1). Mix together the flour, custard powder and baking powder in a mixing bowl. Add the sugar, vanilla sugar, eggs, cooking oil and buttermilk, then whisk all the ingredients with a hand-mixer with whisk attachment, first briefly on the lowest setting, then on the highest setting for 2 minutes until you have obtained a smooth, homogeneous mixture.

3 Carefully fold in the chocolate flakes and morello cherries (photograph 2). Now put the sponge mixture in the greased and floured Bundt pan or kugelhopf mould. Put on the shelf in the bottom third in the preheated oven. **Bake for about 70 minutes.**

4 Leave the cake to rest in the mould for about 10 minutes, then remove it and put on a cake rack to cool.

5 To make the glaze, break the chocolate into pieces and melt with the cooking oil in bain-marie over low heat, stirring all the time. Pour over the cake in such a way that it runs in long "drips" (photograph 3). Leave the glaze to set.

TIPS » You can replace the chocolate glaze with one made with 2 tablespoons cherry juice and 150 g/5 oz (1¼ cups) icing (confectioners') sugar.
» Sprinkle the cake with icing sugar before serving.

Egg liqueur cake

GOOD TO MAKE AHEAD – WITH ALCOHOL (ABOUT 16 SLICES)

Preparation time:
about 20 minutes
Baking time: about 60 minutes

For the Bundt pan or kugelhopf mould (diameter 22 cm/9 in):
a little fat, flour

For the all-in-one sponge:
125 g/4½ oz (1¼ cups) plain (all purpose) flour
125 g/1 oz (3 tablespoons) cornflour (cornstarch)
4 level teaspoons baking powder
250 g/9 oz (2 cups) icing (confectioners') sugar
2 sachets vanilla sugar
250 ml/8 fl oz (1 cup) cooking oil, e.g. sunflower oil
250 ml/8 fl oz (1 cup) egg liqueur
5 eggs (medium)

For dusting:
a little icing (confectioners') sugar

Per slice:
P: 4 g, F: 19 g, C: 35 g,
kJ: 1418, kcal: 339, CU: 3.0

1 Grease and flour the Bundt pan or kugelhopf mould. Preheat the oven:
Top/bottom heat:
about 180 °C/350 °F (Gas mark 4)
Fan oven:
about 160 °C/325 °F (Gas mark 3)

2 To make the sponge mixture, mix together the flour, cornflour (cornstarch) and baking powder in a mixing bowl. Add all the other ingredients and mix with a hand-mixer with whisk attachment on the highest setting for at least 1 minute until foamy. From time to time use a silicone spatula to push the sponge mixture off the sides of the bowl to the middle.

3 Put the sponge mixture in the greased and floured Bundt pan or kugelhopf mould. Put the mould on a shelf in the bottom third of the preheated oven. **Bake for about 60 minutes**.

4 Leave the cake to stand in the mould for about 10 minutes, then remove it, place it on a cake rack and leave to cool. Sprinkle icing (confectioners') sugar on top.

Recipe variation: To make egg liqueur waffles, make a batter as indicated in the recipe with 100 g/ 3½ oz (¾ cup) icing (confectioners') sugar, 2 eggs (medium), 1 packet vanilla sugar, 100 ml/3½ fl oz (½ cup) cooking oil, 100 ml/3½ fl oz (½ cup) egg liqueur, 50 g/2 oz (½ cup) plain (all purpose) flour, 1½ level teaspoons baking powder and 50 g/ 2 oz (½ cup) cornflour (cornstarch). Then for each waffle put 2 tablespoons of the mixture in a greased, hot waffle iron. Cook the waffles until golden yellow and leave to cool next to each other on a cake rack. Sprinkle with icing sugar before serving.

Potato waffles

SAVOURY (ABOUT 10 PIECES) – FRONT OF PHOTOGRAPH

Preparation time:
about 45 minutes

For the waffle iron:
cooking oil

For the all-in-one sponge:
125 g/4½ oz (⅝ cup) butter or
margarine
100 g/3½ oz (1 cup) plain
(all purpose) flour
1 level teaspoon baking powder
1–2 level teaspoons salt
400 ml/14 fl oz (1¾ cups) milk
4 eggs (medium)
instant potato powder for
500 ml/17 fl oz (2¼ cups) liquid
freshly ground pepper
freshly grated nutmeg
250 g/9 oz meat-based salad

Per piece:
P: 7 g, F: 24 g, C: 15 g,
kJ: 1270, kcal: 305, CU: 1.0

1 To make the batter, melt the butter or margarine and leave to cool a little. Preheat the waffle iron to the highest setting. (Be sure to follow the maker's instructions.)

2 Mix together the baking powder and flour in a mixing bowl. Add the salt, milk, eggs and slightly cooled butter or margarine. Mix together all the ingredients with a hand-mixer (whisk attachment), first on the lowest setting, then on the highest setting for about 2 minutes until the mixture is smooth and even.

3 Whisk in the potato puree powder briefly. Season the mixture with pepper and nutmeg.

4 Reduce the temperature of the waffle iron to the medium setting and grease the waffle iron with a pastry brush.

5 For each waffle, put 2 heaped tablespoons of batter in the waffle iron. If necessary spread it out a little and cook until golden brown.

6 Keep the cooked waffles warm on a baking sheet in the oven (top/bottom heat: about 80 °C/ 180 °F).

7 Serve the waffles warm as a snack or lukewarm with a meat-based salad.

TIPS » Potato waffles are delicious served with herb quark or crème fraîche and strips of ham or smoked salmon.
» You can also make the potato waffles in advance and warm them up again in the toaster.

Spicy bacon waffles

GREAT SNACK (ABOUT 14 PIECES) – BACK OF PHOTOGRAPH

Preparation time:
about 55 minutes,
excluding standing time

For the waffle iron:
cooking oil,
e.g. sunflower oil

For the all-in-one sponge:
200 g/7 oz thinly sliced
streaky bacon
1 onion (about 100 g/3½ oz)

1 To make the batter mixture, cut the bacon into small cubes. Peel and finely chop the onion. Rinse the parsley and marjoram, then pat dry. Strip the leaves off the stems and chop them coarsely.

2 Fry the diced bacon in a pan while stirring, add the chopped onion and fry with the bacon. Leave the bacon-onion mixture to cool a little.

3 Put the flour in a mixing bowl. Add the eggs and milk. Then whisk the ingredients with a hand-mixer (whisk attachment) for 2 minutes until you have obtained a smooth, even mixture.

4 Whisk the bacon-onion mixture briefly into the batter. Add the chopped parsley and marjoram. Season the batter with salt and pepper and leave to stand for about 10 minutes.

5 Preheat the waffle iron to the highest setting. (Be sure to follow the maker's instructions.)

6 Reduce the temperature to medium and grease the waffle iron. For each waffle put 2 heaped tablespoons of batter mixture in the waffle iron and cook until golden brown.

7 Use a fork or spatula to take the waffles out of the waffle iron. Put them next to each other on a cake rack and serve immediately while they are hot.

SERVING TIP:
» Serve the bacon waffles with herb yoghurt and red onion rings.

1 bunch each parsley, marjoram
300 g/10 oz (3 cups) rye flour
4 eggs (medium)
800 ml/28 fl oz (3½ cups) milk
salt, pepper

Per piece:
P: 8 g, F: 5 g, C: 17 g,
kJ: 652, kcal: 156, CU: 1.5

Shortcrust pastry

Shortcrust pastry refers to a type of pastry in which all the ingredients are kneaded together to form a dough which is then rolled out. It is suitable, for instance, for making biscuits and fancy cakes. It is also ideal for cutting out shapes because it makes no crumbs and becomes crisp after baking. It is made with flour, sugar, fat and sometimes eggs.

How to make shortcrust pastry

Step 1: Prepare the tin or the baking sheet
Grease the tin or baking sheet generously all over with soft margarine or butter. In the case of biscuits which are to be cut out and then baked on a baking sheet lined with baking parchment, there is no need to grease the baking sheet. If you have only one baking sheet and you have several batches of biscuits to bake one after the other, prepare sheets of baking parchment the same size as the baking sheet and put the biscuits on it; then slide the baking parchment with the biscuits on it onto the baking sheet along its flat side so that the biscuits do not slip (photograph 1).

Step 2: Prepare the ingredients and knead into a dough
Take the fat (margarine or butter) you will be using to make the dough out of the refrigerator well in advance so that it will be soft enough to work with. This will make it easier to knead the dough. When you have set out all the ingredients, first put the flour in a mixing bowl and mix in the baking powder, cocoa powder and so on, depending on the recipe. Then add the other ingredients: the sugar, the butter or margarine and the eggs, if there are any.

Note: Not all shortcrust pastry contains eggs. Mix the ingredients with a hand-mixer with kneading hook, first briefly on the lowest setting, then on the highest setting until the mixture has the right consistency. Then shape the pastry mixture into a ball (photograph 2, if you are using a springform mould) or a roll (if you are using a baking sheet or making biscuits). This will make it easier to roll out. If the pastry feels sticky, wrap it in clingfilm (plastic film) and put in the refrigerator for about 30 minutes.

Step 3: Rolling out the dough
First remove all the bits of dough from the work surface and sprinkle it lightly with flour. It is important to sprinkle as little flour as possible because too much will make the pastry crumbly, which means that the pastry would become hard when baked.
Only knead the refrigerated dough very briefly with your hands, to prevent it from becoming glutinous. When rolling out the pastry, the rolling pin must turn and move lightly across the pastry – do not press it too hard. To make sure the pastry does not stick to the work surface, slide a large knife or a spatula under it (photograph 3). If the pastry sticks while you are rolling it out, wrap it again in clingfilm (plastic wrap) and put back in the refrigerator. This will make the fat in the pastry go hard again and the pastry will no longer stick.

As an alternative to a floured work surface, you can roll out the dough between two layers of plastic wrap or a freezer bag with the sides cut open.

» Transferring thin sheets of pastry onto the baking sheet

Thin sheets of pastry are easier to transfer onto a baking sheet if you first wrap it very carefully round the lightly-floured rolling pin and then unroll it again on the baking sheet (photograph 4). You can also cut the sheet of pastry in half and transfer it in two pieces onto the baking sheet.

» Rolling out pastry for springform moulds of fruit pie tins

When making fruit pies you can bake the pastry either in a spring-form mould or in a fruit pie tin. If you are using a spring-mould, roll two-thirds of the pastry onto the greased base of the springform mould. Knead the rest of the pastry with a tablespoon of flour so that it will hold together better. Shape it into a long, thin sausage and place it as an edge all round the pastry base; then use your fingers to press against the side of the springform mould, making a pastry edge 3 cm/ 1¼ in high (photograph 5). Prick the base several times with a fork to prevent it forming air bubbles.

Step 4: Blind-baking the base

A pastry case which has been baked blind will remain crisp and will not become soggy, even if it has a juicy filling.

To blind-bake, roll out the required amount of pastry on the greased springform mould base. Prick the base several times with a fork to prevent air bubbles from forming, replace the side of the springform mould and blind-bake. Only then should you add the pastry edge as described above – this time you do not need to knead more flour into the pastry.

Pastry for tarts which will have a cold filling (cream, fruit) must be blind-baked: put the rolled out pastry in the prepared springform mould and prick it several times with a fork. Cover the pastry base with baking parchment, cut to size, and fill the mould with dried peas or beans. Now you can blind-bake the pastry – the base remains flat and the edge is supported so that it cannot collapse.

Step 5: Baking the shortcrust pastry

Bake the shortcrust pastry as indicated in the recipe. Leave it on the springform mould base to cool on a cake rack. Freshly baked, warm shortcrust pastry is soft and only becomes short and crisp when it has been allowed to cool thoroughly on all sides as well as underneath. Once cool, remove the baked pastry base immediately from the spring-form mould or out of the tin. A pastry base baked in a springform mould should be loosened from the base with a large knife or palette knife (photograph 6).

Correct storage

If wrapped in clingfilm (plastic film) or placed in a freezer-bag, unbaked shortcrust pastry can be kept in the refrigerator for several days. It freezes well but should be defrosted in its wrapping in the refrigerator. Baked pastry cases can be wrapped in aluminium foil and kept for few days.

Small pastries and biscuits are best stored in sealed containers so that they do not absorb moisture from the air.

Pastry cutter biscuits
(Basic shortcrust pastry recipe)

FOR CHILDREN (ABOUT 55 PIECES/2 BAKING SHEETS)

Preparation time:
about 35 minutes
Baking time: about 12 minutes
per baking sheet
Keeping time: about 3 weeks
in an airtight container

For the baking sheet:
baking parchment

For the shortcrust pastry:
150 g/5 oz (1½ cups) plain
(all purpose) flour
1 pinch baking powder
50 g/2 oz (¼ cup) sugar
1 sachet vanilla sugar
100 g/3½ oz (½ cup) soft
butter or margarine

Per piece:
P: 0.3 g, F: 2 g, C: 3 g,
kJ: 116, kcal: 28, CU: 0.5

1 Line the baking sheet with baking parchment. Preheat the oven:
Top/bottom heat:
about 180 °C/350 °F (Gas mark 4)
Fan oven:
about 160 °C/325 °F (Gas mark 3)

2 Mix the flour and baking powder together in a mixing bowl. Add all the other ingredients and whisk together using a hand-mixer (with kneading hook), first briefly on the lowest setting, then on the highest setting to knead the pastry. Then shape the pastry into a ball (photographs 1 and 2).

3 On a lightly floured work surface, roll out the pastry to a thickness of about 5 mm/³⁄₁₆ in, then cut out the biscuits with your favourite pastry cutters (photograph 3) and place on the baking sheet.

4 Put the baking sheet on the middle shelf in the preheated oven and **bake for about 12 minutes**. Cut out the rest of the biscuits as indicated and put them on the baking parchment.

5 Slide the biscuits and baking parchment off the baking sheet onto a cake rack to cool. Slide the next batch of prepared biscuits and baking parchment onto the baking sheet, then **bake as indicated**.

TIP » Coat the biscuits with an icing (confectioners') sugar-based glaze and sprinkle with hundreds and thousands or chocolate sprinkles.

Recipe variation: For "terraced" biscuits (about 60 biscuits/3 baking sheets, small photograph on the left), prepare a shortcrust pastry with the following ingredients: 300 g/10 oz (1½ cups) plain (all purpose) flour, 2 level teaspoons baking powder, 100 g/3½ oz (½ cup) sugar, 1 packet vanilla sugar, 1 egg (medium) and 150 g/ 5 oz (¾ cup) softened butter or margarine. Wrap the pastry in clingfilm (plastic film) and put in the refrigerator for 30 minutes. Then roll out the pastry in portions to a thickness of about 5 mm/³⁄₁₆ in and cut out the biscuits in the same shapes and quantities but in 3 different sizes (diameters 4 cm/1½ in, 3 cm/1¼ in and 1.5 cm/½ in). Place the biscuits on the baking sheet lined with baking parchment. Bake the biscuits as indicated in the recipe for about 10 minutes for each baking sheet. Slide the baked biscuits and baking parchment from the baking sheet onto a cake rack and leave them there to cool. For the icing, stir 80 g/3 oz (¼ cup) red currant jelly until smooth. Then take 3 biscuits each of a different size and coat the underneath of the two smaller biscuits with this red currant jelly, then arrange them on top of each other to form a small terraced cone. Sprinkle the biscuits with icing (confectioners') sugar. Decorate the top biscuits with a small knob of jelly.
Terraced biscuits will keep for about 2 weeks in an airtight container.

Fancy biscuits

FOR GUESTS (ABOUT 75 PIECES/4 BAKING SHEETS) BACK OF PHOTO

Preparation time:
about 50 minutes
Baking time: about 8 minutes
per baking sheet
Keeping time: about 2 weeks
in an airtight container

For the baking sheet:
baking parchment

For the shortcrust pastry:
250 g/9 oz (2½ cups) plain
(all purpose) flour
1 level teaspoon baking
powder
75 g/3 oz (⅓ cup) sugar
1 sachet vanilla sugar
1 pinch salt
1 egg (medium)
125 g/4½ oz (⅝ cup) soft
butter or margarine

Also:
3–4 tablespoons icing
(confectioners') sugar
100 g/3½ oz (⅜ cup) red jelly,
e.g. red currant jelly

Per piece:
P: 0.4 g, F: 1 g, C: 5 g,
kJ: 144, kcal: 35, CU: 0.5

1 Line the baking sheet with baking parchment. Preheat the oven:
Top/bottom heat:
about 180 °C/350 °F (Gas mark 4)
Fan oven:
about 160 °C/325 °F (Gas mark 3)

2 For the pastry, mix together the flour and the baking powder in a mixing bowl. Add all the other ingredients and mix using a hand-mixer (with the kneading hook), first briefly on the lowest setting, then on the highest setting until the shortcrust pastry has the right texture. Then shape into a ball with your hands.

3 Roll out the pastry thinly (barely 5 mm/³⁄₁₆ in thick) in several portions and cut out 70–80 round biscuits with a diameter of about 4 cm/1½ in). Then cut a small circle (diameter about 1.5 cm/½ in) out of 35–40 of them to create rings. Fill the baking sheet with biscuits, half complete and half rings. Place the biscuits on the baking sheet on the middle shelf of the preheated oven. **Bake for about 8 minutes.**

4 Meanwhile prepare the next batch of biscuits as indicated and put them on the baking parchment.

5 Slide the baked biscuits together with the baking parchment onto a cake rack to cool. Slide the prepared biscuits together with the baking parchment onto the baking sheet and **bake as indicated**.

6 Now sprinkle a little icing (confectioners') sugar on the biscuit rings. Stir the red currant jelly until smooth. Spread a thin layer of jelly on each complete biscuit, then place a ring biscuit on top of it.

TIPS » It is easier to put the biscuits on the baking sheet first and then cut out the centres of the rings.
» If you have a fan oven you can bake 2 batches or baking sheets in the oven at the same time.

Variation: Instead of red currant jelly you can also use melted nut-nougat.

Recipe variation: To make about 140 vanilla biscuits (at the front in the photograph), you can make the shortcrust pastry described and add a few drops of Dr. Oetker Natural Vanilla Extract. Shape the ball of shortcrust pastry into rolls with a diameter of about 3 cm/1½. Wrap these in clingfilm (plastic film) and store in the refrigerator overnight. Then cut the shortcrust pastry rolls into slices about 5 mm/³⁄₁₆ in thick. Place the biscuits on baking parchment as indicated in the recipe and bake for about 12 minutes (per baking sheet). Decorate the cooled biscuits with 50 g/2 oz melted cooking chocolate.
» These vanilla biscuits will keep for about 4 weeks in an airtight container.

Florentine biscuits

TRADITIONAL (ABOUT 100 BISCUITS/4 BAKING SHEETS)

Preparation time:
about 40 minutes, excluding
cooling time
**Baking time: about 20 minutes
per baking sheet
Keeping time: about 2 weeks
in an airtight container**

For the baking sheet:
baking parchment

For the shortcrust pastry:
150 g/5 oz (1½ cups) plain
(all purpose) flour
50 g/2 oz (¼ cup) sugar
1 sachet vanilla sugar
1 egg (medium)
75 g/2½ oz (⅜ cup) soft butter
or margarine

For the topping:
50 g/2 oz (4 tablespoons)
butter
50 g/2 oz (¼ cup) sugar
2 tablespoons runny honey
125 g/4½ oz (½ cup)
whipping cream
50 g/2 oz (scant ¼ cup)
glacé cherries
100 g/3½ oz (⅞ cup)
slivered almonds
100 g/3½ oz (⅞ cup)
chopped hazelnuts
2 tablespoons ground hazelnuts

For the icing:
100 g/3½ oz dark chocolate

Per piece:
P: 1 g, F: 3 g, C: 3 g,
kJ: 188, kcal: 45, CU: 0.5

1 Line the baking sheet with baking parchment. Preheat the oven:
Top/bottom heat:
about 180 °C/350 °F (Gas mark 4)
Fan oven:
about 160 °C/325 °F (Gas mark 3)

2 For the pastry, put the flour and the baking powder in a mixing bowl. Add all the other ingredients and mix using a hand-mixer (with the kneading hook), first briefly on the lowest setting, then on the highest setting until the shortcrust pastry has the right texture. Then shape into a ball with your hands.

3 Roll out the pastry thinly in portions and cut out round biscuits with a diameter of about 5 cm/2 in. Put the biscuits on the baking sheet and place it on the middle shelf in the preheated oven. **Bake for about 8 minutes until golden yellow**.

4 Slide the baked biscuits together with the baking sheet paper onto a cake rack to cool.

5 For the topping, melt the butter, sugar and honey in a small pan over a low heat until it browns a little. Add the whipping cream and stir until the sugar has melted completely.

6 Cut the glazed cherries into pieces and add to the butter and sugar mixture with the flaked almonds, flaked hazelnuts and ground hazelnuts (photograph 1). Simmer gently until the mixture has thickened, stirring all the time. Leave the mixture to

cool for about 10 minutes, then use two teaspoons to decorate each cooled biscuit with a spoonful.

7 Put the baking sheet back on the middle shelf in the preheated oven at the same oven temperature and **bake for a further 12 minutes**.

8 Slide the baked biscuits together with the baking parchment onto a cake rack to cool (photograph 2). Prepare the rest of the biscuits as before and **bake for 12 minutes**.

9 For the chocolate glaze, coarsely chop the chocolate and melt in a bain-marie over low heat, stirring all the time. Spread a thin layer of chocolate on the underside of each biscuit or brush on using a pastry brush (photograph 3). Put the biscuits on the baking parchment until the chocolate has set.

TIPS » If the pastry is too soft, wrap in clingfilm (plastic film) and put in the refrigerator for about 30 minutes.
» If you are using a fan oven, you can bake 2 batches or baking sheets at the same time.
» If you only have 1 baking sheet, prepare the other biscuits on baking parchment, then slide them with the baking parchment onto the baking sheet and bake as indicated.

Variation: To make large Florentine biscuits, cut out 20-25 large circles (diameter 8.5 cm/3½ in) from the pastry, blind-bake as in the recipe, then spread the topping on each biscuit. Bake for 15 minutes more.

Saucer-eye biscuits

SOPHISTICATED (ABOUT 140 BISCUITS/3 BAKING SHEETS)

Preparation time:
about 40 minutes, excluding
cooling time
Baking time: about 15 minutes
per baking sheet
Keeping time: about 2 weeks
in an airtight container

For the baking sheet:
a little fat if necessary
baking parchment

For the shortcrust pastry:
250 g/9 oz (2½ cups) plain
(all purpose) flour
1 level teaspoon baking powder
100 g/3½ oz (½ cup) sugar
1 sachet vanilla sugar
1 pinch salt
3 egg yolks (medium)
150 g/5 oz (¾ cup) soft butter
or margarine

Also:
2 egg whites (medium)
75 g/3 oz (⅝ cup) slivered
almonds
6 tablespoons red jelly,
e.g. red currant jelly
1 tablespoon water

Per piece:
P: 0.4 g, F: 1 g, C: 3 g,
kJ: 105, kcal: 25, CU: 0.2

1 For the pastry, mix together the flour and the baking powder in a mixing bowl. Add all the other ingredients and mix using a hand-mixer (with the kneading hook), first briefly on the lowest setting, then on the highest setting until the shortcrust pastry has the right texture. Then shape into a ball with your hands. Wrap the pastry in clingfilm (plastic film) and put in the refrigerator for 30 minutes.

2 Grease the baking sheet and line with baking parchment. Preheat the oven:
Top/bottom heat:
about 180 °C/350 °F (Gas mark 4)
Fan oven:
about 160 °C/325 °F (Gas mark 3)

3 Form the ball of pastry into 7 rolls each about 40 cm/16 in long, cut each into pieces 2 cm/¾ in thick and shape these pieces into small balls.

4 Beat the egg whites with a fork. Dip one side of each ball into the egg white, then press into the almonds. Place the balls with the side without almonds on the baking sheet and make a depression in each ball with the handle of a mixing spoon (photograph 1).

5 Put the baking sheet on the middle shelf in the preheated oven. **Bake for about 15 minutes.** Meanwhile prepare the rest of the biscuits and arrange on the baking parchment.

6 Slide the baked biscuits together with the baking parchment onto a cake rack to cool. Slide the prepared biscuits together with the baking parchment onto the baking sheet and **bake as indicated**.

7 Bring the jelly briefly to the boil and, using a teaspoon, fill the depressions with it (photograph 2).

TIPS **»** If you have a fan oven you can bake 2 baking sheets at a time.
» The best jelly for these biscuits are red currant or raspberry jelly. But you can also fill the biscuits with yellow jam, first rubbed it through a sieve.
» Should the jelly have set again, simply warm it up.

Recipe variation: To make cats-eye biscuits (photograph 3) dip the balls of pastry in chopped up pine nuts instead of chopped almonds, then fill them with kiwi or gooseberry jam. It is best to rub the jam through a sieve and then bring it to the boil with 1 tablespoon water.

2

3

Heidesand biscuits

TRADITIONAL (ABOUT 160 PIECES/4 BAKING SHEETS)

Preparation time:
about 50 minutes, excluding
cooling time
Baking time: about 15 minutes
per baking sheet
Keeping time: about 3 weeks
in an airtight container

For the baking sheet:
baking parchment

For the shortcrust pastry:
250 g/9 oz (1¼ cups) butter
250 g/9 oz (1¼ cups) sugar
1 sachet vanilla sugar
1 pinch salt
2 tablespoons milk
350 g/12 oz (1¾ cups) plain
(all purpose) flour
1 pinch baking powder

Per piece:
P: 0.2 g, F: 1 g, C: 3 g,
kJ: 107, kcal: 26, CU: 0.5

1 For the pastry, melt the butter in a pan, allow to brown a little and remove from the heat. Leave the butter cool. Then while it is still liquid, transfer the butter into a mixing bowl and put in the refrigerator for about 45 minutes.

2 Once it has set hard again, whisk the butter with the hand-mixer with whisk attachment on the highest setting to make it malleable again. Gradually add the sugar, vanilla sugar, salt and milk. Whisk until the mixture has become creamy and smooth.

3 Mix together the flour and baking powder, then whisk two-thirds of it into the mixture on the medium setting. Knead the pastry with the rest of the flour on the work surface to make a smooth dough. Shape this dough into rolls with a diameter of about 3 cm/1¼ in, then put the rolls in the refrigerator for at least 1 hour until they are hard.

4 Line the baking sheet with baking parchment. Preheat the oven:
Top/bottom heat:
about 180 °C/350 °F (Gas mark 4)
Fan oven:
about 160 °C/325 °F (Gas mark 3)

5 Cut the hard rolls into slices about 5 mm/³⁄₁₆ in thick and put these on the baking sheet. **Bake the biscuits for about 15 minutes.** In the meantime prepare the rest of the biscuits and put them on baking parchment.

6 Slide the baked biscuits together with the baking parchment onto a cake rack to cool. Slide the prepared biscuits together with the baking parchment onto the baking sheet and **bake as indicated**.

TIP » Leave the rolls of shortcrust pastry in the refrigerator overnight and bake the biscuits the following day as indicated in the recipe.

Crème fraîche biscuits

EASY (ABOUT 120 PIECES/3 BAKING SHEETS)

1 To make the shortcrust pastry, put all the ingredients in a mixing bowl and knead into a dough with a hand-mixer, first on the lowest setting, then on the highest setting. Then knead the shortcrust pastry briefly on a lightly floured surface, shape into rolls with a diameter of about 2.5 cm/1 in. Wrap in clingfilm (plastic film) and put in the refrigerator for a few hours or overnight.

2 Grease the baking sheet and line with baking parchment. Preheat the oven:
Top/bottom heat:
about 180 °C/350 °F (Gas mark 4)
Fan oven:
about 160 °C/325 °F (Gas mark 3)

3 Cut the shortcrust pastry rolls into slices 5 mm/3⁄16 in thick, place these on the baking sheet, brush with milk and sprinkle with candy sugar or cinnamon sugar (photographs 1 and 2).

4 Put the baking sheet on the middle shelf in the preheated oven and **bake the biscuits for about 12 minutes**. Meanwhile prepare the rest of the biscuits and put on the baking parchment.

5 Slide the baked biscuits together with the baking parchment onto a cake rack to cool. Slide the prepared biscuits together with the baking parchment onto the baking sheet and **bake as indicated**.

Per piece: P: 0.2 g, F: 2 g, C: 2 g, kJ: 108, kcal: 26, CU: 0.2

Preparation time:
about 30 minutes,
excluding cooling time
Baking time: about 12 minutes
per baking sheet
Keeping time: 2–3 weeks
in an airtight container

For the baking sheet:
a little fat, baking parchment

For the shortcrust pastry:
250 g/9 oz (2½ cups) plain
(all purpose) flour
200 g/7 oz (1 cup) soft butter
or margarine
1 container (150 g/5 oz) crème
fraîche
2 sachets vanilla sugar

Also:
3–4 tablespoons milk
about 50 g/2 oz (¼ cup)
granulated sugar or cinnamon
sugar

Black and white pastries

TRADITIONAL (ABOUT 60 PIECES/2 BAKING SHEETS)

Preparation time:
about 60 minutes, excluding
cooling time
Baking time: about 12 minutes
per baking sheet
Keeping time: about 3 weeks
in an airtight container

For the baking sheet:
baking parchment

For the shortcrust pastry:
250 g/9 oz (2½ cups) plain (all
purpose) flour
1 level teaspoon baking
powder
150 g/5 oz (¾ cup) sugar
1 sachet vanilla sugar
1 pinch salt
1 tablespoon rum
1 egg (medium)
125 g/4½ oz (⅝ cup) soft
butter or margarine

Also:
15 g/½ oz (1 tablespoon) cocoa
powder
15 g/½ oz (1 tablespoon) sugar
1 tablespoon milk

For coating:
1 egg white (medium)

Per piece:
P: 1 g, F: 2 g, C: 6 g,
kJ: 184, kcal: 44, CU: 0.5

1 To make the shortcrust pastry, mix the flour and baking powder together in a bowl. Add all the other ingredients and knead them using a hand-mixer (with kneading hook), at first briefly on the lowest setting, then on the highest setting until the ingredients have formed a dough.

2 For the dark shortcrust pastry, sift the cocoa powder and knead into half the shortcrust pastry. Shape the dark and the light shortcrust pastry into two balls, wrap them separately in clingfilm (plastic film) and put in the refrigerator for 30 minutes.

3 You can make either round biscuits with a snail pattern or square biscuits with a checkerboard pattern:
» For the snail pattern, roll the light-coloured and dark shortcrust pastry into large rectangles, both the same size (30 x 15 cm/12 x 6 in); brush one rectangle thinly with egg white, place the second rectangle on top and brush with egg white as well. Roll up the two rectangles tightly, starting with the long side.
» For the checkerboard pattern, you will need 9 strips 1 cm/⅜ in wide, of the dark shortcrust pastry and 9 similar strips of the light-coloured shortcrust pastry, as well as 2 "shortcrust pastry covers". To make these, roll out the two colours of pastry separately until they are about 1 cm/⅜ in thick. Cut 9 strips, 1 cm/⅜ in wide and 15 cm/ 6 in long, from the light-coloured pastry and 9 similar strips from the dark shortcrust pastry. Brush the strips with egg white and put them

together to make two blocks of shortcrust pastry in a checkerboard pattern (photograph 1). Knead the remaining light-coloured and dark shortcrust pastry separately and roll out thinly to make 2 rectangles, each about 15 x 13 cm/6 x5 in. Wrap the two blocks in these rectangles.
» To make coins, form a roll 3 cm/ 1¼ in in diameter from the dark shortcrust pastry. Roll the light pastry 5 mm/³⁄₁₆ in thick and wrap it round the roll of dark pastry.

4 Place the shortcrust pastry rolls or blocks (photograph 2) in the refrigerator for about 1 hour; this will make them easier to cut.

5 Line the baking sheet with baking parchment. Preheat the oven:
Top/bottom heat:
about 180 °C/350 °F (Gas mark 4)
Fan oven:
about 160 °C/325 °F (Gas mark 3)

6 Cut the cooled shortcrust pastry rolls or blocks into slices 5 mm/ ³⁄₁₆ in thick and arrange these on the baking sheet (photograph 3). Put the baking sheet on the middle shelf in the preheated oven and **bake the shortcrust pastry slices for about 12 minutes**. In the meantime arrange the pastry remaining slices on the baking parchment.

7 Slide the baked biscuits together with the baking parchment onto a cake rack to cool. Slide the prepared biscuits together with the baking parchment onto the baking sheet and **bake as indicated**.

1

2

3

Nut twists

GOOD TO MAKE IN ADVANCE (ABOUT 16 SLICES)

Preparation time:
about 35 minutes
Baking time: about 40 minutes

For the baking sheet:
baking parchment

For the shortcrust pastry:
300 g/10 oz (3 cups) plain (all
purpose) flour
1 level teaspoon baking
powder
100 g/3½ oz (½ cup) sugar
1 sachet vanilla sugar
100 g/3½ oz (½ cup) soft
butter or margarine
1 container (150 g/5 oz) crème
fraîche

For the filling:
200 g/7 oz (2 cups) ground
hazelnuts
100 g/3½ oz (½ cup) sugar
1 egg (medium)
1 egg white (medium)
1 tablespoon rum
4 tablespoons water

For coating:
1 egg yolk (medium)
1 teaspoon milk

For the apricot glaze:
2 tablespoons apricot jam
1 tablespoon water

Per slice:
P: 5 g, F: 17 g, C: 31 g,
kJ: 1225, kcal: 293, CU: 2.5

1 Line the baking sheet with baking parchment. Preheat the oven:
Top/bottom heat:
about 180 °C/350 °F (Gas mark 4)
Fan oven:
about 160 °C/325 °F (Gas mark 3)

2 To make the shortcrust pastry, mix together the flour and baking powder in a mixing bowl. Add all the other ingredients for the short-crust pastry and whisk everything with a hand-mixer (kneading hook), first on the lowest setting, then on the highest setting until all the ingredients have been incorporated and formed a shortcrust pastry. Then shape into a roll with your hands.

3 For the filling, put all the ingredients in a bowl and stir well.

4 Roll out the pastry on a lightly floured work surface to make a rectangle about 40 x 35 cm/ 16 x 14 in and spread the filling on it, leaving an edge about 1 cm/⅜ in wide uncovered all round the rectangle.

5 Roll up the pastry, starting with the long side. Cut the roll in half lengthways with a sharp knife (photograph 1). Make sure when cutting the roll that you cut it exactly in the middle so that the twist has an even appearance. Plait the halves of the roll with their cut surfaces facing upwards (photo-graph 2). Put the resulting twist on the baking sheet and press the ends tightly together.

6 Whisk together the egg yolk and the milk and brush over the twist. Put the baking sheet on the middle shelf in the preheated oven and **bake for about 40 minutes**.

7 Rub the apricot jam through a sieve; then bring it to the boil in a pan with a little water and brush over the nut twist as soon as it comes out of the oven, using a pastry brush (photograph 3).

Hazelnut triangles

FOR GUESTS (ABOUT 30 PIECES)

Preparation time:
about 30 minutes, excluding
cooling time
Baking time: about 25 minutes
Keeping time: about 3 weeks
in an airtight container

For the baking sheet
(40 x 30 cm/16 x 12 in):
a little fat

For the shortcrust pastry:
225 g/8 oz (2¼ cups) plain
(all purpose) flour
1 level teaspoon baking powder
100 g/3½ oz (½ cup) sugar
1 sachet vanilla sugar
1 egg (medium)
1 tablespoon water
100 g/3½ oz (½ cup) soft
butter or margarine

For the topping:
150 g/5 oz (¾ cup) butter
150 g/5 oz (¾ cup) sugar
2 sachets vanilla sugar
3 tablespoons water
100 g/3½ oz (1 cup) ground
hazelnuts
200 g/7 oz (2½ cups) chopped
hazelnuts
3 tablespoons apricot jam

For the icing:
100 g/3½ oz dark chocolate

Per piece:
P: 2 g, F: 15 g, C: 19 g,
kJ: 916, kcal: 219, CU: 1.5

1 Grease the baking sheet. Preheat the oven:
Top/bottom heat:
about 180 °C/350 °F (Gas mark 4)
Fan oven:
about 160 °C/325 °F (Gas mark 3)

2 To make the shortcrust pastry, mix together the flour and baking powder in a mixing bowl. Add all the other ingredients for the shortcrust pastry and whisk everything with a hand-mixer (kneading hook), first on the lowest setting, then on the highest setting until all the ingredients have been incorporated and formed a shortcrust pastry. Then shape into a roll with your hands.

3 For the topping, warm and melt the butter, sugar, vanilla sugar and water gently in a pan, stirring all the time. Stir in the ground and chopped hazelnuts. Remove the pan from the heat and leave the topping to cool for about 10 minutes.

4 Roll out the pastry on the baking sheet. Spread the apricot jam over the rolled-out pastry, then spread the topping evenly over the jam (photograph 1). Put the baking sheet on the middle shelf in the preheated oven and **bake for about 25 minutes**.

5 Put the baking sheet with the baked pastry on a cake rack and leave to cool for about 20 minutes. Then cut into squares of about 8 x 8 cm/ 3 x 3 in and cut each square diagonally to make triangles (photograph 2).

6 To make the glaze, break the chocolate into pieces and melt in a bain-marie over low heat, stirring all the time. Dip the two pointed corners of the triangles in the melted chocolate (photograph 3). Put the nut triangles on a cake rack or baking parchment and allow the glaze to set.

TIPS » Instead of just dipping the two pointed corners in the melted chocolate, you can cover the whole triangle with melted chocolate.
» To make smaller nut corners (about 140 biscuits), cut the sheet of baked pastry into small squares of about 4 x 4 cm/1½ x 1½ in, then cut them in half diagonally.

Recipe variation: To make coconut triangles, replace the hazelnuts with 200 g/7 oz (⅞ cup) grated coconut.

Covered apple cake

POPULAR (ABOUT 20 SLICES)

Preparation time:
about 50 minutes,
excluding cooling time
Baking time: about 25 minutes

For the baking sheet
(40 x 30 cm/16 x 12 in):
a little fat

For the filling:
1.5 kg/3¼ lb sharp apples,
e.g. Boskop
50 g/2 oz (¼ cup) sugar
1 sachet vanilla sugar
1 pinch ground cinnamon
30 g/1 oz (2 tablespoons)
raisins
50 g/2 oz (4 tablespoons)
butter
about 50 g/2 oz (¼ cup) sugar

For the shortcrust pastry:
400 g/14 oz (4 cups) plain
(all purpose) flour
4 level teaspoons baking powder
70 g/3 oz (⅓ cup) sugar
1 sachet vanilla sugar
2 eggs (medium)
4 tablespoons milk
150 g/5 oz (¾ cup) soft butter
or margarine

For coating and sprinkling:
1 egg yolk (medium)
1 tablespoon milk
50 g/2 oz (scant ½ cup)
slivered almonds

Per slice:
P: 4 g, F: 12 g, C: 32 g,
kJ: 1038, kcal: 248, CU: 2.5

1 Grease the baking sheet. Preheat the oven:
Top/bottom heat:
about 180 °C/350 °F (Gas mark 4)
Fan oven:
about 160 °C/325 °F (Gas mark 3)

2 For the filling, peel the apples, cut into quarters, core and cut into sticks or small pieces. Lightly braise the sticks or pieces of apples together with the sugar, vanilla sugar, cinnamon, raisins and butter in a pan, stirring all the time. Then leave to cool and add more sugar to taste.

3 To make the shortcrust pastry, mix together the flour and baking powder in a mixing bowl. Add all the other ingredients for the short-crust pastry and whisk everything with a hand-mixer (kneading hook), first on the lowest setting, then on the highest setting until all the ingredients have been incorporated and formed a shortcrust pastry. Then shape into a roll with your hands.

4 Roll out half the pastry thinly the size of the baking sheet to make the cover, then carefully roll onto the baking parchment (photograph 1). Roll out the rest of the pastry on the baking sheet. Spread the apple filling on top (photograph 2), then unroll the pastry cover over it (photograph 3).

5 Whisk together the egg yolk and milk and brush all over the top. Put the baking sheet in the bottom third of the preheated oven and **bake for about 25 minutes.**

6 Leave the cake on the baking sheet and put on a cake rack to cool.

TIP » You can also bake the cake in a springform mould (diameter 26 cm/10¼ in) but in that case halve the amount of pastry and filling.

Plum cake with a double base

GOOD TO MAKE IN ADVANCE (ABOUT 20 SLICES)

Preparation time:
about 45 minutes
Baking time: about 67 minutes

For the baking sheet
(40 x 30 cm/16 x 12 in):
a little fat

For the shortcrust pastry:
225 g/8 oz (2¼ cups) plain
(all purpose) flour
60 g/2 oz (¼ cup) sugar
1 sachet vanilla sugar
150 g/5 oz (¾ cup) soft butter
or margarine

For the topping:
1.5 kg/3¼ lb plums

For the sponge:
200 g/7 oz (1 cup) soft butter
or margarine
200 g/7 oz (1 cup) sugar
1 sachet vanilla sugar
3 eggs (medium)
200 g/7 oz (2 cups) plain
(all purpose) flour
2 level teaspoons baking
powder

For sprinkling:
50 g/2 oz (¼ cup) sugar

Per slice:
P: 4 g, F: 16 g, C: 38 g,
kJ: 1320, kcal: 316, CU: 3.0

1 Grease the baking sheet. Preheat the oven:
Top/bottom heat:
about 180 °C/350 °F (Gas mark 4)
Fan oven:
about 160 °C/325 °F (Gas mark 3)

2 To make the shortcrust pastry, mix together the flour and baking powder in a mixing bowl. Add all the other ingredients for the shortcrust pastry and whisk everything using a hand-mixer (kneading hook), first on the lowest setting, then on the highest setting until all the ingredients have been incorporated and formed a shortcrust pastry. Then shape into a roll with your hands.

3 Roll out the pastry on the baking sheet and prick several times with a fork. Put the baking sheet on the middle shelf in the preheated oven and **bake for about 12 minutes.**

4 Put the baking sheet on a cake rack and leave the base on it to cool a little.

5 To make the topping, wash the plums, leave to drain, remove the stalks, cut in half and remove the stones.

6 To make the sponge, whisk the margarine or butter in a mixing bowl using a hand-mixer with whisk attachment until soft. Add the sugar and vanilla sugar little by little, whisking all the time until you obtain a smooth, even mixture. Whisk in the eggs, one after the other, for about ½ minute each on the highest setting.

7 Mix together the flour and baking powder and mix in instalments on the medium setting. Spread the sponge mixture over the shortcrust pastry base. Arrange the plums in rows on the sponge mixture. Put the baking sheet back in the oven and **bake at the same temperature for a further 55 minutes.**

8 Put the baking sheet on a cake rack, sprinkle the cake with sugar and leave to cool.

TIPS » You can also prepare the cake the day before you will eat it.
» If the shortcrust pastry is too sticky, wrap it in clingfilm (plastic film) and put it in the refrigerator for a time.
» This cake is also delicious when made either with cherries, rhubarb or apples, cut into segments, with 50 g/2 oz (¼ cup) currants. Spread apricot glaze on the apple cake while still hot. Make the apricot glaze by rubbing 4 tablespoons apricot jam through a sieve, add water and bring to the boil, then brush over the apples.

Buttermilk slices with cherries

REFRESHING (ABOUT 12 SLICES)

Preparation time:
about 45 minutes, excluding cooling time
Baking time: about 15 minutes

For the baking sheet:
a little fat
square cake frame

For the shortcrust pastry:
200 g/7 oz (2 cups) plain (all purpose) flour
1 level teaspoon baking powder
100 g/3½ oz (½ cup) sugar
1 sachet vanilla sugar
1 egg (medium)
1 tablespoon water
100 g/3½ oz (½ cup) soft butter or margarine

For the topping:
12 sheets clear gelatine
500 ml/17 fl oz (2¼ cups) buttermilk
150 g/5 oz (¾ cup) sugar
1 teaspoon lemon zest
500 g/18 oz (2¼ cups) chilled whipping cream

For the cherry compote:
1 jar morello cherries (drained weight 350 g/12 oz)
150 ml/5 fl oz (⅝ cup) cherry juice (from the jar)
15 g/½ oz (1½ tablespoons) cornflour (cornstarch)
25 g/1 oz (2 tablespoons) sugar

Per slice:
P: 6 g, F: 22 g, C: 47 g,
kJ:1738, kcal: 415, CU: 4.0

1 Grease the baking sheet. Preheat the oven:
Top/bottom heat:
about 200 °C/400 °F (Gas mark 6)
Fan oven:
about 180 °C/350 °F (Gas mark 4)

2 To make the shortcrust pastry, mix together the flour and baking powder in a mixing bowl. Add all the other ingredients for the shortcrust pastry and whisk everything using a hand-mixer (kneading hook), first on the lowest setting, then on the highest setting until all the ingredients have been incorporated and formed a shortcrust pastry. Then shape into a roll with your hands.

3 Roll out the dough on a baking sheet to make a square 25 x 25 cm/ 10 x 10 in, prick the base several times with a fork and place a pastry frame the size of the pastry square round it. Put the baking sheet on the middle shelf in the preheated oven and **bake for about 15 minutes**.

4 Put the baking sheet with the baked cake on it on a cake rack and leave to cool with the pastry frame still round it.

5 For the topping, soak the gelatine, following the instructions on the packet. Lightly squeeze the gelatine and dissolve it in a small pan over low heat, stirring all the time.

6 Add the sugar and lemon rind to the buttermilk and stir well. First stir 4 tablespoons buttermilk into the dissolved gelatine, using a whisk, then stir this into the rest of the buttermilk and put in the refrigerator. Whip the cream stiff. As soon as the gelatine-buttermilk mixture begins to set, fold in the whipped cream.

7 Pour this mixture over the cooled base and smooth flat. Make a wavy pattern on the surface with a pastry comb and put the cake in the refrigerator for about 2 hours.

8 In the meantime, make the cherry compote. Drain the cherries thoroughly in a sieve, reserve the juice and measure 150 ml/5 fl oz (⅝ cup) which you put to one side. Whisk 4 tablespoons of juice into the cornflour (cornstarch). Bring the rest of the juice to the boil. Take it off the heat and stir the already dissolved cornflour into it. Bring back to the boil, add the cherries and sugar to taste and leave the compote to cool.

9 Carefully loosen the pastry frame using a knife, then remove it. Cut the cake into slices and spoon a little compote on each slice. Keep the buttermilk slices in the refrigerator until ready to serve them.

TIP » If you are using fresh cherries (400 g/14 oz), increase the amount of sugar to 100 g/3½ oz (½ cup). You can also put ready-made cherry compote from the freezer compartment on the buttermilk slices.

Cider cake slices

SOPHISTICATED – WITH ALCOHOL (ABOUT 20 SLICES)

Preparation time:
about 65 minutes
Baking time: about 55 minutes

For the baking sheet
(40 x 30 cm/16 x 12 in):
a little fat
square cake frame

For the shortcrust pastry:
300 g/10 oz (3 cups) plain
(all purpose) flour
50 g/2 oz (⅓ cup)
cornflour (cornstarch)
1 level teaspoon baking powder
150 g/5 oz (¾ cup) sugar
1 sachet vanilla sugar
1 pinch salt
2 eggs (medium)
150 g/5 oz (¾ cup) soft butter
or margarine

For the apple filling:
2 kg/4½ lb sharp apples,
e.g. Elstar
juice of 1 lemon
120 g/4½ oz (1 cup) custard
powder (vanilla pudding mix)
150 g/5 oz (¾ cup) sugar
2 sachets vanilla sugar
500 ml/17 fl oz (2¼ cups)
white wine
500 ml/17 fl oz (2¼ cups)
clear apple juice

For the wine glaze:
3 sachets clear cake glaze
100 g/3½ oz (½ cup) sugar
375 ml/13 fl oz (1⅝ cups)
white wine
300 ml/10 fl oz (1¼ cups)
clear apple juice

1 Grease the baking sheet. Preheat the oven:
Top/bottom heat:
about 200 °C/400 °F (Gas mark 6)
Fan oven:
about 180 °C/350 °F (Gas mark 4)

2 To make the shortcrust pastry, mix together the flour, cornflour (cornstarch) and baking powder in a mixing bowl. Add all the other ingredients for the shortcrust pastry and whisk everything with a hand-mixer (kneading hook), first on the lowest setting, then on the highest setting until all the ingredients have been incorporated and formed a shortcrust pastry. Then shape into a roll with your hands.

3 Roll out the pastry on the baking sheet (photograph 1), prick the base several times with a fork and place a pastry frame the same size as the baking sheet round the pastry. Put the baking sheet in the preheated oven and **blind-bake for about 15 minutes**.

4 For the filling, peel the apples, cut into quarters, core, cut into small cubes and sprinkle with lemon juice. Prepare the custard following the instructions on the packet but with the ingredients indicated in the recipe: custard powder, sugar, vanilla sugar, wine and apple juice.

5 Immediately stir in the diced apples. Spread the filling on the blind-baked base (photograph 2) and smooth flat. Put the baking sheet back in the oven and **bake for another 40 minutes at the same temperature**.

6 Put the baking sheet with the cake still on it on a cake rack and leave to cool.

7 Make the wine glaze with the glaze, sugar, white wine and apple juice, following the instructions on the packet but with the amounts indicated in the recipe. Pour the glaze over the cooled apple cake and allow to set. Put the cake in the refrigerator.

8 Before serving, carefully loosen the pastry frame with a knife (photograph 3) and remove. Cut the cake into slices.

TIPS » Decorate each slice with a whipped cream rosette and sprinkle chopped pistachio nuts or almonds on each one.
» To prepare the cake without alcohol, replace the white wine with apple juice.

Per slice: P: 3 g, F: 8 g, C: 54 g, kJ: 1388, kcal: 331, CU: 4.5

Red currant meringue cake

FRUITY (ABOUT 12 PIECES)

Preparation time:
about 45 minutes
Baking time: about 72 minutes

For the springform mould
(diameter 26 cm/10¼ in):
a little fat

For the shortcrust pastry:
250 g/9 oz (2½ cups) plain
(all purpose) flour
65 g/2¼ oz (scant ⅓ cup) sugar
1 sachet vanilla sugar
1 pinch salt
1 egg (medium)
125 g/4½ oz (⅝ cup) soft
butter or margarine

Also:
1 tablespoon plain
(all purpose) flour

For the topping:
500 g/18 oz red currants
5 egg whites (medium)
175 g/6 oz (⅞ cup) sugar
100 g/3½ oz (1 cup) ground
almonds
60 g/2 oz (6 tablespoons)
cornflour (cornstarch)

Per piece:
P: 6 g, F: 14 g, C: 44 g,
kJ: 1396, kcal: 334, CU: 3.5

1 Grease the base of the springform mould. Preheat the oven:
Top/bottom heat:
about 200 °C/400 °F (Gas mark 6)
Fan oven:
about 180 °C/350 °F (Gas mark 4)

2 To make the shortcrust pastry, put all the other ingredients for the shortcrust pastry in a mixing bowl and whisk everything using a hand-mixer (kneading hook), first on the lowest setting, then on the highest setting until all the ingredients have been incorporated and formed a shortcrust pastry. Then shape into a roll with your hands.

3 Roll out two-thirds of the short-crust pastry on the base of the prepared springform mould. Then put the springform mould side round it again.

4 Knead 1 tablespoon flour into the rest of the dough and shape into a long roll. Place the roll along the edge of the pastry base and press it against the sides of the springform mould to make an edge about 4 cm/1½ in high. Prick the base several times with a fork.

5 Put the springform mould on the bottom shelf in the preheated oven. **Blind-bake for about 12 minutes.**

6 For the topping, rinse the red currants, leave to drain and pull the red currants off the sprigs. Beat the egg so stiff that if you make an incision with a knife, the cut remains visible. Gradually whisk in the sugar. Carefully fold in the almonds and cornflour (cornstarch), then fold in the red currants.

7 **Reduce the oven temperature by 20 °C/25 °F so that top/bottom heat is about 180 °C/350 °F (Gas mark 4) or fan oven: about 160 °C/325 °F (Gas mark 3).** Spoon the red currant-meringue mixture on the still hot pastry base to form a dome. Put the springform mould back in the oven and **bake the cake for another 60 minutes** (the meringue mixture should be golden brown).

8 Leave the cake in the springform mould and place it on a cake rack to cool for 1–2 hours, then remove carefully from the springform mould.

SERVING TIP » Serve with whipped cream.

TIP » Both the bowl and whisk must be completely free of fat and there should be no trace of egg yolk in the egg white.

Linzer torte

CLASSIC – GOOD TO MAKE IN ADVANCE (ABOUT 12 PIECES)

Preparation time:
about 30 minutes,
excluding cooling time
Baking time: about 30 minutes

For the springform mould
(diameter 26 cm/10¼ in):
a little fat

For the shortcrust pastry:
200 g/7 oz (2 cups) plain
(all purpose) flour
1 level teaspoon baking powder
100 g/3½ oz (½ cup) sugar
1 sachet vanilla sugar
1 pinch ground cloves
1 level teaspoon ground
cinnamon
1 egg (medium)
1 egg white (medium)
100 g/3½ oz (½ cup) soft
butter or margarine
100 g/3½ oz (1 cup) ground
almonds

For the topping:
100 g/3½ oz (⅜ cup)
raspberry jam

For coating:
1 egg yolk (medium)
1 teaspoon milk

Per piece:
P: 4 g, F: 13 g, C: 27 g,
kJ: 1014, kcal: 242, CU: 2.0

1 To make the shortcrust pastry, mix together the flour and baking powder in a mixing bowl. Add all the other ingredients for the short-crust pastry and whisk everything with a hand-mixer (kneading hook), first on the lowest setting, then on the highest setting until all the ingredients have been incorporated and formed a shortcrust pastry. Then shape into a roll with your hands. Wrap the pastry in clingfilm (plastic film) and put in the refrigerator for about 30 minutes.

2 Grease the bottom of the spring-form mould. Preheat the oven:
Top/bottom heat:
about 180 °C/350 °F (Gas mark 4)
Fan oven:
about 160 °C/325 °F (Gas mark 3)

3 Roll out half the pastry to form a circle the same size as the base of the prepared springform mould and cut out 16–20 strips using a pastry wheel (photograph 1). Roll out the rest of the pastry on the bottom of the springform mould and put the side of the springform mould back on.

4 For the topping, spread the jam on the pastry base, leaving an edge about 1 cm/⅜ wide free of jam all round. Arrange the strips of pastry on top to form a trellis pattern (photograph 2). Whisk together the egg yolk and milk and brush over the strips of pastry.

5 Put the springform mould in the bottom third of the preheated oven and **bake for about 30 minutes**.

6 Remove the torte from the oven, carefully release the side of the springform mould and remove it. Then lift the torte off the spring-form mould base and leave to cool on a cake rack.

Recipe variation: To make **Linzer slices** (photograph 3), double the quantities. Roll out half the pastry the same size as the baking sheet and cut into strips. Roll out the rest of the pastry on a greased baking sheet (40 x 30 cm/16 x 12 in). Spread the jam on the pastry base and arrange the strips to form a trellis pattern. Bake the cake as described in the recipe. When cold, cut into slices of the size of your choice.

Friesian crumble tart

FOR GUESTS (ABOUT 12 PIECES)

Preparation time:
about 50 minutes,
excluding cooling time
Baking time: about 15 minutes
per layer

**For the springform mould
(diameter 26 cm/10¼ in):**
a little fat

For the shortcrust pastry:
250 g/9 oz (2½ cups) plain
(all purpose) flour
1 pinch baking powder
2 sachets vanilla sugar
1 container (150 g/5 oz)
crème fraîche
175 g/6 oz (⅞ cup) soft butter
or margarine

For the crumble:
150 g/5 oz (1½ cups) plain (all
purpose) flour
75 g/3 oz (⅓ cup) sugar
1 sachet vanilla sugar
1 pinch ground cinnamon
100 g/3½ oz (½ cup)
soft butter

For the filling:
500 g/18 oz (2¼ cups) chilled
whipping cream (min. 30 % fat)
25 g/1 oz (2 tablespoons) sugar
1 sachet vanilla sugar
450 g/1 lb plum butter

Per piece:
P: 5 g, F: 38 g, C: 56 g,
kJ: 2447, kcal: 585, CU: 4.5

1 Grease the bottom of the sprinform mould. Preheat the oven:
Top/bottom heat:
about 200 °C/400 °F (Gas mark 6)
Fan oven:
about 180 °C/350 °F (Gas mark 4)

2 To make the shortcrust pastry, mix together the flour and baking powder in a mixing bowl. Add all the other ingredients for the short-crust pastry and whisk everything using a hand-mixer (kneading hook), first on the lowest setting, then on the highest setting until all the ingredients have been incor-porated and formed a shortcrust pastry. Divide the pastry into 4 portions of equal size and shape into balls. Roll out one portion on the bottom of the springform mould, prick several times with a fork (photograph 1) and put the ring of the springform mould back on.

3 To make the crumble, mix together the flour, vanilla sugar and cin-namon in a mixing bowl. Add the butter and mix everything using a hand-mixer with whisk attachment to make the crumble of the desired texture. Spread one quarter of the crumble evenly over the pastry base. Put the springform mould in the bottom third of the preheated oven and **bake the base for about 15 minutes. Prepare the other three layers in the same way and bake.**

4 When baked, remove the pastry bases immediately from the spring-form mould and leave to cool separately on a cake rack. Cut one of the layers into 12 slices while it is still warm.

5 For the filling, whisk the whipping cream with the sugar and vanilla sugar until stiff and put in portions in a pastry bag with a star-shaped nozzle (diameter about 8 mm/ ⅓ in). Spread a third of the plum compote on each of the three uncut layers, then pipe onto each one a third of the whipped cream (photo-graph 2). Place the layers on top of each, ending with the layers already cut into slices, to make a tart (photograph 3). Put the tart in the refrigerator for about 1 hour. Sprinkle with icing (confectioners') sugar before serving if you like.

TIP » It is best to cut the tart with a serrated knife before serving.

1

2

3

Cherry crumble tart

FRUITY (ABOUT 12 PIECES)

Preparation time:
about 60 minutes,
excluding cooling time
Baking time: about 52 minutes

For the springform mould
(diameter 26 cm/10¼ in):
a little fat

For the shortcrust pastry:
150 g/5 oz (1½ cups) plain (all
purpose) flour
1 pinch baking powder
100 g/3½ oz (½ cup) sugar
1 sachet vanilla sugar
1 pinch salt
1 egg (medium)
100 g/3½ oz (½ cup) soft butter
or margarine

For the filling:
1 kg/2¼ lb morello cherries
100 g/3½ oz (½ cup) sugar
20 g/¾ oz (2 tablespoons)
cornflour (cornstarch)
about 1 tablespoon sugar

For the crumble:
150 g/5 oz (1½ cups) plain
(all purpose) flour
100 g/3½ oz (½ cup) sugar
1 sachet vanilla sugar
100 g/3½ oz (½ cup) soft butter
or margarine

Per piece:
P: 4 g, F: 15 g, C: 55 g,
kJ: 1578, kcal: 377, CU: 4.5

1 To make the shortcrust pastry, mix together the flour and baking powder in a mixing bowl. Add all the other ingredients for the shortcrust pastry and whisk everything using a hand-mixer (kneading hook), first on the lowest setting, then on the highest setting until all the ingredients have been incorporated and formed a shortcrust pastry. Then shape into a roll with your hands. Wrap the pastry in clingfilm (plastic film) and put in the refrigerator for 20–30 minutes.

2 Grease the bottom of the springform mould. Preheat the oven:
Top/bottom heat:
about 200 °C/400 °F (Gas mark 6)
Fan oven:
about 180 °C/350 °F (Gas mark 4)

3 For the filling, wash the cherries and leave to drain, then remove the stalks and stones. Add the sugar, stir well and leave to stand to draw the juices.

4 Roll out two-thirds of the shortcrust pastry onto the base of the springform mould. Prick the base several times with a fork and put the ring of the springform mould back on. Then put it on a shelf in the bottom third of the preheated oven and **bake for about 12 minutes**.

5 Put the springform mould with the base on a cake rack to cool a little.

6 Bring the cherries together with the juice briefly to the boil, then leave to drain in a sieve, reserving the juice. Measure 250 ml/8 fl oz (1 cup) of the

juice, topping up the quantity with water if necessary, and leave to cool. Take 4 tablespoons of this juice to stir into the cornflour (cornstarch). Bring the rest of the juice to the boil, stir in the cornflour (cornstarch) mixed with the juice and bring briefly to the boil. Now stir in the cherries. Add sugar to taste.

7 For the edge, shape the rest of the dough into a long roll and place it round the pastry base; press it against the sides to form an edge about 2 cm/¾ in high. Spread the cherries on the base.

8 For the crumble, put the flour in a mixing bowl together with all the other crumble ingredients. Whisk all the ingredients together using a hand-mixer with whisk attachment and spread over the filling. Put the springform mould back in the oven and **bake at the same temperature for a further 40 minutes**.

9 Leave the tart in the springform mould for another 15 minutes. Then, using a knife, loosen the tart along the edge and remove the ring from the springform mould. Loosen the base of the tart from the bottom of the springform mould but do not remove it. Put the springform mould bottom on a cake rack to cool.

TIPS » This tart can easily be prepared 1 day in advance.
» You can use two jars of morello cherries (drained weight 350 g/12 oz each). In that case, make the filling without sugar.

Chocolate cheesecake

POPULAR (ABOUT 16 PIECES)

Preparation time:
about 90 minutes, excluding
cooling time
Baking time: about 60 minutes

**For the springform mould
(diameter 26 cm/10¼ in):**
a little fat

For the shortcrust pastry:
300 g/10 oz (3 cups) plain
(all purpose) flour
30 g/1 oz (5 tablespoons)
cocoa powder
2 level teaspoons baking
powder
150 g/5 oz (¾ cup) sugar
1 sachet vanilla sugar
1 egg (medium)
150 g/5 oz (¾ cup) soft butter
or margarine

For the filling:
250 g/9 oz (1¼ cups) butter
or margarine
500 g/18 oz (2 cups) low fat
quark
200 g/7 oz (1 cup) sugar
1 sachet vanilla sugar
3 eggs (medium)
40 g/1½ oz (5 tablespoons)
custard powder (vanilla
pudding mix)

Per piece:
P: 8 g, F: 23 g, C: 39 g,
kJ: 1682, kcal: 402, CU: 3.5

1 To make the pastry, mix together the flour, cocoa powder and baking powder in a mixing bowl. Add the other ingredients for the pastry and knead with a hand-mixer (with kneading hook) first briefly on the lowest setting, then on the highest setting until you have obtained an even mixture. Then shape into a ball with your hands. Wrap the pastry in clingfilm (plastic film) and put in the refrigerator for about 30 minutes.

2 To make the filling, melt the butter or margarine in a pan, then leave to cool.

3 Grease the bottom of the spring-form mould. Preheat the oven:
Top/bottom heat:
about 200 °C/400 °F (Gas mark 6)
Fan oven:
about 180 °C/350 °F (Gas mark 4)

4 Roll out about half the pastry on the springform mould base. Then place the springform ring round it. Shape about half of the remaining pastry into a long roll. Place the roll round the outside of the pastry base and press it against the sides of the springform mould to make an edge about 2 cm/¾ in high.

5 To make the filling, mix together the quark, sugar, vanilla sugar, eggs, custard powder and melted butter or margarine with a whisk until you obtain a smooth, even mixture. Then pour this mixture into the mould and smooth flat. Divide the rest of the pastry into small pieces and distribute over the filling.

6 Put the mould on the shelf in the bottom third of the preheated oven. **Bake for about 60 minutes.**

7 Place the cake in the springform mould on a cake rack to cool.

Variation: For a lighter chocolate cheesecake, reduce the amount of fat in the filling to about 150 g/5 oz (¾ cup) butter or margarine.

Cheesecake

POPULAR (ABOUT 12 PIECES)

Preparation time:
about 40 minutes,
excluding cooling time
Baking time: about 85 minutes

For the springform mould
(diameter 26 cm/10¼ in):
a little fat

For the shortcrust pastry:
150 g/5 oz (1½ cups) plain
(all purpose) flour
½ level teaspoon baking
powder
75 g/3 oz (⅓ cup) sugar
1 sachet vanilla sugar
1 pinch salt
1 egg (medium)
75 g/2½ oz (⅜ cup) soft butter
or margarine

For the filling:
2 egg whites (medium)
200 g/7 oz (⅞ cup) chilled
whipping cream
500 g/18 oz (2 cups) low fat
quark
100 g/3½ oz (½ cup) sugar
2 tablespoons lemon juice
35 g/1¼ oz (4 tablespoons)
cornflour (cornstarch)
2 egg yolks (medium)

Per piece:
P: 9 g, F: 12 g, C: 28 g,
kJ: 1109, kcal: 265, CU: 2.5

1 Grease the bottom of a springform mould. Preheat the oven:
Top/bottom heat:
about 200 °C/400 °F (Gas mark 6)
Fan oven:
about 180 °C/350 °F (Gas mark 4)

2 To make the shortcrust pastry, mix together the flour and baking powder in a mixing bowl. Add all the other ingredients for the short-crust pastry and whisk everything using a hand-mixer (kneading hook), first on the lowest setting, then on the highest setting until all the ingredients have been incor-porated and formed a shortcrust pastry. Then shape into a roll with your hands.

3 Roll out a generous two-thirds of the shortcrust pastry on the bottom of the springform mould and put the springform mould ring back round the base. Prick the base several times with a fork. Put the springform mould on a shelf in the bottom third of the preheated oven. **Blind-bake for about 10 minutes.**

4 After part-baking, put the spring-form mould on a cake rack for the pastry base to cool. **Reduce the oven temperature by 40 °C/100 °F so that bottom/top heat is 160 °C/ 325 °F (Gas mark 3) or fan oven heat 140 °C/275 °F (Gas mark 1).** Shape the rest of the pastry into a long roll. Place the roll round the outside of the pastry base and press it against the sides to make an edge about 3 cm/1¼ in high.

5 To make the filling, beat the egg whites stiff, then whip the cream. Stir the sugar, lemon juice, corn-flour (cornstarch) and egg yolks into the quark. Now fold the stiffly beaten egg whites and whipped cream into the quark mixture. Spread this mixture evenly on the blind-baked pastry base.

6 Put the springform mould back in the oven and continue **to bake for a further 75 minutes.**

7 Turn off the oven but leave the cheesecake in the oven for about 5 minutes with the oven door slightly open; this will prevent the surface from cracking. Then put the cheesecake, still in the springform mould, on a cake rack to cool.

TIP » You can also sprinkle raisins on the pastry base and then put the filling on top.

Recipe variation: To make **cheese-cake with crumble topping**, make a crumble by mixing together 100 g/ 3½ oz (1 cup) plain (all purpose) flour, 75 g/2½ oz (⅜ cup) sugar, 1 packet vanilla sugar and 75 g/ 2½ oz (⅜ cup) softened butter using a hand-mixer with whisk attachment. Then spread the crum-ble evenly over the filling and bake the cheesecake as described in step 6.

Silesian poppy seed tart

TRADITIONAL (ABOUT 16 PIECES)

Preparation time:
about 45 minutes,
excluding cooling time
Baking time: about 60 minutes

**For the springform mould
(diameter 26 cm/10¼ in):**
a little fat

For the shortcrust pastry:
200 g/7 oz (2 cups) plain
(all purpose) flour
1 level teaspoon baking powder
100 g/3½ oz (½ cup) sugar
1 sachet vanilla sugar
1 pinch salt
1 egg (medium)
1 tablespoon cold water
100 g/3½ oz (½ cup) soft butter
or margarine

For the topping:
750 ml/1¼ pints (3½ cups) milk
125 g/4½ oz (⅝ cup) butter
150 g/5 oz (1½ cups) semolina
flour
150 g/5 oz (⅝ cup) freshly
ground poppy seeds
150 g/5 oz (¾ cup) sugar
1 sachet vanilla sugar
125 g/4½ oz (½ cup) low fat
quark
1 egg (medium)
50 g/2 oz (½ cup) ground almonds
50 g/2 oz (⅓ cup) raisins
2 tablespoons rum

For dusting:
a little icing (confectioners')
sugar

1 To make the shortcrust pastry, mix together the flour and baking powder in a mixing bowl. Add all the other ingredients for the short-crust pastry and whisk everything using a hand-mixer (kneading hook), first on the lowest setting, then on the highest setting until all the ingredients have been incorporated and formed a shortcrust pastry. Then shape into a roll with your hands. If the pastry feels sticky, wrap it in clingfilm (plastic film) and put in the refrigerator for about 30 minutes.

2 To make the filling, bring the milk with the butter to the boil in a pan. Mix together the semolina and poppy seeds, remove the pan with the milk from the heat and sprinkle the semolina and poppy seed mixture into the milk, stirring all the time. Leave to soak. Let the poppy seed to cool for about 10 minutes.

3 Grease the bottom of the spring-form mould. Preheat the oven:
Top/bottom heat:
about 180 °C/350 °F (Gas mark 4)
Fan oven:
about 160 °C/325 °F (Gas mark 3)

4 Roll out a generous half of the pastry on the bottom of the prepared

springform mould, then shape the rest of the pastry into a long roll. Place round the outside of the pastry base and press against the sides to make an edge about 3 cm/1¼ in high.

5 Stir the sugar, vanilla sugar, quark, egg, almonds, raisins and rum into the poppy seed mixture. Now spoon this mixture into the springform mould and smooth the surface to make it even. Put the springform mould on a shelf (lined with baking parchment because some fat may ooze out) in the bottom third of the oven. **Bake for about 60 minutes.**

6 Leave the tart to cool in the spring-form mould on a cake rack.

7 Loosen the tart from the springform mould and remove it. Sprinkle with icing (confectioners') sugar before serving. If you like you can "stencil" a pattern using a cake rack.

TIPS » This tart is also delicious when served slightly warm.
» Instead of ground poppy seeds you can use whole poppy seeds.
» You can add a touch of sophistication by including a pear in the filling: peel the pear, cut into quarters, core, grate and stir into the filling.

Per piece: P: 8 g, F: 20 g, C: 38 g, kJ: 1561, kcal: 373, CU: 3.0

Engadine walnut tart

GOOD TO MAKE IN ADVANCE (ABOUT 12 PIECES)

Preparation time:
about 55 minutes,
excluding cooling time
Baking time: about 45 minutes

For the springform mould
(diameter 26 cm/10¼ in):
a little fat

For the shortcrust pastry:
275 g/9½ oz (2¾ cups) plain
(all purpose) flour
1 level teaspoon baking powder
100 g/3½ oz (½ cup) sugar
1 sachet vanilla sugar
1 pinch salt
1 egg (medium)
150 g/5 oz (¾ cup) soft butter
or margarine

For the filling:
250 g/9 oz (3 cups) shelled
walnuts
225 g/8 oz (1⅛ cups) sugar
200 g/7 oz (⅞ cup) whipping
cream
1–2 tablespoons runny honey
1 egg white (medium)

For coating:
1 egg yolk (medium)
1 tablespoon water

For dusting:
icing (confectioners') sugar

Per piece:
P: 7 g, F: 30 g, C: 50 g,
kJ: 2093, kcal: 500, CU: 4.0

1 To make the shortcrust pastry, mix together the flour and baking powder in a mixing bowl. Add all the other ingredients for the shortcrust pastry and whisk everything using a hand-mixer (kneading hook), first on the lowest setting, then on the highest setting until all the ingredients have been incorporated and formed a shortcrust pastry. Then shape into a roll with your hands. Wrap the pastry in clingfilm (plastic film) and store in the refrigerator until you are ready to use it.

2 Grease the bottom of the springform mould. Preheat the oven:
Top/bottom heat:
about 200 °C/400 °F (Gas mark 6)
Fan oven:
about 180 °C/350 °F (Gas mark 4)

3 To make the filling, coarsely chop the walnuts. Melt the sugar in a pan over medium heat until it is caramelised (only start stirring with a wooden or metal spoon when the sugar begins to melt). Then continue stirring until the sugar has turned light brown. Stir in the chopped walnuts and cream one after the other and bring to the boil. Stir in the honey. Leave the mixture to cool a little. Then stir in the egg white.

4 Roll out half the pastry on the bottom of the springform mould. Then put the ring of the springform mould back on. Roll out two-thirds of the remaining pastry between a cut-open freezer-bag or to sheets of clingfilm (plastic film) to make a circle. Use the bottom of

the springform mould as a template for the lid by placing it on the rolled-out pastry and cutting round it with a pastry wheel or knife.

5 Shape the rest of the dough into a long roll and place it round the outside of the pastry base; then press it against the sides of the springform mould to make an edge about 2 cm/¾ in high.

6 Spread the filling evenly over the pastry base. Remove the freezer-bag or clingfilm from the top of the pastry lid, then turn the lid over so that the other side is upwards and place it on the filling; now remove the remaining freezer bag or clingfilm. Press the pastry lid down lightly round the edge and prick several times with a fork. Whisk together the egg yolk and water and brush over the pastry lid. Put the springform mould on a shelf in the bottom third of the preheated oven and **bake for about 45 minutes.**

7 Loosen the ring and remove it. Now loosen the tart from the bottom of the springform mould but leave it there; put the springform mould base on a cake rack to cool. Allow the tart to infuse for at least 1 day.

8 Sprinkle with icing (confectioners') sugar before serving. You can make a pattern if you like by sprinkling the sugar through a paper stencil.

TIP ›› The tart will keep for 1 week if well wrapped.

Cheese pastries

SAVOURY (1 BAKING SHEET)

Preparation time:
about 30 minutes
Baking time: about 10 minutes

For the baking sheet
(40 x 30 cm/16 x 12 in):
baking parchment

For the shortcrust pastry:
400 g/14 oz (4 cups) plain (all
purpose) flour
3 level teaspoons baking
powder
½ level teaspoon salt
250 g/9 oz (1 cup) low fat
quark
250 g/9 oz (1¼ cups) soft
butter

For coating and dusting:
3 tablespoons condensed milk
50 g/2 oz (⅓ cup) grated
Parmesan cheese
2 tablespoons caraway seeds

In all:
P: 95 g, F: 235 g, C: 305 g,
kJ: 15757, kcal: 3767, CU: 25.5

1 Line the baking sheet with baking parchment. Preheat the oven:
Top/bottom heat:
about 200 °C/400 °F (Gas mark 6)
Fan oven:
about 180 °C/350 °F (Gas mark 4)

2 To make the shortcrust pastry, mix together the flour and baking powder in a mixing bowl. Add all the other ingredients for the shortcrust pastry and whisk everything using a hand-mixer (kneading hook), first on the lowest setting, then on the highest setting until all the ingredients have been incorporated and formed a shortcrust pastry. Then shape into a roll with your hands. If the pastry feels sticky, wrap it in clingfilm (plastic film) and put it in the refrigerator for about 30 minutes.

3 Roll out the pastry in several portions to a thickness of about 5 mm/³⁄₁₆ in (photograph 1). Cut out strips and squares (photograph 2) with a pastry wheel, brush with condensed milk, then sprinkle with grated Parmesan cheese and caraway seeds (photograph 3). Put the baking sheet on the middle shelf of the preheated oven and **bake for about 10 minutes**.

4 Slide the pastries together with the baking parchment onto a cake rack to cool.

Recipe variation: Snails with red fromage frais filling (50 pieces/2 baking sheets). Make a shortcrust pastry with 200 g/7 oz (2 cups) hard flour, ½ teaspoon baking powder, ½ level teaspoon salt, 1 egg (medium), 80 g/3 oz (⅜ cup) softened butter or margarine and 3 tablespoons cold water. Wrap the pastry in clingfilm (plastic film) and place in the refrigerator for about 1 hour. To make the fromage frais filling, drain 40 g/1½ oz sun-dried tomatoes in oil, chop up finely and mix together with 100 g/3½ oz (⅜ cup) double cream fromage frais, 2 teaspoons tomato puree and 20 g/¾ oz (2 tablespoons) grated Parmesan; season with pepper. Roll out the dough on a floured work top to make rectangle about 50 x 30 cm/20 x 12 in. Spread the filling on the pastry rectangle, leaving an uncovered edge 1 cm/⅜ in wide all round. Roll up the dough starting from the long side. Cut the roll in half to make 2 rolls. Wrap the rolls in clingfilm (plastic film) and place in the refrigerator for at least 3 hours. Then line the baking sheet with baking parchment. Preheat the oven: Top/bottom heat: about 200 °C/400 °F (Gas mark 6) or Fan oven: about 180 °C/350 °F (Gas mark 4). Cut the rolls into slices 1 cm/⅜ in thick using a serrated knife and place on the baking sheet. Bake the baking sheets on the middle shelf of the preheated oven one after the other (or both at once if you have a fan oven). Bake each baking sheet of snails for about 20 minutes.

2

3

Yeast dough

Yeast dough is a very special dough because it is "alive". Tiny organisms ensure that the dough remains elastic and the baked item becomes light and fluffy. Yeast dough is made with flour, yeast, sometimes fat, sugar, sometimes eggs and (usually lukewarm) liquid. Yeast dough is particularly suitable for cakes baked on a baking sheet, small pastries and items such as plaited buns, bread and rolls.

How to make yeast dough

Step 1: Prepare the yeast dough with dried yeast or fresh yeast
Whether you use dried or fresh yeast – if prepared correctly, the result will excellent.
Baking with dried yeast does not require any special preparations. Baking with fresh dough is very "traditional". When using fresh yeast it is necessary to make a leaven which is not necessary if you use dried yeast.
You will find dried yeast in shops in the baking section and fresh yeast (sometimes) in the freezer section.

» Baking with dried yeast
Put the flour in a mixing bowl, add the dried yeast and mix well with a fork to ensure the dried yeast is incorporated evenly (photograph 1). Now add the ingredients listed in the recipe. Fluids should be lukewarm or about 37 °C/99 °F because only then will the yeast be able to develop its full power. Using a hand-mixer with a kneading hook, knead all the ingredients first briefly on the lowest setting, then on the highest setting for about 5 minutes to make a smooth dough (photograph 2). Finally carefully knead the heavier ingredients such as fruit and nuts into the dough.

» Baking with fresh yeast
When baking with fresh yeast, you must make a leaven with the fresh yeast. Crumble the yeast and stir into the lukewarm water with a little sugar (photograph 3), then allow to stand at room temperature for about 15 minutes. Salt and fat in particular slow down the yeast's activity, so they should only come into contact with the yeast when the

dough itself is kneaded. Add the other ingredients only after the yeast has been mixed with the flour. Then continue as indicated for the dough made with dried yeast and finally knead any fruit or nuts into the dough.

Step 2: Let the dough rise (1st rising)
To enable the yeast cultures to do their work, the dough cannot be baked immediately. Place the bowl with the dough in a warm place and cover with a tea towel; leave to rise for 20–30 minutes until the dough has visibly increased in volume (photographs 4 and 5).
A good place to put the dough to rise is near a radiator or in the oven with top and bottom heat set at a maximum of 50 °C/120 °F and the oven door held open with a wooden spoon. The dough can also be placed in the microwave to rise. This is done by covering the bowl with a moist tea towel, switching the microwave to 80-90 watts and leave the dough to rise for about 8 minutes. If the microwave does

not have a turntable, turn the dough after 4 minutes.

You can also leave the dough to rise in the refrigerator. In this case, make the dough with cold ingredients, brush the dough in the mixing bowl with a little cooking oil, cover with moist tea towel and leave to rise in the refrigerator overnight.

Step 3: Preparing the baking tin or baking sheet

While the dough is rising, grease the baking tin or baking sheet generously and evenly with spreadable margarine or butter, using a pastry brush. Do not use oil – it would run down the sides of the tin. For chunks of dough or small pastries, line the baking sheet with baking parchment – it is not necessary to grease it.

Step 4: Let the dough rise a second time (2nd rising)

The dough must rise a second time after the first rising. In the meantime preheat the oven. For the second rising, sprinkle the dough with a little flour, take it out of the mixing bowl and knead it briefly again with your hands on the lightly floured work surface (photograph 6). Then continue working the dough as indicated in the recipe. Now put the dough in the tin or on the baking sheet, cover with the tea towel and put it in a warm place again until it has visibly increased in volume.

Step 5: Bake the yeast dough

After the second rising the dough must immediately be put in the preheated oven and baked.

When the dough has baked, leave it in the tin for a further 10 minutes. Then turn the tin out onto a cake rack and leave to cool. Larger chunks of dough baked on a baking sheet should be left on it and the whole baking sheet is put on a cake rack. Small pastries such as plaited buns should be removed from the baking sheet and put on a cake rack to cool.

How to store baked yeast dough

Baked yeast dough is best consumed fresh but it can also be frozen. In this case it should be defrosted in the freezer bag at room temperature before being briefly crisped up in the oven at baking temperature.

Raw yeast dough can also be frozen and kept for 6–8 months. In this case, prepare the dough without rising, shape it on the floured work top into a flat rectangle, put it in a freezer bag and freeze. To use it, leave it to defrost in the bag overnight in the refrigerator, then follow the instructions in the recipe – the next step will be the 1st rising.

Sophisticated kugelhopf cake

TRADITIONAL (ABOUT 16 SLICES)

Preparation time:
about 35 minutes,
excluding rising time
Baking time: about 50 minutes

For the Bundt pan or kugelhopf
mould (diameter 22 cm/9 in):
a little fat

For the yeast dough:
200 g/7 oz (⅞ cup) whipping
cream
100 g/3½ oz (½ cup) butter or
margarine
400 g/14 oz (4 cups) plain
(all purpose) flour
1 sachet dried yeast
125 g/4½ oz (⅝ cup) sugar
1 sachet vanilla sugar
a few drops Dr. Oetker
Natural Lemon Extract
1 pinch salt
3 eggs (medium)
150 g/5 oz (¾ cup) raisins
100 g/3½ oz (⅔ cup) currants
100 g/3½ oz (⅞ cup) peeled,
chopped almonds

Also:
a little icing (confectioners')
sugar

Per slice:
P: 6 g, F: 14 g, C: 38 g,
kJ: 1298, kcal: 310, CU: 3.0

1 For the dough, warm the cream in a small pan and melt the butter or margarine in it.

2 To make the dough, carefully mix together the flour and dried yeast in a mixing bowl. Then add the other ingredients (except for the raisins, currants and almonds) and add the warm cream-fat mixture. Mix all the ingredients using a hand-mixer (kneading hook), first briefly on the lowest setting, then on the highest setting for about 5 minutes to make a smooth dough.

3 Briskly knead the raisins, currants and almonds into the dough. Put the dough in a warm place until it has visibly increased in volume.

4 Grease the kugelhopf mould. Preheat the oven:
Top/bottom heat:
about 180 °C/350 °F (Gas mark 4)
Fan oven:
about 160 °C/325 °F (Gas mark 3)

5 Knead the dough briefly using a hand-mixer (kneading hook) on the highest setting, put the dough in the kugelhopf mould and put the dough again in a warm place to rise until it has visibly increased in volume. Put the mould on a shelf in the bottom third of the preheated oven and **bake for about 50 minutes**.

6 Leave the cake in the tin for about 10 minutes, then turn it out and leave to cool on a cake rack. Sprinkle with icing (confectioners') sugar.

Variation: Instead of almonds, raisins and currants, you make the kugelhopf using 100 g/3½ oz (½ cup) finely chopped glacé cherries, 200 g/7 oz (1⅓ cups) dried, chopped apricots and 50 g/2 oz (⅓ cup) chopped pistachio nuts.

Apple turnovers

FOR CHILDREN (ABOUT 14 PIECES/2 BAKING SHEETS)

Preparation time:
about 65 minutes,
excluding rising time
Baking time: about 20 minutes
per baking sheet

For the baking sheet:
baking parchment

For the yeast dough:
200 ml/7 fl oz (⅞ cup) milk
50 g/2 oz (4 tablespoons)
butter or margarine
375 g/13 oz (3¾ cups) plain
(all purpose) flour
1 sachet dried yeast
50 g/2 oz (¼ cup) sugar
1 sachet vanilla sugar
1 pinch salt
1 egg (medium)

For the filling:
500 g/18 oz apples, e.g.
Jonagold or Elstar
50 g/2 oz (⅓ cup) raisins
40 g/1½ oz (3 tablespoons)
sugar
20 g/¾ oz (2 tablespoons)
butter

For coating and sprinkling:
milk
slivered almonds

For the icing:
100 g/3½ oz (¾ cup) icing
(confectioners') sugar
1 tablespoon lemon juice
10 g/⅓ oz (2 teaspoons) butter

1 For the dough, warm the milk in a small pan and melt the butter or margarine in it.

2 To make the dough, carefully mix together the flour and dried yeast in a mixing bowl. Then add the other ingredients and the warm cream-fat mixture. Mix all the ingredients using a hand-mixer (kneading hook), first briefly on the lowest setting, then on the highest setting for about 5 minutes to make a smooth dough.

3 Cover the dough in a warm place and leave to rise until it has visibly increased in volume.

4 For the filling, peel the apples, cut into quarters, core and cut into small chunks. Braise the apples in a pan together with the raisins, sugar and butter, stirring all the time, then leave to cool.

5 Sprinkle the dough with a little flour and knead again briefly on the lightly floured work surface. Roll out the dough thinly and cut out 14 circles (diameter about 12 cm/ 4¾ in) (photograph 1). Put the filling on one half of each circle.

6 Brush the edges of each circle with milk (photograph 2), then fold one half over the other. Press the edges firmly together with a fork or a pastry scraper (photograph 3).

7 Line the baking sheet with baking parchment. Preheat the oven:
Top/bottom heat:
about 200 °C/400 °F (Gas mark 6)
Fan oven:
about 180 °C/350 °F (Gas mark 4)

8 Brush the apple turnovers with the milk, sprinkle with almonds if you like and put half the apple turnovers on the baking sheet.

9 Put all the apple turnovers in warm place to rise again until they have visibly increased in volume.

10 Put the baking sheet on the middle shelf in the preheated oven. **Bake for about 20 minutes.**

11 Slide the baked apple turnovers together with the baking parchment onto a cake rack to cool. **Then bake the rest of the apple turnovers as indicated.**

12 For the glaze, sift the icing (confectioners') sugar, then add to the lemon juice to make a thick mixture. Melt the butter and stir into the lemon and icing sugar mixture.

13 Brush immediately over the apple turnovers while they are still hot and leave to cool.

TIP » If you are using a fan oven you can bake 2 baking sheets at a time.

Per piece: P: 5 g, F: 8 g, C: 41 g, kJ: 1085, kcal: 259, CU: 3.5

Custard Chelsea buns

GOOD FOR FREEZING (ABOUT 30 PIECES/3–4 BAKING SHEETS)

Preparation time:
about 50 minutes,
excluding rising time
Baking time: about 15 minutes
per baking sheet

For the baking sheet:
baking parchment

For the yeast dough:
125 ml/4 fl oz (½ cup) milk
100 g/3½ oz (½ cup) butter or
margarine
500 g/18 oz (5 cups) plain
(all purpose) flour
1 sachet dried yeast
50 g/2 oz (¼ cup) sugar
1 sachet vanilla sugar
2 eggs (medium)

For the filling:
80 g/3 oz (⅔ cup) custard
powder (vanilla pudding mix)
750 ml/1¼ pints (3½ cups)
milk
80 g/3 oz (⅜ cup) sugar
100 g/3½ oz (⅔ cup) raisins

For the apricot glaze:
4 tablespoons apricot jam
2 tablespoons water

Per piece:
P: 3 g, F: 4 g, C: 25 g,
kJ: 655 kcal: 156, CU: 2.0

1 For the dough, heat up the milk in a small pan. Melt the butter or margarine in it.

2 To make the dough, carefully mix together the flour and dried yeast in a mixing bowl. Then add the other ingredients and add the warm cream-fat mixture. Mix all the ingredients using a hand-mixer (kneading hook), first briefly on the lowest setting, then on the highest setting for about 5 minutes to make a smooth dough. Cover the dough and put in a warm place to rise until it has visibly increased in volume.

3 For the filling, make a custard with custard powder, milk and sugar, following the instructions on the packet but using only 750 ml/1¼ pints (3½ cups) milk. Leave to cool, stirring occasionally. Then stir in the raisins.

4 Line the baking sheet with baking parchment. Preheat the oven:
Top/bottom heat:
about 200 °C/400 °F (Gas mark 6)
Fan oven:
about 180 °C/350 °F (Gas mark 4)

5 Sprinkle the dough with a little flour, take out of the mixing bowl and knead again briefly on the lightly floured work surface.

6 Roll out the dough to make a rectangle (about 60 x 40 cm/24 x 16 in) and spread the custard filling over it. Roll up the dough, starting with the long side (photograph 1) and cut into slices about 2 cm/¾ in thick. Arrange 6–8 slices a little distance from each other on the baking sheet (photograph 2) and put the other slices on the baking parchment.

7 Put the slices again in a warm place to rise until they have visibly increased in volume. Put the baking sheet on the middle shelf in the preheated oven. **Bake for about 15 minutes.**

8 For the apricot glaze, rub the jam through a sieve, bring to the boil briefly with the water, stirring all the time, then brush onto the custard Chelsea buns as soon as they come out of the oven (photograph 3). **Bake the remaining custard Chelsea buns as indicated** and brush with apricot glaze.

9 Leave the custard Chelsea buns to cool on a cake rack.

TIP » If you have a fan oven you can bake 2–3 baking sheets at a time.

Plaited brioche loaf

TRADITIONAL – FOR GUESTS (ABOUT 12 SLICES)

Preparation time:
about 35 minutes,
excluding rising time
Baking time: about 30 minutes

For the baking sheet:
baking parchment

For the yeast dough:
250 g/9 oz (1 cup) whipping cream
500 g/18 oz (5 cups) plain (all purpose) flour
1 sachet dried yeast
80 g/3 oz (⅜ cup) sugar
1 sachet vanilla sugar
1 teaspoon grated lemon zest
1 pinch salt, 2 eggs (medium)
1 egg white (medium)

For coating:
1 egg yolk (medium)
1 tablespoon milk

Per slice:
P: 7 g, F: 9 g, C: 39 g,
kJ: 1108, kcal: 265, CU: 3.5

1 To make the dough, warm the cream. Then carefully mix together the flour and dried yeast in a mixing bowl. Add the other ingredients and the warm cream. Mix all the ingredients using a hand-mixer (kneading hook), first briefly on the lowest setting, then on the highest setting for about 5 minutes to make a smooth dough. Cover the dough and put in a warm place to rise until it has visibly increased in volume.

2 Sprinkle with a little flour and knead briefly on the lightly floured work surface. Divide the dough into 4 portions to make 4 rolls about 30 cm/12 in long.

3 Weave the rolls into each other to make a plait (photograph 1 and drawing). To do this put the 4 rolls next to each other. Push the top ends of the rolls together. Now put roll 4 over roll 3, under roll 2 and over roll 1. Pull all the rolls a little to the right, then pick up the far right roll (3) and put over roll 2, under roll 1 and over roll 4. Repeat this process until the plait is complete, making sure you always start from the right. Press the ends firmly together.

4 Line the baking sheet with baking parchment, place the plaited bun on it. Preheat the oven:
Top/bottom heat:
about 180 °C/350 °F (Gas mark 4)
Fan oven:
about 160 °C/325 °F (Gas mark 3)

5 Beat together the egg yolk and the milk and brush over the plaited bun. Put the plaited bun in a warm place again to rise until it has visibly increased in volume.

6 Put the baking sheet on the middle shelf of the preheated oven and **bake for about 30 minutes**.

7 Slide the baked biscuits together with the baking parchment onto a cake rack to cool.

Recipe variations: To make a **plaited brioche loaf with raisins**, briefly knead 200 g/7 oz (1⅓ cups) raisins into the dough after the first rising.
» For a **plaited brioche loaf with exotic dried fruit** (photograph on the left), knead 200 g/7 oz (1⅓ cups) coarsely chopped exotic dried fruit into the dough after the first rising.

1.

2.

3.

4.

1

Plaited poppy seed loaf

POPULAR – SUITABLE FOR FREEZING (ABOUT 20 SLICES)

Preparation time:
about 60 minutes,
excluding rising time
Baking time: about 60 minutes

For the baking sheet:
baking parchment

For the yeast dough:
200 ml/7 fl oz (⅞ cup) water
150 g/5 oz (¾ cup) butter or
margarine
500 g/18 oz (5 cups) plain
(all purpose) flour
1 sachet dried yeast
75 g/3 oz (⅓ cup) sugar
1 sachet vanilla sugar

For the filling:
300 g/10 oz (1¼ cups) poppy seeds
400 ml/14 fl oz (1¾ cups) milk
40 g/1½ oz (5 tablespoons)
custard powder (vanilla
pudding mix)
100 ml/3½ fl oz (½ cup) milk
2 eggs (medium)
75 g/3 oz (⅓ cup) sugar
75 g/3 oz rusks

For the crumble:
100 g/3½ oz (1 cup) plain (all
purpose) flour
100 g/3½ oz (⅞ cup) slivered
almonds
100 g/3½ oz (½ cup) sugar
100 g/3½ oz (½ cup) soft butter

For the apricot glaze and icing:
4 tablespoons apricot jam
1 tablespoon water
100 g/3½ oz (¾ cup) icing
(confectioners') sugar
2–3 tablespoons water

1 For the dough, heat up the water in a small pan and melt the butter or margarine in it.

2 Now carefully mix together the flour and dried yeast in a mixing bowl. Then add the other ingredients and the warm water-fat mixture. Mix all the ingredients using a hand-mixer (kneading hook), first briefly on the lowest setting, then on the highest setting for about 5 minutes to make a smooth dough. Cover the dough and put in a warm place to rise until it has visibly increased in volume.

3 For the filling, put the poppy seeds in the milk and bring briefly to the boil. Then remove the pan from the heat and leave the poppy seeds to swell for about 10 minutes. Stir the custard powder into the milk and add to the poppy seed mixture together with the eggs and sugar. Bring briefly to the boil while stirring, then leave to cool. Put the rusks in a freezer bag, seal it, then crush with a rolling pin to turn into fine crumbs. Fold the crumbs into the poppy seed mixture.

4 Line the baking sheet with baking parchment. Preheat the oven:
Top/bottom heat:
about 180 °C/350 °F (Gas mark 4)
Fan oven:
about 160 °C/325 °F (Gas mark 3)

5 Sprinkle the dough with a little flour, take out of the bowl and

knead again briefly on the lightly floured work surface. Roll out to make a rectangle about 40 x 30 cm/ 16 x 12 in.

6 Spread the poppy seed mixture on it, leaving an edge about 1 cm/⅜ in wide uncovered. Roll up the dough, starting with the long side, and put the roll on the baking sheet with the seam upward.

7 To make the crumble, put the flour in a mixing bowl together with the almonds, sugar and softened butter and mix using a hand-mixer with whisk attachment to make a crumble of the right texture.

8 Sprinkle the cake with a little water, then scatter the crumble on top and press down. Leave the cake to rise once more until it has visibly increased in volume. Put the baking tin in the bottom third of the oven and **bake for about 60 minutes**.

9 To make the apricot glaze, rub the jam through a sieve and bring to the boil briefly with the water.

10 Brush immediately over the plaited poppy seed loaf while it is still hot and leave to cool on a cake rack.

11 To make the icing, sift the icing (confectioners') sugar, add water and stir to make a thick icing.

12 Brush this over the plaited poppy seed loaf.

Per slice: P: 9 g, F: 20 g, C: 50 g, kJ: 1808, kcal: 432, CU: 4.0

Apple, crumble or plum cake

POPULAR – TRADITIONAL (ABOUT 20 SLICES)

Preparation time:
about 35 minutes,
excluding rising time
Baking time: about 25 minutes

For the baking sheet
(40 x 30 cm/16 x 12 in):
a little fat

For the yeast dough:
200 ml/7 fl oz (⅞ cup) milk
50 g/2 oz (4 tablespoons)
butter or margarine
375 g/13 oz (3¾ cups) plain
(all purpose) flour
1 sachet dried yeast
50 g/2 oz (¼ cup) sugar
1 sachet vanilla sugar
1 pinch salt, 1 egg (medium)

For the apple cake:
about 1.5 kg/3¼ lb sharp apples
20 g/¾ oz (5 tablespoons)
slivered almonds
20 g/¾ oz (1½ tablespoons)
raisins

For the apricot glaze:
3 tablespoons apricot jam
1 tablespoon water

or For the crumble cake:
300 g/10 oz (3 cups) plain (all
purpose) flour
150 g/5 oz (¾ cup) sugar
1 sachet vanilla sugar
175 g/6 oz (¼ cup) soft butter
or margarine
25 g/1 oz (2 tablespoons) butter

or For the plum cake:
2½ kg/5½ lb plums
a little sugar

1 For the dough, warm the milk in a small pan and melt the butter or margarine in it.

2 Carefully mix together the flour and dried yeast in a mixing bowl. Then add the other ingredients and the warm milk-fat mixture. Mix all the ingredients using a hand-mixer (kneading hook), first briefly on the lowest setting, then on the highest setting for about 5 minutes to make a smooth dough.

3 Put the dough in a warm place to rise until it has visibly increased in volume. Grease the baking sheet.

4 Sprinkle a little flour on the dough, remove from the bowl, knead again briefly on the lightly floured work surface and shape into a roll. Roll out the dough on the baking sheet and continue to make the apple, crumble or plum cake.

5 Preheat the oven:
Top/bottom heat:
about 200 °C/400 °F (Gas mark 6)
Fan oven:
about 180 °C/350 °F (Gas mark 4)

a To make the apple cake, peel the apples, cut into quarters, core and cut into thick slices. Arrange the apple slices on the dough, sprinkle with almonds and raisins. Put the dough in a warm place again to rise until it has increased visibly in volume. Put the baking sheet on the middle shelf in the preheated oven.

Bake for about 25 minutes. For the apricot glaze, rub the jam through a sieve and bring to the boil with water, stirring all the time. Brush over the apple cake as soon as it comes out of the oven and put the cake – still on the baking sheet – on a cake rack to cool.

b To make the crumble cake, mix together the flour, sugar, vanilla sugar and butter or margarine with a hand-mixer with whisk attachment to make the crumble of the desired texture. Melt the butter and brush over the dough. Spread the crumble on top. Put the dough in a warm place again to rise until it has visibly increased in volume. Put the baking sheet on the middle shelf in the preheated oven and **bake for about 15 minutes**. Put the cake – still on the baking sheet – on a cake rack to cool.

c To make the plum cake, wash the plums, drain well, pat dry, remove the stones and, if necessary, make an incision, then arrange them with their inside facing upward in such a way that they overlap. Put the dough in a warm place again to rise until it has visibly increased in volume. Put the dough on the middle shelf in the preheated oven and **bake for about 25 minutes**. Put the cake – still on the baking sheet – on a cake rack to cool. Sprinkle the slightly cooled plum cake with a little sugar.

pple cake per slice:
3 g, F: 4 g, C: 28 g,
J: 690, kcal: 165, CU: 2.5

Crumble cake per slice:
P: 4 g, F: 12 g, C: 36 g,
kJ: 1129, kcal: 270, CU: 3.0

Plum cake per slice:
P: 3 g, F: 3 g, C: 30 g,
kJ: 725, kcal: 174, CU: 2.5

Thuringian crumble cake

SOPHISTICATED (ABOUT 20 SLICES) PHOTOGRAPH FRONT

Preparation time:
about 35 minutes,
excluding rising and cooling time
Baking time: about 20 minutes

For the baking sheet
(40 x 30 cm/16 x 12 in):
a little fat

For the yeast dough:
200 ml/7 fl oz (⅞ cup) milk
50 g/2 oz (4 tablespoons)
butter or margarine
375 g/13 oz (3¾ cups) plain
(all purpose) flour
1 sachet dried yeast
50 g/2 oz (¼ cup) sugar
1 sachet vanilla sugar
1 egg (medium)

For coating:
20 g/¾ oz (2 tablespoons)
butter

For the crumble:
300 g/10 oz (3 cups) plain
(all purpose) flour
150 g/5 oz (¾ cup) sugar
1 sachet vanilla sugar
200 g/7 oz (1 cup) soft butter
or margarine
10 g/⅓ oz (1½ tablespoons)
cocoa powder

For drizzling:
125 ml/4 fl oz (½ cup) milk
60 g/2 oz (¼ cup) butter

For coating and sprinkling:
100 g/3½ oz (½ cup) butter
50 g/2 oz (¼ cup) icing
(confectioners') sugar

1 For the dough, heat the milk in a small pan and melt the butter or margarine in it.

2 Carefully mix together the flour and dried yeast in a mixing bowl. Then add the other ingredients and add the warm milk-fat mixture. Mix all the ingredients using a hand-mixer (kneading hook), first briefly on the lowest setting, then on the highest setting for about 5 minutes to make a smooth dough. Cover the dough and put in warm place to rise until it has visibly increased in volume.

3 Grease the baking sheet. Preheat the oven:
Top/bottom heat:
about 200 °C/400 °F (Gas mark 6)
Fan oven:
about 180 °C/350 °F (Gas mark 4)

4 Sprinkle a little flour on the dough, take it out of the bowl, knead again briefly on the lightly floured work surface and shape into a roll. Roll the dough on the baking sheet. Melt the butter and brush over the dough.

5 For the crumble, put the flour, sugar, vanilla sugar and softened butter or margarine in a mixing bowl. Whisk all the ingredients together using a hand-mixer with whisk attachment to make a crumble of the desired texture. Sprinkle half the crumble over the dough. Stir the cocoa powder into the rest of the

crumble and fill the gaps with it to create a black and white pattern.

6 Put the dough in a warm place again to rise until it has increased visibly in volume. Put the baking sheet on the middle shelf in the preheated oven and **bake for about 20 minutes**.

7 Now heat the milk and melt the butter in it. Drizzle on the still hot cake. Put the cake together with the baking sheet on a cake rack to cool.

8 For the coating, melt the butter and brush over the cake, then sprinkle with icing (confectioners') sugar.

Recipe variation: To make a **Thuringian coconut cake** (at the back of the photograph), make the dough as indicated in the recipe (up to and including step 4). To make the coconut topping, melt 200 g/7 oz (1 cup) butter in a pan. Add 150 g/2 oz (¼ cup) sugar and 1 sachet of vanilla sugar and bring it all to the boil. Then add 200 g/7 oz (2½ cups) grated coconut and allow to brown lightly, stirring all the time. Leave the coconut topping to cool, then stir in 3 eggs (medium). Spread the coconut topping on the dough and bake for 25 minutes at the temperature indicated. Brush the still hot cake with 150 ml/5 fl oz (⅝ cup) hot milk. Leave the cake to cool. If you like, sprinkle 50 g/2 oz melted chocolate on the cake.

Per slice: P: 5 g, F: 20 g, C: 39 g, kJ: 1477, kcal: 353, CU: 3.0

Almond-coated yeast cake

POPULAR (ABOUT 20 SLICES)

Preparation time:
about 50 minutes,
excluding rising time
Baking time: about 15 minutes

**For the baking sheet (40 x 30 cm/
16 x 12 in) with high sides
(about 2 cm/¾ in):**
a little fat

For the yeast dough:
200 ml/7 fl oz (⅞ cup) milk
50 g/2 oz (4 tablespoons)
butter or margarine
375 g/13 oz (3¾ cups) plain
(all purpose) flour
1 sachet dried yeast
50 g/2 oz (¼ cup) sugar
1 sachet vanilla sugar
1 pinch salt
1 egg (medium)

For the topping:
150 g/5 oz (¾ cup) butter
100 g/3½ oz (½ cup) sugar
1 sachet vanilla sugar
1–2 tablespoons honey
4 tablespoons whipping cream
200 g/7 oz (1⅔ cups) slivered
almonds

For the filling:
80 g/3 oz (⅔ cup) custard
powder (vanilla pudding mix)
750 ml/1¼ pints (3½ cups)
milk
100 g/3½ oz (½ cup) sugar
100 g/3½ oz (½ cup) butter

Per slice:
P: 6 g, F: 21 g, C: 34 g,
kJ: 1477, kcal: 353, CU: 3.0

1 For the dough, heat the milk in a small pan and melt the butter or margarine in it.

2 Carefully mix together the flour and dried yeast in a mixing bowl. Then add the other ingredients and the warm milk-fat mixture. Mix all the ingredients using a hand-mixer (kneading hook), first briefly on the lowest setting, then on the highest setting for about 5 minutes to make a smooth dough. Cover the dough and put in a warm place to rise until it has visibly increased in volume.

3 For the topping, gently heat up the butter with the sugar, vanilla sugar, honey and cream, stirring all the time, and bring briefly to the boil. Stir in the almonds. Allow the mixture to cool, while stirring now and again.

4 Grease the baking sheet and preheat the oven:
Top/bottom heat:
about 200 °C/400 °F (Gas mark 6)
Fan oven:
about 180 °C/350 °F (Gas mark 4)

5 Sprinkle the dough lightly with flour and knead again briefly on the lightly floured work surface, shape into a roll and roll out on the baking sheet. Spread the topping on the dough. Place the dough in a warm place again to rise until it has visibly increased in volume.

6 Put the baking sheet on the middle shelf in the preheated oven and **bake for about 15 minutes.**

7 Leave the cake – still on the baking sheet – to cool on a cake rack. Then slide the cake from the baking sheet onto the work surface. Cut the cake vertically into four quarters (photograph 1), then cut each quarter in two horizontally (photograph 2).

8 For the filling, make a custard with the custard powder, milk and sugar, following the instructions on the packet but using only 750 ml/ 1¼ pints (3½ cups) milk. Stir the butter into the hot custard. Then refrigerate and stir occasionally. Fill the slices with the cooled custard (photograph 3).

Recipe variation: To make a **coconut-coated yeast cake with caramel sauce,** replace the almonds used to make the topping by 200 g/ 7 oz (2½ cups) grated coconut. Prepare the filling as follows: mix together 3 sachets caramel cream pudding powder with 125 g/4½ oz (⅝ cup) sugar. Then gradually add at least 100 ml/3½ fl oz (½ cup) of the 750 ml/1¼ pints (3½ cups) milk and stir in 250 g/9 oz (1 cup) whipping cream. Bring the rest of the milk and cream mixture to the boil, remove from the heat and stir in the custard powder mixed with the 100 ml/3½ fl oz (½ cup) milk. Allow the custard mixture to simmer for at least 1 minute. Put the custard mixture in a bowl, cover with clingfilm (plastic film) and refrigerate. Now whisk the cooled custard mixture again with the hand-mixer with whisk attachment and fill the cake with it as described above.

Butter cake

EASY (ABOUT 20 SLICES)

Preparation time:
about 20 minutes,
excluding rising time
Baking time: about 15 minutes

For the baking sheet
(40 x 30 cm/16 x 12 in):
a little fat

For the yeast dough:
200 ml/7 fl oz (⅞ cup) milk
50 g/2 oz (4 tablespoons) butter
375 g/13 oz (3¾ cups) plain (all purpose) flour
1 sachet dried yeast
50 g/2 oz (¼ cup) sugar
1 sachet vanilla sugar
1 pinch salt
1 egg (medium)

For the topping:
100 g/3½ oz (½ cup) cold butter
75 g/2½ oz (⅜ cup) sugar
1 sachet vanilla sugar
100 g/3½ oz (1¼ cups) slivered almonds

Per slice:
P: 4 g, F: 10 g, C: 22 g,
kJ: 817, kcal: 195, CU: 2.0

1 For the dough, heat up the milk in a small pan and melt the butter in it.

2 Carefully mix together the flour and dried yeast in a mixing bowl. Then add the other ingredients and the warm milk-butter mixture. Mix all the ingredients using a hand-mixer (kneading hook), first briefly on the lowest setting, then on the highest setting for about 5 minutes to make a smooth dough. Cover the dough and put in a warm place to rise until it has visibly increased in volume.

3 Grease the baking sheet. Preheat the oven:
Top/bottom heat: about 200 °C/400 °F (Gas mark 6)
Fan oven: about 180 °C/350 °F (Gas mark 4)

4 Sprinkle a little flour over the dough, take it out the mixing bowl and knead it again briefly on the lightly floured work surface. Roll out the dough on the baking sheet.

5 For the topping, make a few slight depressions in the dough with the handle of a wooden spoon and distribute flakes of butter evenly across the dough. Mix together the sugar and vanilla sugar, sprinkle over the dough and distribute the almonds evenly across it. Put the dough in a warm place to rise until it has visibly increased in volume.

6 Put the baking sheet on the middle shelf in the preheated oven and **bake for about 15 minutes**.

7 Put the cake – still on the baking sheet – on a cake rack to cool.

Recipe variations: For a butter cake with a nutty crust (photograph 1): sprinkle 100 g/½ oz (⅝ cup) chopped hazelnuts or walnuts over the dough. Only then distribute the flakes of butter and sugar on top. Finally drizzle 8 tablespoons whipping cream over the dough. Put the dough in a warm place again to rise until it has visibly increased in volume and bake as indicated in the recipe.
» For a butter cake with apples (photograph 2): peel 1.5 kg/3¼ lb apples (for instance Elstar), cut into quarters and core. Chop them up small and bring to the boil with 4 tablespoons lemon juice, 2 tablespoons water, 75 g/3 oz (⅜ cup) sugar and 1 packet Bourbon vanilla sugar. Cook gently over low heat for about 15 minutes. Allow the apples to cool a little, then spread on the rolled out dough. If you like dot with 100 g/3½ oz (½ cup) flakes of butter. Mix together 50 g/2 oz (¼ cup) sugar with 1–2 teaspoons ground cinnamon and sprinkle on top. Put the dough in a warm place again to rise until it has visibly increased in volume. Bake as indicated in the recipe for about 25 minutes.

Eierschecke (egg-custard cake)

CLASSIC (ABOUT 20 SLICES)

Preparation time:
about 40 minutes, excluding rising time
Baking time: about 30 minutes

For the baking sheet
(40 x 30 cm/16 x 12 in) with high sides (about 2 cm/¾ in):
a little fat

For the yeast dough:
125 ml/4 fl oz (½ cup) milk
100 g/3½ oz (½ cup) butter or margarine
300 g/10 oz (3 cups) plain (all purpose) flour
1 sachet dried yeast
50 g/2 oz (¼ cup) sugar
1 sachet vanilla sugar
a few drops Dr. Oetker Lemon Extract
1 pinch salt
1 egg (medium)

For the quark topping:
40 g/1½ oz (5 tablespoons) custard powder (vanilla pudding mix)
40 g/1½ oz (3 tablespoons) sugar
500 ml/17 fl oz (2¼ cups) milk
500 g/18 oz (2 cups) low-fat quark
50 g/2 oz (⅓ cup) raisins

For the egg custard:
4 egg whites (medium)
125 g/4½ oz (⅝ cup) soft butter
125 g/4½ oz (⅝ cup) sugar
4 egg yolks (medium)
15 g/½ oz (1½ tablespoons) cornflour (cornstarch)

1 For the dough, warm the milk in a small pan and melt the butter or margarine in it.

2 To make the dough, carefully mix together the flour and dried yeast in a mixing bowl. Then add the other ingredients and the warm milk-fat mixture. Mix all the ingredients using a hand-mixer (kneading hook), first briefly on the lowest setting, then on the highest setting for about 5 minutes to make a smooth dough. Cover the dough and put in a warm place to rise until it has visibly increased in volume.

3 For the quark topping, make a custard with custard powder, sugar and milk, following the instructions on the packet. Transfer the custard to a bowl, place a sheet of clingfilm (plastic film) directly on the surface of the custard and leave to cool.

4 Grease the baking sheet. Preheat the oven:
Top/bottom heat:
about 180 °C/350 °F (Gas mark 4)
Fan oven:
about 160 °C/325 °F (Gas mark 3)

5 Stir the quark and raisins into the cooled custard. Sprinkle a little flour on the dough, take out of the bowl, knead again briefly on the lightly floured work surface, shape into a roll and roll out on the baking sheet. Spread the quark topping over the dough.

6 For the egg-custard, beat the egg whites until stiff. Whisk the softened butter using a hand-mixer with whisk attachment until smooth. Gradually stir in the sugar and continue stirring until the mixture has become completely even. Now stir in the egg yolks one by one.

7 Put the stiffly beaten egg whites on the egg yolk mixture, sift the cornflour (cornstarch) on top and fold both in very carefully. Spoon the egg custard on the quark filling and smooth flat.

8 Put the baking sheet on a shelf in the bottom third of the preheated oven and **bake for about 30 minutes**.

9 Put the cake – still on the baking sheet – on a cake rack to cool.

TIPS » Soak the raisins for the quark filling in 2 tablespoons rum before incorporating them in the mixture.
» If you do not have a baking sheet with high sides, you can bake the cake in a roasting tin (40 x 30 cm/ 16 x 12 in), or you can also use a pastry frame the same size as the baking sheet to put on a normal baking sheet.

Per slice: P: 8 g, F: 13 g, C: 28 g, kJ: 1106, kcal: 264, CU: 2.5

Onion slices

SAVOURY (ABOUT 8 SLICES)

Preparation time:
about 70 minutes,
excluding rising time
Baking time: about 35 minutes

For the baking sheet
(40 x 30 cm/16 x 12 in) with high
sides (about 2 cm/¾ in):
a little fat

For the yeast dough:
250 ml/8 fl oz (1 cup) milk
400 g/14 oz (4 cups) plain
(all purpose) flour
1 sachet dried yeast
1 teaspoon sugar
1 level teaspoon salt
6 tablespoons cooking oil,
e.g. sunflower oil

For the topping:
1.5 kg/3¼ lb Spanish onions
300 g/10 oz streaky bacon
4 tablespoons cooking oil,
e.g. sunflower oil
a little salt
freshly ground pepper
1 level teaspoon ground
caraway seeds
200 g/7 oz medium mature
Gouda cheese
4 eggs (medium)
1 container (150 g/5 oz)
crème fraîche

Per slice:
P: 20 g, F: 36 g, C: 40 g,
kJ: 2322, kcal: 566, CU: 3.0

1 To make the dough, heat the milk in a small pan. Carefully mix together the flour and dried yeast in a mixing bowl. Then add the other ingredients and the warm milk. Mix all the ingredients using a hand-mixer (kneading hook), first briefly on the lowest setting, then on the highest setting for about 5 minutes to make a smooth dough. Cover the dough and put in a warm place to rise until it has visibly increased in volume.

2 For the topping, peel the onions, cut into quarters and into thin slices. Cut the bacon into very small cubes. Heat the oil in a large pan, add the sliced onions and fry lightly, stirring all the time. Add the diced bacon and fry briefly with the onions, then season with salt, pepper and caraway. Leave the cool a little.

3 Grease the baking sheet. Preheat the oven:
Top/bottom heat:
about 200 °C/400 °F (Gas mark 6)
Fan oven:
about 180 °C/350 °F (Gas mark 4)

4 Sprinkle a little flour on the dough, take it out the bowl and knead again briefly on the lightly floured work surface. Roll out the dough on the baking sheet and press the edges lightly against the sides.

5 Grate the cheese and stir into the onion-bacon mixture together the eggs and crème fraîche. Spread this mixture on the dough, then put in a warm place to rise until it has visibly increased in volume. Place the baking sheet on a shelf in the bottom third of the preheated oven. **Bake for about 35 minutes**.

SERVING TIP » Serve the onion slices hot or cold.

TIPS » The onion slices can also be prepared the day before. To do this, prepare the dough with cold ingredients, then brush a little oil on the dough to prevent it from drying out. Cover the bowl and leave to rise in the refrigerator overnight. The next day continue from step 2.
» You can also sprinkle caraway seeds on the onion slices just before serving.

Recipe variation: To make **leek slices**, replace the onions with 1.5 kg/ 3¼ lb leeks. Prepare the leeks, rinse and drain them, then cut into thin rings. Fry the leeks with the bacon as you did the onions. Season with salt, pepper and nutmeg.

Fatless sponge

Fatless sponge with its airy texture is particularly good for flans and rolls with crème patissière, whipped cream and fruit. It is made from beaten eggs and sugar to which flour is then added.

How to make a fatless sponge

Step 1: Prepare the tin
Lightly grease the bottom of the tin or baking sheet with spreadable margarine or butter using a pastry brush.
In the case of a springform mould you only need to grease the bottom (photograph 1) so that the pastry mixture does not slide down and form a domed surface on top. Then line the baking sheet or bottom of the tin with baking parchment. Fold the baking parchment along the sloping side to make an edge which will prevent the sponge pastry running out or being too thin along the edge.
In the case of a springform mould, place the springform mould on the baking parchment, draw round it, then cut out the circle. Place the baking parchment circle on the bottom of the springform mould and smooth down. Alternatively, remove the springform mould ring, put a sheet of baking parchment on the bottom, then put back the ring to secure the baking parchment.

Step 2: Beat the eggs until foamy
Put the eggs, with or without hot water depending on the recipe, in a bowl and whisk with a hand-mixer with whisk attachment on the highest setting for about a minute until foamy. The addition of water, as recommended in some recipes, increases the volume of the beaten eggs.

Step 3: Mix together the sugar and vanilla sugar and add it
Mix together the vanilla sugar and sugar, sprinkle both into the mixture while stirring for 1 minute, then whisk the mixture for another 2 minutes. It is important to stop whisking at the time indicated because if you do not whisk it for long enough the volume will be too small while if you whisk it too long the beaten eggs will increase too much in volume and the fatless sponge pastry will collapse during the baking process. Then add the flavouring or spices.

Step 4: Mix the flour and baking powder
If cornflour (cornstarch) or cocoa powder are also listed in the ingredients as well as the flour and baking powder, mix everything well together, then whisk all the ingredients on the lowest setting into the egg mixture. Now you can briefly whisk in the other heavier ingredients. It is important to whisk the flour and other heavy ingredients as briefly as possible so as not to reduce the volume of the egg-sugar mixture. In Viennese pastry a small amount of slightly cooled, melted butter is folded in which makes the sponge even moister and fine-textured.

Step 5: Put the sponge in the tin or mould
The fatless sponge mixture should be transferred to the prepared tin, mould or baking sheet immediately after being made. A pastry scraper will be very helpful here. You can use a pastry scraper or cake slice to smooth the surface of the sponge.

Step 6: Bake the sponge
Fatless sponge pastry must be baked immediately after it has been prepared, otherwise this airy pastry will collapse. Before removing the sponge from the oven, check that it is done. All you need to do this is the palm of your hand: place your hand lightly on the cake: if the sponge no longer feels moist and the pastry feels soft and cottonwool-like, the sponge is done. The springy surface will immediately bounce up again when pressed lightly. If the sponge feels dry and solid, it means it has been baked for too long.

When the cake is done, carefully loosen the sponge from the sides of the springform mould and remove the ring. Turn the sponge out (photograph 2) onto a cake rack lined with baking parchment, remove the springform mould base and leave the sponge to cool together with the baking parchment. If you have baked a sponge base on a baking sheet, turn it out onto a sheet of baking parchment sprinkled with sugar and leave it to cool on it. Then carefully remove the baking parchment it was baked on. In addition: fatless sponge containing egg yolks, like those in this book, do not need to be rolled because the cooled pastry does not break.

Filling and decorating

Step 1: Cut the sponge base horizontally
Cutting sponge bases evenly horizontally is not so difficult. Place the sponge base on a sheet of paper or cake platter in such a way that the underneath side, which is perfectly smooth, faces upward. Whether you are going to use the linen thread method or a large knife, it is important first to make a cut 1 cm/⅜ in deep all round the cake with a pointed knife (photograph 3) so that the layers are of equal thickness.

If you are using a linen thread, place it round the cake inside the cut, cross the two ends and pull tight – the result is that the thread will cut through the cake (photograph 4). Note that it is much easier to cut the base when it has been baked earlier. To ensure that the base does not break when you lift it, use a sheet of baking parchment or a cake platter to help you (photograph 5). Fold the front of the paper downwards to reinforce it and slide it very carefully under the top layer. The paper will slide more easily if you hold the top layer of sponge now and again with you index finger.
When the baking parchment is under the whole of the top layer, lift the top layer with the baking parchment, keeping it as horizontal as possible so that the sponge base does not break.

If you prefer to cut the sponge with a knife, you must make sure that the blade is longer than the sponge base. Place the knife horizontally in the cut and cut as far as the middle while you rotate the base.

Step 2: Fill the cake or torte, put it together and ice it
You can fill the cake with jam and/or butter-cream or cream sauce. Use a knife, a pastry scraper or a cake slice to ice the cake.
Spread the filling on the bottom layer. Using the baking parchment

or cake slice, place the middle layer on top. Make sure the edges of the individual layers line up "edge to edge". Spread the filling on top of the middle layer and put the next layer on top.

When all the layers are in place, spread a thin layer of filling over the top and the sides and then finish with the icing or cream. It is best to use a knife with a wide blade or a palette to spread the icing or cream on the sides (photograph 1).

Step 3: Decorate the sides and top of the cake

It is the decoration which really gives a cake its irresistible appearance. Sprinkle the sides with chocolate flakes, flaked and roast almonds, ground walnuts or grated coconut. To make sure that the flakes end up on the sides of the cake and not on the kitchen floor, put them close to the side of the cake, then carefully smooth them against the sides with the help of a pastry scraper or knife. Cut the cake into individual slices with a cake divider or knife.

There are cake dividers to make 16 and 18 slices, but if you prefer thicker slices, you can divide it into 12 slices with a knife.

The final touch

The real crowning of a cake is undoubtedly decorating it with a piping bag. To use the piping bag, fold the sides of the bag about 5 cm/2 in towards the outside. Put the piping bag in a mixing beaker and half fill with butter-cream. Turn the sides up again. Using a pastry scraper, carefully push the butter-cream towards the nozzle (photograph 2) – this makes the air escape and the piping bag will be easier to twist as the butter-cream emerges.

If you need more butter-cream, you can add it to the bag as you go. To apply decoration, hold the piping bag vertically with your right hand at the top. Carefully press the butter-cream out, guiding the piping bag with your left hand (photograph 3).

How to store a cream cake

Cream and butter-cream cakes can be kept for 1–2 days in the refrigerator. If you want to freeze a cream tart, it is recommended to freeze it lightly first and then wrap it so that the decoration is not damaged. If you want to eat the cake little by little, freeze the cake in portions. Once it has been defrosted it cannot be frozen again.

TIPS » Do not hold the piping bag with your whole hand because the heat of your hand would make the butter-cream turn liquid.
» Guide the bag or rather the attachment to the nozzle with your thumb and index finger. This will help you decorate the cake with sensitivity.

Storage times: A cream cake should be eaten after 3 months or at the most 6 months. Leave the cake to defrost in its wrapping in the refrigerator.

Basic recipe
Fatless sponge for a springform mould

EASY

1 Grease the bottom of a springform mould and line with baking parchment. Preheat the oven:
Top/bottom heat:
about 180 °C/350 °F (Gas mark 4)
Fan oven:
about 160 °C/325 °F (Gas mark 3)

2 For the sponge, put the eggs in a mixing bowl and whisk with a hand-mixer with whisk attachment on the highest setting for 1 minute until foamy. Mix the sugar and vanilla sugar, sprinkle into the eggs while stirring for 1 minute, then whisk for a further 2 minutes.

3 Mix the flour, baking powder and cornflour (and cocoa powder if used in the recipe), then stir into the mixture with the hand-mixer on the lowest setting. Pour the mixture into the mould and smooth the surface. Put the springform mould on a shelf in the bottom third of the preheated oven and **bake for about 25 minutes**.

4 Take the sponge out of the mould and turn out onto a cake rack lined with baking parchment to cool. Carefully pull the baking parchment away from under the sponge.

TIP » Cut the sponge once horizontally and fill with whipped cream or butter-cream.

Recipe variation: For a nut-flavoured sponge make a sponge with 3 eggs (medium), 2 tablespoons water, 100 g/3½ oz (½ cup) sugar, 1 sachet vanilla sugar, 100 g/3½ oz plain (all purpose) flour, 1 level teaspoon baking powder and 50 g/2 oz (½ cup) ground hazelnuts or almonds. Bake the sponge as in the recipe for about 30 minutes.

Preparation time:
about 20 minutes
Baking time: about 25 minutes

For the springform mould
(diameter 26 cm/10¼ in):
a little fat, baking parchment

For the fatless sponge:
3 eggs (medium)
100 g/3½ oz (½ cup) sugar
1 sachet vanilla sugar
80 g/3 oz (⅞ cup) plain
(all purpose) flour
1 level teaspoon baking powder
25 g/1 oz (3 tablespoons)
cornflour (cornstarch)

For a dark sponge, in addition:
1 tablespoon cocoa powder

In all (light sponge):
P: 29 g, F: 22 g, C: 187 g,
kJ: 4470, kcal: 1067, CU: 15.5

Black Forest Gateau

TRADITIONAL – WITH ALCOHOL (ABOUT 12 PIECES)

Preparation time:
about 75 minutes, excluding
cooling time
Baking time: about 40 minutes

For the springform mould
(diameter 26 cm/10¼ in):
a little fat, baking parchment

For the fatless sponge:
3 eggs (medium)
100 g/3½ oz (½ cup) sugar
1 sachet vanilla sugar
80 g/3 oz (⅞ cup) plain
(all purpose) flour
1 level teaspoon baking
powder
25 g/1 oz (3 tablespoons)
cornflour (cornstarch)
10 g/⅓ oz (1½ tablespoons)
cocoa powder
a good pinch ground cinnamon

For the shortcrust pastry:
125 g/4½ oz (1¼ cups) plain
(all purpose) flour
10 g/⅓ oz (1½ tablespoons)
cocoa powder
1 pinch baking powder
50 g/2 oz (¼ cup) sugar
1 sachet vanilla sugar
1 egg (medium)
50 g/2 oz (4 tablespoons) soft
butter or margarine

For the filling:
1 jar morello cherries
(drained weight 350 g/12 oz)
250 ml/8 fl oz (1 cup) cherry
juice (from the jar)
or
500 g/18 oz morello cherries

1 Grease the bottom of the spring-form mould and line with baking parchment. Preheat the oven:
Top/bottom heat:
about 180 °C/350 °F (Gas mark 4)
Fan oven:
about 160 °C/325 °F (Gas mark 3)

2 For the sponge, put the eggs in a mixing bowl and whisk with a hand-mixer (whisk attachment) on the highest setting for 1 minute until foamy. Mix together the sugar and vanilla sugar, sprinkle into the eggs while stirring for 1 minute, then whisk for 2 minutes more. Mix the flour, baking powder, cocoa powder and cinnamon and whisk briefly on the lowest setting. Transfer the sponge mixture into the spring-form mould and put on a shelf in the bottom third of the oven. **Bake for about 25 minutes.**

3 Take the sponge cake out of the mould and put on a cake rack lined with baking parchment. Leave to cool. Wash the springform mould and grease the bottom.

4 For the shortcrust pastry, mix the flour, cocoa powder and baking powder in a bowl. Add all the other ingredients and mix using a hand-mixer (with the kneading hook), first briefly on the lowest setting, then on the highest set-ting until the shortcrust pastry has the right texture. Then shape into a ball with your hands. Roll out the pastry on the bottom of the springform mould and prick

several times with a fork. Put the ring back on the mould.

5 Put the springform mould on a shelf in the bottom third of the oven and **bake the shortcrust pastry base at the same temperature as the sponge for about 15 minutes.**

6 Loosen the shortcrust pastry from the bottom of the mould as soon as it comes out of the oven but leave it on the bottom of the mould to cool on a cake rack. Peel the baking parchment off the sponge and cut once horizontally into two layers.

7 To make the filling, drain the cherries thoroughly and reserve the juice. Pour off 250 ml/8 fl oz (1 cup) and put to one side. Or wash the morello cherries, drain thoroughly, remove the stalks, stone, stir in the sugar and leave to stand for a few minutes to draw the juices. Put the fresh cherries in a bowl and bring to the boil; transfer to a sieve, reserve the juice and leave to cool. Pour off 250 ml/8 fl oz (1 cup) and top up with water if necessary. Reserve 12 cherries to decorate the cake and put them on kitchen paper.

8 Mix together the cornflour (corn-starch) and sugar, add 4 table-spoons of the cherry juice and stir well. Bring the rest of the juice to the boil. Take off the heat and stir in the cornflour, sugar and juice mixture. Bring to the boil again, stir in the cherries and leave to cool. Add the Kirsch.

9 Add the gelatine to the water and stir; leave to soak for 5 minutes and heat up, stirring all the time, until the gelatine has dissolved completely. Whip the cream almost stiff. First stir about 2 tablespoons of whipped cream into the dissolved gelatine, then whisk the gelatine mixture immediately into the whipped cream and whisk until stiff. Mix together the icing (confectioners') sugar and vanilla sugar and stir into the cream-gelatine mixture.

10 Put the shortcrust pastry base on a cake platter. Spread the cherry mixture on top, leaving a an edge 1 cm/ ⅜ in wide free all round. Spread one-third of the whipped cream mixture on top. Now put the bottom sponge layer on top and spread half the remaining whipped cream mixture over it. Next put the top layer on it and press down lightly. Put 3 tablespoons of the whipped cream mixture in a piping bag with a star-shaped nozzle and put to one side. Spread the rest of the whipped cream mixture on the top and sides of the cake so that it is completely covered. Decorate with the whipped cream in the piping bag and garnish with the chocolate flakes and cherries you have put aside. Leave the cake in the refrigerator for at least two hours.

and 75 g/3 oz (⅓ cup) sugar
30 g/1 oz (3 tablespoons) cornflour (cornstarch)
about 25 g/1 oz (2 tablespoons) sugar
about 3 tablespoons Kirsch liqueur

1 sachet clear powdered gelatine
5 tablespoons cold water
800 g/1¾ lb (3½ cups) chilled whipping cream
40 g/1½ oz (⅜ cup) sifted icing (confectioners') sugar
1 sachet vanilla sugar

For the decoration:
grated chocolate curls or grated chocolate

Per piece:
P: 7 g, F: 28 g, C: 48 g,
kJ: 2039, kcal: 487, CU: 4.0

Cappuccino cream torte

FOR GUESTS – WITH ALCOHOL (ABOUT 16 PIECES)

Preparation time:
about 45 minutes, excluding
cooling time
Baking time: about 25 minutes

For the springform mould
(diameter 26 cm/10¼ in):
a little fat
baking parchment

For the fatless sponge:
3 eggs (medium)
100 g/3½ oz (¼ cup) sugar
1 sachet vanilla sugar
80 g/3 oz (⅞ cup) plain
(all purpose) flour
1 level teaspoon baking powder
25 g/1 oz (3 tablespoons)
cornflour (cornstarch)

For the filling:
6 sheets clear gelatine
800 g/1¾ lb (3¼ cups) chilled
whipping cream
2 sachets (6 heaped
teaspoons) instant espresso
coffee powder, unsweetened
3 tablespoons lukewarm water
50 g/2 oz (¼ cup) sugar
1 sachet vanilla sugar
a good tablespoon orange
liqueur
2 tablespoons apricot jam

For garnishing:
50 g/2 oz dark coating
chocolate
a little cocoa powder

Per piece:
P: 4 g, F: 18 g, C: 22 g,
kJ: 1133, kcal: 271, CU: 2.0

1 Grease the bottom of the spring-form mould and line with baking parchment. Preheat the oven:
Top/bottom heat:
about 180 °C/350 °F (Gas mark 4)
Fan oven:
about 160 °C/325 °F (Gas mark 3)

2 To make the sponge, put the eggs in a mixing bowl and whisk with a hand-mixer with whisk attachment on the highest setting for 1 minute until foamy. Mix the sugar and vanilla sugar, sprinkle into the eggs while stirring for 1 minute, then whisk for 2 minutes.

3 Mix together the flour, baking powder and cornflour (cornstarch) and whisk briefly into the egg and sugar mixture on the lowest setting. Transfer the sponge into the springform mould, smooth down the surface and put on the shelf in the preheated oven. **Bake for about 25 minutes.**

4 Take the sponge cake out of the springform mould, put on a cake rack lined with baking parchment and leave to cool. Now remove the baking parchment and cut the cake horizontally into two layers.

5 For the filling, soak the gelatine following the instructions on the packet. Whip the cream until stiff. Stir the water into the cappuccino powder in a small pan. Lightly squeeze the gelatine, then add to the cappuccino powder and water mixture, stirring over low heat until it has dissolved. Mix the sugar and vanilla sugar

and stir into the gelatine mixture. First stir 2 tablespoons of whipped cream into the gelatine mixture, then stir the gelatine mixture into the rest of the whipped cream.

6 Put the bottom layer of the sponge pastry on a cake platter, drizzle orange liqueur over it and spread apricot jam on top. Then put two-thirds of the whipped cream on top to form a dome (photograph 1). Put the top layer on top the whipped cream dome and press down lightly (photograph 2). Spread the rest of the whipped cream on the top and sides of the cake and make depressions in the cream using the back of a tablespoon. Refrigerate the cake for at least 2 hours.

7 To decorate the cake, coarsely chop the cooking chocolate, melt in a bain-marie over low heat, stirring all the time, then put it in a paper piping bag or small freezer bag. Cut off a small corner and pipe motifs on the baking parchment. Allow these to cool, then arrange on the cake as decorations and sprinkle cocoa powder on top.

Variation: Add 10 g/⅓ oz (1½ table-spoons) cocoa powder to the sponge mixture. Prepare the filling as indicated in the recipe and put one third on the bottom prepared layer, place the top layer on top, cover with one-third of the cream mixture and use the rest of the cream to decorate the cake with the piping bag. Garnish with chocolate-coated coffee beans and sprinkle with cocoa powder.

Butter cream torte

TRADITIONAL – SUITABLE FOR FREEZING (ABOUT 16 PIECES

Preparation time:
about 70 minutes, excluding cooling time
Baking time: about 25 minutes

**For the springform mould
(diameter 26 cm/10¼ in):**
a little fat
baking parchment

For the fatless sponge:
4 eggs (medium)
125 g/4½ oz (⅝ cup) sugar
1 sachet vanilla sugar
100 g/3½ oz (1 cup) plain
(all purpose) flour
1 level teaspoon baking powder
50 g/2 oz (⅓ cup) cornflour
(cornstarch)

For the chocolate butter cream:
100 g/3½ oz dark chocolate
(about 72 % cocoa content)
40 g/1½ oz (5 tablespoons)
custard powder (chocolate
pudding mix)
80 g/3 oz (⅜ cup) sugar
500 ml/17 fl oz (2¼ cups) milk
300 g/10 oz (1½ cups) soft butter
or

**For the light-coloured
butter cream:**
40 g/1½ oz (5 tablespoons)
custard powder, vanilla, cream,
almond or caramel flavoured
80 g/3 oz (⅜ cup) sugar
500 ml/17 fl oz (2¼ cups) milk
250 g/9 oz (1¼ cups) soft butter
or

For the mocha butter cream:
40 g/1½ oz (5 tablespoons)
custard powder(chocolate
pudding mix)

1 Grease the bottom of the spring-form mould and line with baking parchment. Preheat the oven:
Top/bottom heat:
about 180 °C/350 °F (Gas mark 4)
Fan oven:
about 160 °C/325 °F (Gas mark 3)

2 To make the sponge, put the eggs in a mixing bowl and whisk with a hand-mixer with whisk attachment on the highest setting for 1 minute until foamy. Mix together the sugar and vanilla sugar, sprinkle into the eggs while stirring for 1 minute, then continue whisking for 2 minutes.

3 Mix together the flour, baking powder and cornflour (cornstarch) and whisk into the egg mixture on the lowest setting. Transfer the sponge into the springform mould and smooth the surface flat (photograph 1). Put the mould on a shelf in the bottom third of the oven and **bake for about 25 minutes**.

4 Take the sponge out of the spring-form mould, put on a cake rack lined with baking parchment and leave to cool. Then peel off the baking parchment baked with the cake (photograph 2) and cut the sponge horizontally into three layers.

5 To make the chocolate butter cream, break the chocolate into small pieces. Make a custard with the custard powder, sugar and milk, following the instructions on the packet, but with 80 g/3 oz (⅜ cup) sugar. Stir the pieces of chocolate into the hot custard and continue stirring until

they are completely melted. Allow the custard to cool (but do not put in the refrigerator) and stir occasionally.

Or to make **light-coloured butter-cream**, make a custard with the custard powder, sugar and milk, following the instructions on the packet, but with 80 g s3 oz (⅜ cup) sugar. Allow the custard to cool (but do not put in the refrigerator) and stir occasionally.

Or for **mocha butter-cream**, make a custard with the custard powder, sugar, instant espresso powder and milk, following the instructions on the packet, but with 80 g/3 oz (⅜ cup) sugar. Allow the custard to cool (but do not put in the refrigerator) and stir occasionally.

6 Whisk the butter with the hand-mixer with whisk attachment until smooth. Then add the cooled custard to the softened butter a tablespoon at a time. Make sure that both the butter and custard are at room temperature or the butter-cream may curdle.

7 Put the bottom layer on a cake platter, spread the jam on top, then cover with a generous quarter of the butter-cream. Put the next layer on top, press down lightly and spread just under half the remaining butter-cream on it. Finally put the top layer on top and press lightly.

8 Now coat the top and sides of the cake with a thin, even layer of the remaining butter-cream. Use the

rest of the butter-cream to decorate the cake with a piping bag, fitted with a star-shaped nozzle. Decorate further with sugar beads and chocolate.

TIPS » Put plastic wrap directly on the surface while the pudding cools (photograph 3). No layer of skin will form and the pudding will not need to be stirred as it cools.
» If you like, garnish the outer edge of the cake with flaked, roasted almonds.
» If you make the light-coloured butter-cream with caramel flavoured custard powder, you can use brown sugar instead of white.

80 g/3 oz (⅜ cup) sugar
2 tablespoons instant espresso powder
500 ml/17 fl oz (2¼ cups) milk
250 g/9 oz (1¼ cups) soft butter

For coating and decorating:
about 3 tablespoons apricot jam
some pearl sugar (optional)
about 30 g/1 oz chocolate curls or grated chocolate

Per piece:
P: 4 g, F: 21 g, C: 32 g,
kJ: 1427, kcal: 341, CU: 2.5

Mandarin-quark slices

FOR CHILDREN (ABOUT 10 SLICES)

Preparation time:
about 45 minutes,
excluding cooling time
Baking time: about 10 minutes

For the baking sheet
(40 x 30 cm/16 x 12 in):
a little fat
baking parchment

For the fatless sponge:
3 eggs (medium)
3 tablespoons hot water
150 g/5 oz (¾ cup) sugar
1 sachet vanilla sugar
100 g/3½ oz (1 cup) plain
(all purpose) flour
1 level teaspoon baking powder
50 g/2 oz/ (⅓ cup) cornflour
(cornstarch)

For the filling:
2 cans mandarin oranges
(drained weight 175 g/6 oz each)
100 ml/3½ fl oz (½ cup) mandarin
orange juice (from the can)
6 sheets clear gelatine
500 g/18 oz (2 cups) low fat quark
150 g/5 oz (¾ cup) sugar
1 sachet vanilla sugar
1 teaspoon grated lemon zest
2 tablespoons lemon juice
200 g/7 oz (⅞ cup) chilled
whipping cream

For sprinkling:
a little icing (confectioners') sugar

Per slice:
P: 11 g, F: 8 g, C: 57 g,
kJ: 1488, kcal: 355, CU: 5.0

1 Grease the baking sheet and line with baking parchment. Fold the baking parchment to make a pleat along the edge facing the sloping side of the baking sheet, creating an upright edge. Preheat the oven:
Top/bottom heat:
about 200 °C/400 °F (Gas mark 6)
Fan oven:
about 180 °C/350 °F (Gas mark 4)

2 To make the sponge, put the eggs with the hot water in a mixing bowl and whisk with a hand-mixer with whisk attackment on the highest setting for 1 minute until foamy. Mix together the sugar and vanilla sugar, sprinkle into the eggs while stirring for 1 minute, then continue whisking for 2 minutes. Mix together the flour, baking powder and cornflour (cornstarch) and stir briefly into the egg mixture on the lowest setting.

3 Spread the sponge on the baking sheet and put on the middle shelf in the preheated oven. **Bake for about 10 minutes**.

4 Carefully loosen the sponge along the edges of the baking sheet and transfer onto a sheet of baking parchment, sprinkled with sugar, then carefully remove the baking parchment from the underside. Allow the sponge to cool, then cut vertically in half to make 2 rectangles about 30 x 20 cm (12 x 8 in).

5 For the filling, drain the mandarins in a sieve, reserve the juice and measure off 100 ml/3½ fl oz (½ cup) of

this juice. Then soak the gelatine, following the instructions on the packet.

6 Mix together the quark, sugar, vanilla sugar, lemon rind and lemon juice. Heat up the 100 ml/3½ fl oz (½ cup) of juice you have measured. Squeeze the gelatine lightly and dissolve into the hot juice, stirring all the time. Stir about 4 tablespoons of quark mixture into the dissolved gelatine with a whisk, then stir this into the rest of the quark mixture.

7 Whip the cream until stiff. When the quark mixture begins to set, fold in the whipped cream and mandarins. Spread the filling one of the sponge layers, put the other one on top (with the underside facing upwards) and press down lightly. Smooth the sides and leave the sponge in the refrigerator for about 2 hours.

8 Sprinkle with icing (confectioners') sugar before serving.

Recipe variation: For **pineapple quark slices**, use 1 tin of pineapple chunks (drained weight 340 g/ 12 oz) instead of 2 tins of mandarins. Drain the pineapple and cut into smaller pieces. Fresh pineapple cannot be used in combination with gelatine or jelly because one of the enzymes in the raw fruit affects the gelatinisation of the gelatine, in other words it will no longer set.

Yoghurt slices

REFRESHING (ABOUT 20 SLICES)

Preparation time:
about 60 minutes, excluding
cooling time
Baking time: about 10 minutes

For the baking sheet
(40 x 30 cm/16 x 12 in):
a little fat
baking frame

For the fatless sponge:
4 eggs (medium)
150 g/5 oz (¾ cup) sugar
1 sachet vanilla sugar
150 g/5 oz (1½ cups) plain
(all purpose) flour
1 level teaspoon baking
powder

For the topping:
about 500 g/18 oz fresh fruit,
e.g. strawberries, raspberries,
grapes or cherries
12 sheets clear gelatine
500 g/18 oz (2¼ cups) yoghurt
150–200 g/6–7 oz (1–1⅓ cups)
sifted icing (confectioners')
sugar (depending on the
sweetness of the fruit)
1 sachet vanilla sugar
juice of 1½ lemon
400 g/14 oz (1¾ cups) chilled
whipping cream (min. 30 % fat)

For coating:
4 tablespoons apricot jam

Per slice:
P: 4 g, F: 9 g, C: 31 g,
kJ: 968, kcal: 231, CU: 2.5

1 Grease the bottom of the baking sheet and preheat the oven:
Top/bottom heat:
about 200 °C/400 °F (Gas mark 6)
Fan oven:
about 180 °C/350 °F (Gas mark 4)

2 To make the sponge, put the eggs in a mixing bowl and whisk with a hand-mixer with whisk attachment on the highest setting for 1 minute until foamy. Mix together the sugar and vanilla sugar, sprinkle into the eggs while stirring for 1 minute, then continue whisking for another 2 minutes. Mix together the baking powder and flour and whisk briefly on the lowest setting.

3 Spread the sponge on the baking sheet and put the baking sheet on the middle shelf in the preheated oven. **Bake for about 10 minutes.**

4 Put the baking sheet on a cake rack and leave the sponge to cool on it.

5 For the topping, prepare the fruit, wash, drain thoroughly, remove the stalks and – depending on the fruit – the stones. Cut into small pieces. If you like, keep a few berries to decorate the yoghurt slices.

6 Soak the gelatine following the instructions on the packet. Stir together the yoghurt, icing (confectioners') sugar, vanilla sugar and lemon juice. Squeeze the gelatine lightly and dissolve in a small pan over low heat, stirring all the time.

7 First stir in 4 tablespoons of the yoghurt mixture into the dissolved gelatine, using a whisk; then whisk this into the rest of the yoghurt mixture. Beat the cream until thick. When the mixture begins to thicken, fold in the cream and fruit.

8 For coating, stir the jam until smooth and spread on the sponge base. Now put the pastry frame round the sponge. Spread the yoghurt/fruit mixture on the jam-coated sponge base and put in the refrigerator for about 2 hours.

9 Carefully loosen and remove the pastry frame before serving. Cut the sponge into slices and decorate with the berries you have put aside.

TIPS » Do not prepare the slices more than 1 day in advance.
» You can also use tinned fruit (drained weight about 480 g/17 oz).

Lemon and cream roll

REFRESHING (ABOUT 16 SLICES)

Preparation time:
about 45 minutes, excluding
cooling time
Baking time: about 10 minutes

For the baking sheet
(40 x 30 cm/16 x 12 in):
a little fat
baking parchment

For the fatless sponge:
4 eggs (medium)
1 egg yolk (medium)
80 g/3 oz (⅜ cup) sugar
1 sachet vanilla sugar
80 g/3 oz (⅞ cup) plain
(all purpose) flour
½ level teaspoon baking
powder

For the filling:
4 sheets clear gelatine
400 g/14 oz (1¾ cups) chilled
whipping cream
4 tablespoons lemon juice
70 g/3 oz (⅔ cup) sifted icing
(confectioners') sugar
1 teaspoon grated lemon zest

Also:
icing (confectioners') sugar

Per slice:
P: 3 g, F: 10 g, C: 17 g,
kJ: 720, kcal: 172, CU: 1.5

1 Grease the baking sheet and line with baking parchment. Fold the baking parchment to make a pleat along the edge facing the sloping side of the baking sheet, thus creating an upright edge. Preheat the oven
Top/bottom heat:
about 200 °C/400 °F (Gas mark 6)

2 To make the sponge, put the eggs and egg yolk in a mixing bowl and whisk using a hand-mixer with whisk attachment on the highest setting for 1 minute until foamy. Mix together the sugar and vanilla sugar, sprinkle over while stirring for 1 minute, then whisk for another 2 minutes.

3 Mix together the flour and baking powder and whisk into the egg mixture on the lowest setting. Spread the sponge evenly on the baking sheet. Put the baking sheet on the middle shelf in the preheated oven. **Bake for about 10 minutes**.

4 Loosen the sponge along the edges and turn out onto baking parchment, previously sprinkled with sugar, and leave to cool with the baking parchment.

5 To make the filling, soak the gelatine following the instructions on the packet. Beat the cream almost stiff. Squeeze the gelatine lightly and dissolve in a small pan over low heat,

stirring all the time until it dissolves. Stir the lemon juice, icing (confectioners') sugar and lemon rind into the dissolved gelatine.

6 First stir 2 tablespoons of cream with a hand whisk into the gelatine mixture, then whisk the gelatine mixture immediately into the cream and continue whisking until the cream is very stiff.

7 Carefully peel off the baking parchment baked with the sponge. Spread the lemon cream on the sponge, roll up starting from the long side and put in the refrigerator for at least 2 hours.

8 Sprinkle with icing (confectioners') sugar before serving.

Recipe variation: For a simple sponge roll, make a sponge with 5 eggs (medium), 1 egg yolk (medium), 75 g/3 oz (⅜ cup) sugar, 1 packet vanilla sugar, 90 g/3 oz (⅞ cup) plain (all purpose) flour and ½ teaspoon baking powder. Bake, turn out and leave to cool. Puree about 375 g/13 oz (1⅛ cups) jam or rub through a sieve. Carefully remove the baking parchment baked with the sponge (photograph 1) and spread the jam on the sponge (photograph 2). Roll up the sponge, starting from the long side (photograph 3) and sprinkle with icing (confectioners') sugar.

1

2

3

Carrot cake

WITH ALCOHOL (ABOUT 15 SLICES)

Preparation time:
about 30 minutes, excluding
cooling time
Baking time: about 60 minutes

For the tin
(25 x 11 cm/10 x 4½ in):
a little fat
a little flour

For the fatless sponge:
200 g/7 oz carrots
4 egg whites (medium)
4 egg yolks (medium)
160 g/5½ oz (¾ cup) sugar
1 sachet vanilla sugar
1 pinch salt
2–3 tablespoons rum
50 g/2 oz (½ cup) plain
(all purpose) flour
2½ level teaspoons baking
powder
300 g/10 oz (4 cups) ground
almonds

For the icing:
200 g/7 oz (1⅓ cups) icing
(confectioners') sugar
3–4 tablespoons rum
20 g/¾ oz (1½ tablespoons)
butter

For garnishing:
some marzipan carrots
(optional)

Per slice:
P: 6 g, F: 14 g, C: 29 g,
kJ: 1153, kcal: 275, CU: 2.5

1 For the sponge, first peel the carrots, then grate them finely on a kitchen grater. Grease and flour the mould. Preheat the oven:
Top/bottom heat:
about 180 °C/350 °F (Gas mark 4)
Fan oven:
about 160 °C/325 °F (Gas mark 3)

2 To make the pastry, beat the egg whites in a mixing bowl until they form stiff peaks and put to one side. Whisk the egg yolks together with the sugar, vanilla sugar and salt in another mixing bowl with a hand-mixer (whisk attachment) on the highest setting for about 5 minutes until the mixture has become foamy.

3 Stir in the rum briefly. Mix together the flour and baking powder, add half the almonds and whisk on the lowest setting.

4 Fold in the stiffly beaten egg whites. Now stir in the rest of the almonds and grated carrots, whisking very briefly. Transfer the pastry mixture into the greased and floured tin. Put the tin on the lowest shelf in the preheated oven. **Bake for about 60 minutes.**

5 Leave the cake in the tin for about 10 minutes to cool on a cake rack, then take the cake out of the tin and leave to cool on the rack.

6 To make the glaze, sift the icing (confectioners') sugar, add the rum and stir to make a thick mixture. Melt the butter, stir into the glaze mixture and pour over the cake. If you like, you can decorate the cake with marzipan carrots when the glaze is still soft and leave to set.

TIPS » You can also make the cake without rum which you can replace by the same amount of orange juice.
» You can also bake the carrot cake in a spring-mould (diameter 26 cm/10¼ in).

Quark & oil dough

Quark & oil dough is very similar to yeast dough and it tastes almost the same – but it is easier and quicker to make because it does not need to rise. It is made from flour, baking powder, quark, oil, sometimes sugar, milk and sometimes eggs.

The quality of the oil you use for your quark & oil dough will determine how good the dough is. It is best to use a neutral, pure vegetable oil such as sunflower oil, corn oil or soya oil which cannot be replaced by solid fat.

Like yeast dough, quark & oil dough is ideally suited for baking on a baking sheet but it is also perfect for small sweet and savoury pastries.

How to make quark & oil dough

Step 1: Prepare the baking sheet or baking tin

First grease the baking sheet or baking tin evenly using a pastry brush – it is best to use spreadable margarine or butter. Do not use oil because it would run down the sides of the tin. If you are baking small pastries, you do not need to grease the baking sheet; all you need to do is line it with baking parchment.

Step 2: Prepare the dough

Mix together the flour and baking powder (photograph 1). Then add, depending on the recipe, sugar, vanilla sugar, salt, quark, milk and/or egg and oil and mix everything using a hand-mixer with kneading hook (photograph 2), first on the lowest setting, then on the highest setting to make a smooth dough. Do not knead too long or the dough may become sticky.

Sprinkle a little flour on the kneaded dough, take it out of the mixing bowl and shape into a roll on the lightly floured work surface (photograph 3).

Step 3: Baking quark & oil dough

Bake the quark & oil dough as described in the recipe. When it is done, immediately take it out of the tin or off the baking sheet and leave to cool on a cake rack.

How to store
quark & oil dough

If you want to keep quark and oil dough pastry a little longer – although it does taste nicer fresh – you can freeze it and defrost it at room temperature in the wrapping.

Pizza with quark & oil dough

FOR GUESTS (ABOUT 8 PIECES/1 BAKING SHEET)

1 Grease the bottom of the baking sheet. Preheat the oven:
Top/bottom heat:
about 200 °C/400 °F (Gas mark 6)
Fan oven:
about 180 °C/350 °F (Gas mark 4)

2 For the pastry, mix together the flour and the baking powder in a mixing bowl. Add all the other ingredients and mix using a hand-mixer (with the kneading hook), first briefly on the lowest setting, then on the highest setting to make a smooth dough (do not knead too long because that would make the dough sticky).

3 Then shape the dough into a roll on the lightly floured work surface. Roll out the dough on a baking sheet.

4 For the topping, mix together the chopped tomatoes and spices, then season with salt and pepper. Cut the mozzarella into slices. Drain the tuna fish, peel the onion, cut in half and then in fine rings. If you like, cut the salami slices in half. Cut the ham into cubes. Cut the olives in half.

Per piece: P: 26 g, F: 36 g, C: 31 g, kJ: 2319, kcal: 552, CU: 2.5

5 Spread the tomato mixture evenly on the dough, leaving an edge about 1 cm/⅜ in wide uncovered. Sprinkle about one-third of the grated cheese on top.

6 Garnish about one quarter of the pizza with the mozzarella slices and pesto, one quarter with tuna fish and onion slices, one quarter with cooked ham and one quarter with salami and olives. Sprinkle the rest of the grated cheese on top, except on the quarter with mozzarella topping.

7 Put the baking sheet in the bottom third in the preheated oven and **bake for about 25 minutes.**

TIP » Sprinkle the warm pizza with basil leaves.

Preparation time:
about 40 minutes
Baking time: about 25 minutes

For the baking sheet
(40 x 30 cm/16 x 12 in):
a little fat

For the quark & oil dough:
300 g/10 oz (3 cups) plain (all purpose) flour
3 level teaspoons baking powder
1 pinch salt
150 g/5 oz (⅔ cup) low fat quark
100 ml/3½ fl oz (½ cup) milk
100 ml/3½ fl oz (½ cup) cooking oil, e.g. sunflower oil

For the topping:
1 can chopped tomatoes (drained weight 400 g/14 oz)
½ teaspoon hot paprika powder
½ teaspoon dried oregano
1 teaspoon dried basil
salt
freshly ground pepper

200 g/7 oz (⅞ cup) mozzarella cheese
1 can tuna fish in oil (drained weight 135 g/4½ oz)
1 small onion
100 g/3½ oz cooked ham
40 g/1½ oz salami slices
50 g/2 oz (scant ¼ cup) stoned black olives
200 g/7 oz (2 cups) grated Gouda cheese
6 teaspoons green pesto

Mandarin orange and sour cream cake

FOR CHILDREN (ABOUT 20 SLICES)

Preparation time:
about 45 minutes, excluding
cooling time
Baking time: about 40 minutes

For the baking sheet
(40 x 30 cm/16 x 12 in):
a little fat, baking frame

For the quark & oil dough:
300 g/10 oz (3 cups) plain
(all purpose) flour
3 level teaspoons baking
powder
75 g/3 oz (⅓ cup) sugar
1 sachet vanilla sugar
1 pinch salt
125 g/4½ oz (½ cup) low-fat
quark
100 ml/3½ fl oz (½ cup) milk
100 ml/3½ fl oz (½ cup) cooking
oil, e.g. sunflower oil

For the topping:
4 cans mandarin oranges
(drained weight 175 g/6 oz each)
80 g/3 oz (⅔ cup) custard
powder (vanilla pudding mix)
100 g/3½ oz (½ cup) sugar
750 ml/1¼ pints (3½ cups) milk
500 g/18 oz (2¼ cups) sour cream
50 g/2 oz (scant ½ cup) slivered
almonds

For the icing:
200 g/7 oz (1 cup) icing
(confectioners') sugar
3 tablespoons lemon juice

Per slice:
P: 5 g, F: 14 g, C: 43 g,
kJ: 1365, kcal: 326, CU: 3.5

1 Grease the baking sheet and pre-heat the oven:
Top/bottom heat:
about 180 °C/350 °F (Gas mark 4)
Fan oven:
about 160 °C/325 °F (Gas mark 3)

2 For the pastry, mix together the flour and the baking powder in a mixing bowl. Add all the other ingredients and mix using a hand-mixer (with the kneading hook), first briefly on the lowest setting, then on the highest setting to make a smooth dough (do not knead too long because that would make the dough sticky). Then shape the dough into a roll. Roll out the dough on the baking sheet and put a pastry frame – the same size as the baking sheet – round it.

3 For the topping, drain the manda-rins thoroughly in a sieve. Make a custard with the custard powder, sugar and milk, following the in-structions on the packet but with the quantities indicated here. Stir in the sour cream and spread the warm mixture on the dough. Distribute the mandarins on the sour cream custard mixture and sprinkle the almonds on top. Put the baking sheet in the bottom third in the preheated oven and **bake for about 40 minutes.**

4 Put the baking sheet on a cake rack and leave the cake to cool on it. Then carefully loosen the pastry frame along the edges with a knife and remove it.

5 For the glaze, sift the icing (confec-tioners') sugar and stir in enough lemon juice to make a thick mix-ture. Sprinkle the glaze on the cake with a teaspoon.

TIP » If you have no pastry frame, you can bake the cake in a roasting tin or on a baking sheet with a high edge.

Variation: If you like, rub 4 table-spoons of apricot jam through a sieve, bring to the boil in a small pan with 2 tablespoons water and spread on the cake while it is still warm. In this case do not sprinkle the almonds before baking but roast the almonds in a pan without fat, leave to cool on a plate and sprinkle on the cake before serving.

Cheese and ham croissants

SOPHISTICATED – SUITABLE FOR FREEZING (8 PIECES)

Preparation time:
about 30 minutes
Baking time: about 25 minutes

For the baking sheet:
baking parchment

For the quark & oil dough:
250 g/9 oz (2½ cups) plain
(all purpose) flour
3 level teaspoons baking
powder
125 g/4½ oz (½ cup) low fat
quark
50 ml/1½ fl oz (3 tablespoons)
milk
50 ml/1½ fl oz (3 tablespoons)
cooking oil, e.g. sunflower oil
1 egg white (medium)
½ level teaspoon salt

For the filling:
100 g/3½ oz cooked ham
100 g/3½ oz (1 cup) grated
Gouda cheese

For coating and sprinkling:
1 egg yolk (medium)
1 tablespoon milk
coarsely ground pepper
sesame seeds

Per piece:
P: 13 g, F: 14 g, C: 26 g,
kJ: 1197, kcal: 286, CU: 2.0

1 Line the baking sheet with baking parchment and preheat the oven:
Top/bottom heat:
about 180 °C/350 °F (Gas mark 4)
Fan oven:
about 160 °C/325 °F (Gas mark 3)

2 For the pastry, mix together the flour and the baking powder in a mixing bowl. Add all the other ingredients and mix using a hand-mixer (with the kneading hook), first briefly on the lowest setting, then on the highest setting to make a smooth dough (do not knead too long because that would make the dough sticky).

3 Then shape the dough into a ball on the floured work surface. Roll out the ball of dough on the floured surface to make a circle with a diameter of about 35 cm/14 in, then cut out 8 "slices" (photograph 1).

4 Cut the ham into small, thin strips and distribute evenly on the slices of dough (photograph 2), then sprinkle the grated cheese on top. Press the filling lightly into the dough. Roll up the slices, starting from the round side, shape into croissants (photograph 3) and put on the baking sheet.

5 Mix together the egg yolk and the milk, spread this mixture on the croissants and sprinkle pepper and sesame seeds on top. Put the baking sheet on the middle shelf in the preheated oven. **Bake for about 25 minutes.**

Recipe variation: To make **vegetable rolls**, cut the ends of 1 courgette (zucchini) (150 g/5 oz). Rinse it, pat dry and cut into small dice. Peel 1 onion, chop finely and fry in 1 tablespoon cooking oil until transparent. Add the chopped courgette, fry with the onion and season with salt and pepper. Grate 150 g/5 oz Appenzeller cheese finely, stir into the courgette mixture and leave to cool. Prepare the dough as indicated in the recipe, roll a rectangle of about 40 x 30 cm/16 x 12 in and then cut into smaller rectangles about 15 x 10 cm/6 x 4 in. Put an equal amount of filling on the rectangles, roll up the dough starting from the short side and put on a baking sheet with the seam facing downwards. Stir together 1 egg yolk in 1 tablespoon milk. Brush this mixture over the dough rolls and sprinkle sesame seeds on top. Bake the rolls at the temperature indicated in the recipe for about 25 minutes.

Choux pastry

Choux pastry differs from all other types of pastry and dough in that it is stirred in a pan over low heat until the pastry detaches itself from the bottom of the pan.

Pastries made from choux pastry are not only very light and airy but also slightly crisp when freshly baked. During the baking process large holes appear – as in profiteroles, one of the best-known pastries made with choux pastry – which can then be filled with sweet or savoury fillings. Pie bases made from choux pastry are also delicious. Choux pastry is made from water or milk, fat, flour, sometimes cornflour (cornstarch), baking powder and eggs.

How to make choux pastry

Step 1: Prepare the baking sheet or springform mould
Grease the baking sheet or springform mould and line with baking parchment. Alternatively you can also grease the baking sheet or springform mould evenly with spreadable margarine or butter,

using a pastry brush. Then sprinkle a little flour on the baking sheet or the bottom of the springform mould. To do this, sift a little flour (not too much!) on one edge of the baking sheet or springform mould and then tap the other (unfloured) side on the work surface. This will distribute the flour evenly. Tap off any excess flour.

Step 2: Bring the fat and liquid to the boil
Put the milk or water, depending on the recipe, in a small pan – it is best to use a pan with a long handle because it is easier to hold it while you are stirring the flour. Let the mixture come to the boil, then take the pan off the heat.

Step 3: Stir in the flour
Now add the flour already mixed with the cornflour (cornstarch), if it is listed in the ingredients, all at once to the hot liquid (photograph 1). Stir the ingredients with a stirring spoon to make a ball of smooth dough (photograph 2). Then put the pan back on the heat and cook the dough for about

1 minute, stirring all the time. This stirring over high heat makes the dough firmer. As soon as a thin white film begins to form on the bottom of the pan, it means the dough is ready. Remove the pan from the heat and put the ball of dough in a mixing bowl.

Step 4: Stir in the eggs
Stir all but one of the eggs, one after the other, into the hot dough using a hand-mixer (with kneading hook) on the highest setting. Whisk the last egg and stir only enough of it into the dough for it to become very shiny and drip from the spoon (photograph 3). The dough should not be too soft or the pastry will spread too much.

Step 5: Add the baking powder to the dough
You can only stir the baking powder into the dough when it has cooled. Then proceed with the dough as in the recipe.

Step 6: Bake the choux pastry
Bake the choux pastry as indicated in the recipe. The slightest air current during the baking process

will cause the choux pastry to collapse. This is why you should only open the door very carefully to check the pastry at the end of the baking process. You can tell the pastry is done if it has risen, looks airy and light and not too dark. When

"Puffed up!"
Choux pastry is something quite special: it already starts being cooked when the ingredients are stirred in the pan over high heat. This is also the reason why the baking powder can only be added when the dough has cooled: its leavening agents would come into action too early so that the pastry would already have "puffed up" before baking. The result would a flat pastry which had not been able to rise.

you cut it open, the hollow inside should not be moist any more.

In addition: choux pastry which is to be filled – such as profiteroles and eclairs – must be cut open immediately with a knife or scissors after being taken out of the oven; then the halves are put next to each other to cool. This will prevent the pastry from breaking and will enable you to fill them easily.

TIP » You have just used the piping bag and there are still a few bits of choux pastry in the bag? Just pipe the rest of the choux pastry as small balls onto the baking sheet together with the other pastries! You can use these little choux pastries to decorate other cakes or pastries or as a garnish in sweet and savoury soups.

How to store choux pastry
If the choux pastry contains a filling, it is best consumed on the day they are made. Because this kind of pastry gets soggy very quickly. Choux pastry without filling (for instance cream puffs before they are filled with cream) will keep better if stored in a freezer. Afterwards, defrost at room temperature while leaving it in the wrapping. Then warm it for about 5 minutes at the baking temperature indicated in the recipe. Leave to cool before filling so that the cream does not melt.

Cream puffs

TRADITIONAL – POPULAR (8 PIECES) FRONT OF PHOTOGRAPH

Preparation time:
about 30 minutes, excluding
cooling time
Baking time: about 25 minutes

For the baking sheet:
a little fat
baking parchment

For the choux pastry:
125 ml/4 fl oz (½ cup) water
25 g/1 oz (2 tablespoons)
butter or margarine
75 g/2½ oz (¾ cup) plain
(all purpose) flour
15 g/½ oz (1½ tablespoons)
cornflour (cornstarch)
2–3 eggs (medium)
1 pinch baking powder

For the filling:
500 g/18 oz morello cherries
50 g/2 oz (¼ cup) sugar
15 g/½ oz (1½ tablespoons)
cornflour (cornstarch)
a little sugar
500 g/18 oz (2¼ cups) chilled
whipping cream (min. 30 % fat)
25 g/1 oz (½ cup) sifted icing
(confectioners') sugar
1 sachet vanilla sugar

For dusting:
20 g/¾ oz (2½ tablespoons)
sifted icing (confectioners')
sugar

Per piece:
P: 5 g, F: 24 g, C: 35 g,
kJ: 1623, kcal: 388, CU: 3.0

1 Grease the baking sheet and line with baking parchment. Preheat the oven:
Top/bottom heat:
about 200 °C/400 °F (Gas mark 6)
Fan oven:
about 180 °C/350 °F (Gas mark 4)

2 To make the choux pastry, bring the water to the boil in a small pan together with the butter or margarine. Remove the pan from the heat. Mix together the flour and cornflour (cornstarch) and stir all at once into the hot liquid. Stir all the ingredients together with a cooking spoon until you have a ball of smooth dough. Then heat for about 1 minute, stirring all the time (photograph 1) and transfer to a mixing bowl.

3 Stir two eggs into the dough, one after the other, using a hand-mixer (with the kneading hook) on the highest setting. Whisk the last egg and stir only enough of it into the dough for it to become very shiny and hang in a long strip from the spoon. Only stir the baking powder into the dough when it has cooled.

4 Put the choux pastry in portions in a pastry-bag with a large nozzle or make 8 small heaps of dough on the baking sheet with two teaspoons or pipe them on the baking sheet. Put the baking sheet on the middle shelf in the preheated oven and **bake for about 25 minutes**. Do not open the oven during the first 15 minutes of baking time, or they may relax.

5 Cut off the top of each cream puff to make a lid (photograph 2) and leave to cool on a cake rack.

6 To make the filling, wash the morello cherries, drain thoroughly, remove the stalks and stones. Stir in the sugar and leave to stand for a while to draw the juices. Put the cherries and the juice in a pan and bring to the boil briefly. Then put in a sieve, reserve the juice, measure 125 ml/4 fl oz (½ cup) of the juice and, if necessary, top up with water. Stir 4 tablespoons of the juice into the cornflour (cornstarch). Bring the rest of the juice to the boil. Remove the juice from the heat and stir the cornflour (cornstarch) diluted with the juice into the hot juice. Bring the juice and cornflour (cornstarch) mixture back to the boil briefly. Stir in the cherries and add sugar to taste. Allow the mixture to cool.

7 Whip the cream stiff with the icing (confectioners') sugar and vanilla sugar. Then transfer in portions in a piping bag with a star-shaped nozzle. Put the cherry filling in the cream puffs, pipe the cream on top, put the lid back on and sprinkle with icing sugar.

TIPS » Serve the cream puffs fresh.
» Instead of fresh morello cherries you can also use morello cherries from a jar (drained weight 350 g/ 12 oz). But in that case, do not add any sugar.

Recipe variations: To make **cream puffs with cranberries and straciatella cream filling** (photograph in the middle), whip 400 g/14 oz (1¾ cups) refrigerated whipping cream (min. 30 % fat) with 1 sachet vanilla sugar. Stir in 150 g/5 oz of thickened wild cranberries (from a jar) and 50 g/2 oz grated chocolate.

To make **cream puffs with fruity quark filling** (at the back in the photograph), whip 250 g/9 oz (1 cup) refrigerated whipping cream (min. 30 % fat) with 1 sachet vanilla sugar and fold in 250 g/9 oz (1 cup) fruit quark.

Flockentorte (Layered choux pastry cake)

A LITTLE EXPENSIVE (ABOUT 12 PIECES)

Preparation time:
about 60 minutes, excluding cooling time
Baking time: 75–90 minutes

For the springform mould (diameter 26 cm/10¼ in):
a little fat

For the baking sheet:
a little fat, baking parchment

For the shortcrust pastry:
150 g/5 oz (1½ cups) plain (all purpose) flour
40 g/1½ oz (3 tablespoons) sugar
1 sachet vanilla sugar
100 g/3½ oz (½ cup) soft butter or margarine

For the choux pastry:
125 ml/4 fl oz (½ cup) water
25 g/1 oz (2 tablespoons) butter or margarine
75 g/2½ oz (¾ cup) plain (all purpose) flour
15 g/½ oz (1½ tablespoons) cornflour (cornstarch)
2–3 eggs (medium)
1 pinch baking powder

For the filling:
1 jar morello cherries (drained weight 350 g/12 oz)
200 ml/7 fl oz (⅞ cup) cherry juice (from the jar)
1 sachet red cake glaze
2 tablespoons sugar
400 g/14 oz (1¾ cups) chilled whipping cream (min. 30% fat)
25 g/1 oz (¼ cup) sifted icing (confectioners') sugar

1 Grease the springform mould. Draw one circle on three separate sheets of baking parchment of each 26 cm/ 10 in in diameter. Grease the baking sheet and line with a sheet of baking parchment. Preheat the oven:
Top/bottom heat:
about 200 °C/400 °F (Gas mark 6)
Fan oven:
about 180 °C/350 °F (Gas mark 4)

2 For the shortcrust pastry, put all the ingredients in a mixing bowl and mix using a hand-mixer (with the kneading hook), first briefly on the lowest setting, then on the highest setting to make the shortcrust pastry. Then shape the dough into a ball using your hands. Roll out the pastry on the bottom of the springform mould, prick the pastry several times with a fork, then put the ring back on the springform mould. Put the springform mould on the middle shelf of the preheated oven and **bake for about 15 minutes**.

3 Loosen the shortcrust pastry off the base of the springform mould im- mediately after being taken out of the oven, then put it – still on the springform mould base – on a cake rack to cool. Then put the shortcrust pastry base on a cake platter.

4 To make the choux pastry, bring the water to the boil in a small pan with the butter or margarine. Remove the pan from the heat. Mix together the flour and cornflour (cornstarch) and add all at once to the hot liquid. Stir all the ingredients with a stirring spoon until you obtain a smooth

lump of dough. Return the pan to the heat and cook the choux pastry for 1 minute, stirring all the time, then transfer into a mixing bowl.

5 Stir two eggs, one after the other, into the choux pastry using a hand- mixer (kneading hook) on the highest setting. Whisk the last egg and stir only enough of it into the dough for it to become very shiny and hang in a long strip from the spoon. Only stir in the baking powder when the choux pastry has cooled down.

6 Bake three layers from the choux pastry. To do this, spread one-third of the pastry on each of the three circles you have drawn on the baking parchment (photograph 1). Make sure that the pastry layer is not too thin at the edges or the pastry there will become too dark. Put the baking sheet on the middle shelf of the preheated oven and **bake this choux pastry layer at the same temperature for 20–25 minutes**. Do not open the oven door during the first 15 minutes in the oven or the pastry will collapse.

7 Next slide the other prepared layers together with the baking parchment onto the baking sheet and **bake one after the other as indicated** in the recipe. Slide the layers still with the baking parchment onto separate cake racks to cool.

8 To make the filling, drain the morello cherries in a sieve, reserve the juice and measure off 200 ml/ 7 fl oz (⅞ cup) of the juice; top up

with water if necessary. Prepare the glaze with the sugar, following the instructions on the packet but with 200 ml/7 fl oz (⅞ cup) of liquid, then stir in the cherries. Refrigerate the mixture and season with sugar to taste. Whip the cream stiff with the icing (confectioners') sugar and vanilla sugar.

9 Spread a thin layer of red currant jelly on the shortcrust pastry base and cover with a choux pastry layer (photograph 2). Now spread half the cherries on top and cover with half the whipped cream. Then cover with the second choux pastry layer and spread the rest of the cherries and whipped cream on top. Break the third layer into coarse pieces and arrange on the cream (photograph 3), then sprinkle with icing (confectioners') sugar.

TIP » Cut the cake into slices with a serrated knife or an electric one.

1 sachet vanilla sugar

For coating:
red currant jelly

For dusting:
30 g/1 oz (¼ cup) icing (confectioners') sugar

Per piece:
P: 4 g, F: 21 g, C: 39 g,
kJ: 1546, kcal: 369, CU: 3.5

Cheese puffs

SAVOURY (24 PIECES) LEFT IN THE PHOTOGRAPH

Preparation time:
about 45 minutes, excluding
cooling time
Baking time: about 20 minutes

For the baking sheet:
a little fat
baking parchment

For the choux pastry:
125 ml/4 fl oz (½ cup) water
1 pinch salt
25 g/1 oz (2 tablespoons)
butter or margarine
75 g/2½ oz (¾ cup) plain
(all purpose) flour
15 g/½ oz (1½ tablespoons)
cornflour (cornstarch)
2–3 eggs (medium)
½ level teaspoon baking
powder
75 g/3 oz (¾ cup) grated
Emmental cheese

For the filling:
200 g/7 oz (⅞ cup) full fat
cream cheese
1 container (150 g/5 oz) crème
fraîche
a little salt
freshly ground black pepper
100 g/3½ oz air-cured ham
sweet paprika powder

Per piece:
P: 4 g, F: 7 g, C: 3 g,
kJ: 388, kcal: 93, CU: 0.5

1 Grease the baking sheet and line with baking parchment. Preheat the oven:
Top/bottom heat:
about 200 °C/400 °F (Gas mark 6)
Fan oven:
about 180 °C/350 °F (Gas mark 4)

2 To make the choux pastry, bring the water to the boil in a small pan with the salt and butter or margarine. Remove the pan from the heat. Mix together the flour and cornflour (cornstarch) and add all at once to the hot liquid. Stir all the ingredients with a spoon until you obtain a smooth lump of dough. Return the pan to the heat and cook the choux pastry for about 1 minute, stirring all the time, then transfer into a mixing bowl.

3 Stir two eggs, one after the other, into the choux pastry using a hand-mixer (with kneading hook) on the highest setting. Whisk the last egg and stir only enough of it into the dough for it to become very shiny and hang in a long strip from the spoon. Only stir in the baking powder when the choux pastry has cooled down. Finally fold in the grated cheese.

4 Make walnut-sized heaps of choux pastry on the baking sheet using two teaspoons. Put the baking sheet on the middle shelf in the preheated oven and **bake for about 20 minutes**. Do not open the oven door during the first 15 minutes of baking or the pastry will collapse.

5 Cut off the top of the choux pastry puffs as soon as you take them out of the oven and put them on a cake rack to cool.

6 For the filling, stir together the fromage frais and crème fraîche and season with salt and pepper. Cut the ham into very small cubes, stir into the fromage frais and crème fraîche mixture and fill the choux pastries with it. Replace the tops and sprinkle with paprika.

Recipe variations: To make **choux pastries with salmon and quark filling** (photograph on the right), cut 150 g/5 oz smoked salmon into small cubes. Stir together 250 g/9 oz quark (40 % fat), 2 teaspoons creamy horseradish, 1 container (125 g/4½ oz) crème fraîche and the herbs. Fold in the salmon and season with salt and pepper. Fill the choux pastries with this mixture and put the tops back on. Garnish with dill if you like.

For **choux pastries with a vegetarian filling** (in the middle in the photograph), mix together 200 g/7 oz (⅞ cup) fromage frais with 1 container (150 g/5 oz) crème fraîche. Stir in 1 finely chopped red pepper (about 150 g/5 oz) and season with salt and pepper. Fill the bottom halves of the choux pastries with this mixture and sprinkle with 2 tablespoons chopped chives. Put the lids back on.

Viennese apple strudel

TRADITIONAL (ABOUT 12 SLICES)

Preparation time:
about 50 minutes,
excluding standing time
Baking time: about 50 minutes

For the baking sheet:
a little fat

For the pan:
baking parchment

For the strudel pastry:
**200 g/7 oz (2 cups) plain
(all purpose) flour
1 pinch salt
75 ml/3 fl oz (⅜ cup)
lukewarm water
50 g/2 oz (4 tablespoons)
melted butter or margarine
or
3 tablespoons cooking oil,
e.g. sunflower oil**

For the filling:
**1–1.5 kg/3¼ lb apples,
e.g. Cox's Orange, Elstar
a few drops Dr. Oetker
Natural Lemon Extract
75 g/3 oz (⅜ cup) butter
or margarine
50 g/2 oz (¾ cup) breadcrumbs
50 g/2 oz (⅓ cup) raisins
100 g/3½ oz (½ cup) sugar
1 sachet vanilla sugar
50 g/2 oz (⅜ cup) peeled
chopped almonds**

Per slice:
P: 3 g, F: 12 g, C: 28 g,
kJ: 1141, kcal: 273, CU: 3.0

1 For the pastry, put the flour in a mixing bowl. Add all the other ingredients and mix using a hand-mixer (with the kneading hook), first briefly on the lowest setting, then on the highest setting to make a smooth dough. Boil the water in a small pan, pour the water away and dry the pan.

2 Place the dough on baking parchment in the hot pan. Cover the pan with a lid and leave the dough to rise for about 30 minutes.

3 Grease the baking sheet. Preheat the oven:
Top/bottom heat:
about 180 °C/350 °F (Gas mark 4)
Fan oven:
about 160 °C/325 °F (Gas mark 3)

4 For the filling, peel the apples, cut into quarters, core and cut into thin sticks. Stir in the lemon essence. Melt the butter or margarine. Cut the dough in half and roll out each half on a large floured tea towel.

5 Spread a little fat on the rolled-out dough, then pull to make a rectangle (about 35 x 25 cm/14 x 10 in, photograph 1). Cut off the edges if they are too thick. Spread two-thirds of the fat on the rolled-out sheet of dough and sprinkle the breadcrumbs on top (leave an edge about 2 cm/¾ in wide uncovered all round, photograph 2).

6 Sprinkle the sticks of apple, raisins, sugar, vanilla sugar and almonds one after the other on the dough. Fold the uncovered edges of the short sides over the filling. Using the cloth to help you, roll up the dough, covered with filling, starting from the long side (photograph 3) and press the ends together firmly.

7 Place the strudel on the baking sheet with the seam downwards and spread a little fat over the top. Put the baking sheet in the bottom third of the preheated oven and **bake for about 50 minutes**.

8 After about 30 minutes spread the rest of the fat over the strudel. When the strudel is done, take it out of the oven and leave to cool on the baking sheet placed on a cake rack or serve warm.

TIPS » Add a touch of sophistication to the filling by stirring in 1 tablespoon rum.
» Fresh vanilla custard, seasoned with a little cinnamon, is also delicious with strudel.
» Bake 1 large strudel instead of 2 small ones.

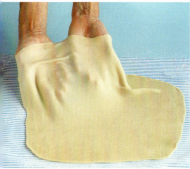

Topfenstrudel (quark strudel)

FOR GUESTS (ABOUT 12 SLICES)

Preparation time:
about 40 minutes,
excluding standing time
Baking time: about 45 minutes

For the baking sheet:
a little fat

For the pan:
baking parchment

For the strudel pastry:
125 g/4½ oz (1¼ cups) plain (all purpose) flour
1 pinch salt
1 egg (medium)
2 tablespoons lukewarm water
scant 2 tablespoons cooking oil, e.g. sunflower oil

For the filling:
40 g/11/2½ oz (3 tablespoons) soft butter or margarine
40 g/1½ oz (3 tablespoons) sugar
1 egg (medium)
1 tablespoon lemon juice
250 g/9 oz (1 cup) low fat quark
40 g/1½ oz (3 tablespoons) vanilla-flavoured custard powder
2 tablespoons whipping cream
1 can apricot halves (drained weight 240 g/8½ oz)
50 g/2 oz (⅓ cup) raisins

40 g/1½ oz (3 tablespoons) butter
a little icing (confectioners') sugar

Per slice:
P: 5 g, F: 9 g, C: 22 g,
kJ: 806, kcal: 192, CU: 2.0

1 For the pastry, put the flour in a mixing bowl. Add all the other ingredients and mix using a hand-mixer (with the kneading hook), first briefly on the lowest setting, then on the highest setting until you have a smooth dough. Boil water in a small pan, pour away the water and dry the pan. Put the dough on baking parchment in the hot pan. Cover the pan with a lid and leave the dough to rise for 30 minutes.

2 Grease the baking sheet and preheat the oven:
Top/bottom heat:
about 180 °C/350 °F (Gas mark 4)
Fan oven:
about 160 °C/325 °F (Gas mark 3)

3 For the filling, stir softened butter or margarine until smooth. Gradually add the sugar, egg, lemon juice, quark, custard powder and cream. Drain the apricots thoroughly in a sieve and chop up finely. Cut the dough in half and roll each half on a floured tea towel to make a rectangle about 40 x 30 cm/16 x 12 in.

4 Melt the butter. Brush the two halves of dough with a little melted butter. Spread each rectangle with half the filling (leave an edge about 3 cm/1¼ wide uncovered all round) and sprinkle half the raisins and chopped apricots on top of each rectangle. Fold the uncovered edges Using the tea towel to help you, roll up the rectangles, starting from the short side, and press the ends together firmly to seal the filling.

5 Place the strudel on the baking sheet with the seam facing downwards, brush a little butter over the strudel and put the baking sheet in the bottom third of the preheated oven. **Bake for about 45 minutes**.

6 After about 30 minutes, brush the rest of the butter over the strudel. When the strudel is done, take out of the oven and leave to cool on the baking sheet placed on a cake rack, or serve warm. Sprinkle with icing (confectioners') sugar if you like.

TIPS » Serve the strudel with warm vanilla custard.
» To crisp up frozen strudel, brush the defrosted strudel with melted butter and bake in the preheated oven at the baking temperature indicated in the recipe for 10 minutes.

Recipe variation: To make a **quark strudel with dried fruit**, prepare the dough as indicated in the recipe and roll out. Finely chop 125 g/ 4½ oz (¾ cup) mixed dried fruit. Whisk together 1 egg yolk (medium), 35 g/1¼ oz (4 tablespoons) sugar, 1 sachet vanilla sugar and 1–2 tablespoons lemon juice until very creamy, then stir in the dried fruit, 200 g/ 7 oz (⅞ cup) full fat cream fromage frais and 125 g/4½ oz (½ cup) low-fat quark. Beat 2 egg whites (medium) very stiff and fold into the mixture. Spread the filling on the rolled out dough as indicated in the recipe. Roll up the strudel, brush the strudel with 1 egg yolk (medium) and bake as in the recipe.

Dutch cherry cake

A LITTLE EXPENSIVE (ABOUT 12 PIECES)

Preparation time:
about 60 minutes, excluding
thawing, cooling and
standing time
Baking time: about 15 minutes
per layer

For the baking sheet:
baking parchment

For the pastry:
1 sachet (450 g/1 lb) frozen
puff pastry (10 square sheets)

For the cherry filling:
1 jar morello cherries
(drained weight 350 g/12 oz)
250 ml/8 fl oz (1 cup) cherry
juice (from the jar)
25 g/1 oz (3 tablespoons)
cornflour (cornstarch)
2 sachets vanilla sugar

For the cream filling:
600 g/20 oz (2½ cups) chilled
whipping cream (min. 30 % fat)
25 g/1 oz (2 tablespoons) sugar
1 sachet vanilla sugar

For the icing:
100 g/3½ oz (⅜ cup)
red currant jelly
100 g/3½ oz (¾ cup) sifted
icing (confectioners') sugar
3–4 teaspoons lemon juice

Per piece:
P: 4 g, F: 24 g, C: 44 g,
kJ: 1749, kcal: 418, CU: 3.5

1 Put the sheets of puff pastry next to each other on the work surface and defrost, following the instructions on the packet. Prepare three sheets of baking parchment the same size as the baking sheet.

2 Line the baking sheet with baking parchment. Preheat the oven:
Top/bottom heat:
about 200 °C/400 °F (Gas mark 6)
Fan oven:
about 180 °C/350 °F (Gas mark 4)

3 First make one layer by arranging 3 sheets of puff pastry on top of each other in a staggered position in the middle of one piece of baking parchment. Fold the projecting corners slightly inwards and roll to make a circle with a diameter of about 28–30 cm/11–12 in. Prick the dough very closely many times with a fork and leave to rise for about 15 minutes. Prepare the other two layers in the same way.

4 Slide the baking parchment with the first layer onto the baking sheet and put on the middle shelf in the preheated oven. **Bake the layer for about 15 minutes.** Bake the other two layers in the same way.

5 As soon as a layer is done, take it out of the oven and slide it together with the baking parchment off the baking sheet (photograph 1), then leave to cool on a cake rack without the baking parchment.

6 For the cherry filling, drain the morello cherries thoroughly in a

sieve and measure off 250 ml/8 fl oz (1 cup) of the juice, topping up with water if necessary. Mix together the cornflour (cornstarch) and vanilla sugar, stir in 4 tablespoons of the cherry juice and bring the rest of the juice to the boil. Take the juice off the boil, stir in the cornflour diluted in the cherry juice and bring to the boil again. Now stir in the cherries and leave the mixture to cool.

7 For the cream filling, whip the cream with the sugar and vanilla sugar. Put 5 tablespoons of the whipped cream in a piping bag with a large star-shaped nozzle. Now spread the cherry filling on the bottom layer (leaving an edge about 1 cm/⅜ in wide uncovered all round, photograph 2), then pipe a ring of whipped cream round the cherries (photograph 3). Next cover all the cherry filling with whipped cream and put the next layer of puff pastry on top. Pipe another ring of whipped cream round the edge, then spread the rest of the cream inside this ring.

8 To make the glaze, bring the jelly to the boil in a small pan, stirring all the time. Pour this glaze over the third layer and allow to set. Stir the lemon juice into the icing (confectioners') sugar to make a syrupy mixture and spread over the jelly glaze, then leave to set again. Cut this layer into 12 pieces and arrange on top of the whipped cream layer.

TIP ›› You can use the rest of the puff pastry to serve separately.

Fried egg nests

FRUITY (10 PIECES/2 BAKING SHEETS)

Preparation time:
about 40 minutes,
excluding thawing and
cooling time
Baking time: about 15 minutes
per baking sheet

For the baking sheet:
baking parchment

For the pastry:
1 sachet (450 g/1 lb) frozen
puff pastry (10 square sheets)

For the filling:
25 g/1 oz vanilla-flavoured
custard powder
2 tablespoons sugar
250 ml/8 fl oz (1 cup) milk
1 can apricot halves
(drained weight 240 g/8½ oz)
2 tablespoons milk

50 g/2 oz (scant ½ cup)
slivered almonds

For coating:
2 tablespoons apricot jam
1 tablespoon water

Per piece:
P: 5 g, F: 14 g, C: 31 g,
kJ: 1137, kcal: 271, CU: 2.5

1 Place the sheets of puff pastry next to each other on the work surface and defrost, following the instructions on the package. Mix together the custard powder, sugar and milk, following the instructions on the packet but using the ingredients listed here. Leave the pudding to cool, stirring occasionally. Preheat the oven:
Top/bottom heat:
about 220 °C/425 °F (Gas mark 7)
Fan oven:
about 200 °C/400 °F (Gas mark 6)

2 Line the baking sheet with baking parchment. Put the apricots in a sieve to drain, then put 10 apricot halves aside. Chop the rest of the apricot halves into small cubes.

3 Put half the puff pastry squares on the baking sheet and brush the top edges with milk. Stir the chopped apricots into the cooled custard mixture. Put 2 teaspoons of this custard mixture in the middle of each puff pastry square. Then put one apricot half on top with the cut side facing down. Finally complete the "nests" by sprinkling slivered almonds along the edges of the puff pastry squares.

4 Put the baking sheet on the middle shelf in the preheated oven and **bake for about 15 minutes**. Prepare the remaining nests in the same way on a sheet of baking parchment.

5 Slide the nests that have just been baked together with the baking parchment off the baking sheet onto a cake rack. Now slide the second lot of nests you have prepared onto the baking sheet and bake in the same way. Remove from the oven and leave to cool on a cake rack.

6 To make the glaze, mix the jam and a little water together in a small pan and bring to the boil. Brush this mixture onto the nests and leave to set.

TIPS » If you cannot find a pack of square sheets of puff pastry, you can buy a packet (450 g/1 lb) of rectangular ones. Cut each rectangular sheet so as to make 12 squares. Put 12 apricot halves to one side and chop the rest into small cubes. Then continue as indicated in the recipe.
» If you have a fan oven you can bake 2 baking sheets at the same time.

Meringue confections

Meringue confections are light, airy delicacies which consist mainly of stiffly beaten egg white and sugar. Meringues can be varied by the addition of ingredients such as nuts, grated coconut and various condiments. Another plus point: if you have any egg white left over after cooking or baking, you can magic up a delicious sweet with very few ingredients in the twinkling of an eye. Macaroons and baisers are among the best known meringue confections.

How to prepare meringue confections

Step 1: Prepare the baking sheet
Line the baking sheet with baking parchment. If you grease the baking sheet lightly before lining it with baking parchment, it will prevent the baking parchment from slipping when you pipe or spoon the beaten egg white onto the baking parchment.

Step 2: Beat the egg white stiff
To beat the egg white really stiff you must make sure that the bowl and whisk are completely fat free. In addition, when separating the eggs, make sure that the egg white is completely clear and that there is not a trace of egg yolk in it. Now take a hand-mixer with a whisk (photograph 1) and beat the egg white on the highest setting until stiff enough for a knife cut to remain visible. Note: only beat the egg whites stiff just before you are going to use them.

Step 3: Fold in the sugar
The sugar and flavourings are added gradually while whisking the egg whites on the highest setting. The egg whites which are now very stiff must be used immediately. If you let stiffly-beaten egg whites stand, they will lose their firmness and it will not be possible to beat them stiff again.

Step 4: Process the egg whites further according to the recipe
In sweet meringue confections the solid ingredients, such as grated coconut, are added at this point. It is important to note that they should be folded in, not stirred in because that would reduce the volume of the beaten egg whites. The mixture can now be processed further according to the recipe (photograph 2).

Step 5: Bake (dry) the meringue confections
Meringue confections are dried rather than baked in the preheated oven. An electric oven is better for baking or rather drying meringue because the low temperatures required can be kept constant without great variations in temperature (unlike in a gas oven). When the meringues are ready, slide them with the baking parchment onto a cake rack to cool (photograph 3). Macaroons should not be baked for too long or they will become too dry. They should still feel soft underneath when you take them off the baking sheet. They will reach the right firmness while cooling on the cake rack.

How to store correctly
Macaroons will remain crisp on the outside and retain their flavour if they are stored in an airtight container. Meringues cannot be frozen.

Baiser

EASY (BASIC RECIPE/ABOUT 80 PIECES)

1 Grease the baking sheet and line with baking parchment. Preheat the oven:

Top/bottom heat:
about 120 °C/230 °F (Gas mark ½)

Fan oven:
about 100 °C/200 °F (Gas mark ¼)

2 To make the meringue mixture, beat the egg whites using a hand-mixer with whisk attachment on the highest setting until they are firm enough for a cut made by a knife to remain visible (photograph 1). Add the sugar gradually while whisking on the highest setting.

3 Then put the egg white mixture in a piping bag with a star-shaped nozzle and pipe shapes onto the baking sheet (photograph 2); or use 2 tea-spoons to make the shapes on the baking sheet.

4 Put the baking sheet in the bottom third of the preheated oven and **bake for about 70 minutes**. The meringue mixture only needs to rise a little and turn slightly creamy-coloured.

5 Then slide the meringues together with the baking parchment onto a cake rack to cool.

Preparation time:
about 25 minutes
Baking time: about 70 minutes

For the baking sheet:
a little fat
baking parchment

For the meringue mixture:
4 egg whites (medium)
200 g/7 oz (1 cup) caster (superfine) sugar

Per piece:
P: 0.2 g, F: 0 g, C: 2 g,
kJ: 45, kcal: 11, CU: 0.2

Amarettini

Preparation time:
about 25 minutes
Baking time: about 30 minutes
per baking sheet

For the baking sheet:
a little fat, baking parchment

For the meringue mixture:
1 egg white (medium)
100 g/3½ oz (½ cup) caster (superfine) sugar, 1 sachet vanilla sugar
1 tablespoon Amaretto
(almond liqueur)
100 g/3½ oz (1 cup) ground almonds

For dusting:
20 g/¾ oz (2½ tablespoons) icing
(confectioners') sugar

Per piece:
P: 0.2 g, F: 0.5 g, C: 1 g,
kJ: 45, kcal: 11, CU: 0.1

1 Grease the baking sheet and line with baking parchment. Preheat the oven:
Top/bottom heat:
about 150 °C/300 °F (Gas mark 2)
Fan oven:
about 130 °C/250 °F (Gas mark ½)

2 To make the meringue mixture, beat the egg whites using a hand-mixer with whisk attachment on the highest setting until they are firm enough for a cut made by a knife to remain visible. Then gradually add the sugar, vanilla sugar and Amaretto while briefly whisking on the highest setting. Fold in the almonds.

3 Put the egg white mixture in a piping bag with a nozzle (diameter 6 mm/ ¼ in) and pipe the amarettini as little heaps 1 cm/⅜ in across on the baking sheet. Put the baking sheet in the bottom third of the preheated oven.

4 **Bake the amarettini for about 30 minutes.** Prepare the rest of the amarettini in the same way on a piece of baking parchment.

5 Slide the amarettini together with the baking parchment onto a cake rack; sprinkle with icing (confectioners') sugar while still warm, leave to cool, then remove the baking parchment. Now slide the baking parchment with the second batch of amarettini onto the baking sheet and bake. Take out of the oven together with the baking parchment, sprinkle with icing (confectioners') sugar and leave to cool.

TIP » If you have a fan oven you can bake 2–3 baking sheets at the same time.

Wasp nests

Preparation time:
about 25 minutes
Baking time: about 25 minutes
per baking sheet

For the baking sheet:
a little fat, baking parchment

125 g/4½ oz chocolate
3 egg whites (medium)
250 g/9 oz (1¼ cups) caster
(superfine) sugar
1 sachet vanilla sugar
250 g/9 oz (3 cups) peeled
chopped almonds

1 Grease the baking sheet and line with parchment. Preheat the oven:
Top/bottom heat:
about 140 °C/275 °F (Gas mark 1)
Fan oven:
about 120 °C/230 °F (Gas mark ½)

2 For the meringue mixture, grate the chocolate finely on a grater. Whisk the egg whites in a bowl using a hand-mixer with whisk attachment on the highest setting; continue whisking until they are firm enough for a cut made by a knife to remain visible. Add the sugar and vanilla sugar little by little and whisk briefly on the highest setting.

3 Carefully fold in the chocolate and almonds while whisking on the lowest setting. Using 2 teaspoons, make small heaps on the baking sheet lined with baking parchment. Put in the bottom third of the preheated oven. **Bake for about 25 minutes.** Prepare the rest of the wasp nests in the same way.

4 Slide the wasp nests together with the baking parchment off the

baking sheet onto a cake rack. Then slide the baking parchment with the second batch of wasp nests onto the baking sheet and bake. Leave the wasp nests to cool on a cake rack.

Per piece:
P: 1 g, F: 3 g, C: 5 g,
kJ: 218, kcal: 52, CU: 0.5

Coconut macaroons

POPULAR (ABOUT 80 PIECES/ABOUT 2 BAKING SHEETS)

Preparation time:
about 25 minutes
Baking time: about 25 minutes
per baking sheet

For the baking sheet:
a little fat
baking parchment

For the meringue mixture:
200 g/7 oz (⅞ cup) grated
coconut
4 egg whites (medium)
200 g/7 oz (1¼ cups) caster
(superfine) sugar
1 sachet vanilla sugar
1 pinch ground cinnamon

Per piece:
P: 0.3 g, F: 2 g, C: 3 g,
kJ: 109, kcal: 26, CU: 0.2

1 Put the grated coconut in a pan without fat and roast until golden yellow (photograph 1), stirring occasionally; then put on a plate and leave to cool. Grease the baking sheet and line with baking parchment. Preheat the oven:
Top/bottom heat:
about 140 °C/275 °F (Gas mark 1)
Fan oven:
about 120 °C/230 °F (Gas mark ½)

2 Beat the egg whites stiff using a hand-mixer with whisk attachment on the highest setting until they are firm enough for a cut made by a knife to remain visible. Add the sugar, vanilla sugar and cinnamon little by little, then continue whisking briefly on the highest setting. Fold the grated coconut carefully into the beaten egg whites.

3 Using 2 teaspoons, make small heaps of the egg white mixture on the baking sheet (photograph 2). Put the baking sheet in the bottom third of the preheated oven. **Bake for about 25 minutes.** Prepare the rest of the macaroons in the same way on a piece of baking parchment.

4 Slide the baked macaroons together with the baking parchment onto a cake rack and leave to cool. Then slide the second batch of macaroons on the baking parchment onto the baking sheet and bake. Leave to cool on the baking parchment on a cake rack.

TIP » If you like, you can drizzle 50 g/2 oz melted chocolate on the macaroons.

Recipe variation: To make hazelnut macaroons (photograph 3), make the egg white mixture as indicated in the recipe. But instead of the grated coconut, fold in 200 g/7 oz (2 cups) chopped and 150 g/5 oz (1½ cups) ground hazelnuts. Make heaps of this egg white mixture as described in the recipe and bake.

Deep-fried pastry

The best-known deep-fried pastry is made from yeast dough and known as doughnuts or "Berliners". But puff pastry, shortcrust pastry or quark & oil pastry are also delicious deep-fried. First choose the kind of pastry you want, then prepare the pastry as described in the recipe. To deep-fry you can use either a chip pan or a saucepan large enough for the pastry to "swim" in.

How to deep-fry pastry

Step 1: The right kind of fat
Fry the pastry in pure neutral-flavoured vegetable oil which can be heated to a high temperature. Neutral-flavoured cooking-oil such as sunflower oil is just as suitable as solid vegetable fat, for instance coconut oil.
Depending on the size of the chip pan or saucepan you will need 750 g–1 kg/1½–2¼ lb solid vegetable fat or 750 ml–1 litre/1¼–1¾ pints (3½–4¼ cups) cooking oil. The pan should be about two-thirds full with fat or oil. When deep-frying in a chip pan, make sure you follow the manufacturer's instructions. Cooking oil and solid fat should not be mixed together.

Step 2: Heat the oil or fat and determining its temperature
Fill the chip pan or saucepan with enough oil or fat so that the individual pastries can "swim" in it freely.
Now heat the oil or fat and check that it is the right temperature – if the oil or fat is too hot, the pastry will brown too quickly, it will not increase in volume and it will remain doughy inside. If the fat is not hot enough the pastry will absorb too much oil or fat. In addition, the fat or oil can begin to foam so much that when you put the pastry in the more delicate pieces could be torn apart. If this happens, you must increase the temperature.
You can establish that the temperature is correct by putting the handle of a wooden spoon in the hot fat or oil. If bubbles form round the spoon, the oil or fat has reached the right temperature, namely about 175 °C/350 °F (photograph 1).

Step 3: Fry the pastry
Now put the prepared pastries in the fat or oil as described in the recipe – do not put too many in at a time because this would cool the oil or fat. Check the temperature of the oil or fat regularly with the wooden spoon to check that it is still correct. When the pastries have turned a beautiful golden brown, take them out of the pan and put on kitchen paper to drain so that the excess fat is not absorbed by the pastry (photograph 2). Then leave the pastries to cool on a cake rack.

Step 4: Clean the frying oil or fat
Any small particles of pastry that might remain in the oil or fat would burn the next time you heated it, so contaminating it. For this reason you must clean the oil or fat after every use. To do this, pour it through a metal sieve lined with kitchen paper (photograph 3).

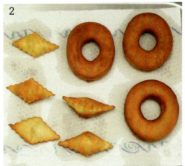

The same bath for all
Different pastries can be deep-fried one after the other in the same oil or fat without the taste being transferred from one to the other. But the oil or fat should not be used more than six to ten times.

How to store deep-fried pastries
Deep-fried pastries taste best when fresh. You should not keep them for more than one day and even so you should crisp them up briefly in the oven, preheated at the top and bottom to 150 °C/300 °F (Gas mark 2). Deep-fried pastries can also be frozen. In this case let them defrost at room temperature in their wrapping, then crisp briefly in the oven, preheated at the top and bottom to 150 °C/300 °F (Gas mark 2). Depending on the type of pastry, sprinkle with icing (confectioners') sugar or cover with a glaze.

Quark balls

POPULAR (ABOUT 25 PIECES)

1 For the yeast dough, carefully mix together the flour and dried yeast in a mixing bowl. Add all the other ingredients for the dough (except the raisings) and mix using a hand-mixer (with the kneading hook), first briefly on the lowest setting, then on the highest setting for about 5 minutes until you have obtained a smooth dough. Cover the dough and put in a warm place until it has visibly increased in volume.

2 Meanwhile put the oil or fat in a chip pan or saucepan and heat to 175 °C/350 °F so that it forms small bubbles when you put the handle of a wooden spoon in it.

3 Knead the dough briefly again, then knead the raisins into the dough with the hand-mixer on the medium setting.

4 Shape small balls with a teaspoon dipped in the oil and deep-fry in the hot oil until lightly brown. Lift the quark balls out of the oil with a skimming ladle and drain thoroughly on kitchen paper. Sprinkle the quark balls with icing (confectioners') sugar and serve lukewarm.

Preparation and baking time: about 40 minutes, excluding rising time

For the yeast dough:
200 g/7 oz (2 cups) plain (all purpose) flour
1 sachet dried yeast
75 g/3 oz (⅓ cup) sugar
1 sachet vanilla sugar
1 pinch salt
a few drops Dr. Oetker Natural Lemon Extract
1 egg (medium)
50 g/2 oz (4 tablespoons) soft butter or margarine
250 g/9 oz (1 cup) low fat quark
75 g/3 oz (½ cup) raisins

deep-frying oil
a little icing (confectioners') sugar

Per piece:
P: 3 g, F: 4 g, C: 12 g,
kJ: 402, kcal: 96, CU: 1.0

173

Berliners (doughnuts)

Preparation and baking time:
about 60 minutes,
excluding rising time

For the yeast dough:
125 ml/4 fl oz (½ cup) milk
100 g/3½ oz (½ cup) butter or
margarine
500 g/18 oz (5 cups) plain
(all purpose) flour
1 sachet dried yeast
30 g/1 oz (3 tablespoons) sugar
1 sachet vanilla sugar
1 tablespoon rum
1 level teaspoon salt
2 eggs (medium)
1 egg yolk (medium)

For the deep-frier:
deep-frying oil

For the filling:
300 g/10 oz (1 cup) jam of your
choice or 250 g/9 oz (1 cup)
plum butter or jelly

For the coating:
a little sugar

Per piece:
P: 5 g, F: 11 g, C: 43 g,
kJ: 1250, kcal: 299, CU: 3.5

1 To make the dough, heat the milk in a small pan, add the butter or margarine and melt it in the hot milk.

2 Mix the flour and dried yeast carefully together in a mixing bowl. Add all the other ingredients, the warm milk and fat mixture and mix everything using a hand-mixer (with the kneading hook), first briefly on the lowest setting, then on the highest setting for about 5 minutes until you have a smooth dough. Cover the dough and put in a warm place to rise until it has visibly increased in volume.

3 Meanwhile put the oil or fat in a chip pan or saucepan and heat to 175 °C/350 °F so that it forms small bubbles when you put the handle of a wooden spoon in it (photograph 1).

4 Sprinkle a little flour over the dough and knead again briefly on the work surface. Now roll out the dough onto the lightly floured work surface until it is about 1 cm/⅜ in thick and cut out about 14–16 circles with a diameter of about 7 cm/2¾ in. Now put the circles between two floured tea towels to rise until they have visibly increased in volume.

5 Put the doughnuts in the hot fat in instalments and deep-fry until golden brown on both sides. Then lift then out of the fat with a skimming ladle (photograph 2) and leave to drain on kitchen paper.

6 To make the filling, rub the jam through a sieve or stir plum butter or jelly until smooth. Then put it in a piping bag with long, thin nozzle. Stick the nozzle into the light-coloured band on the side of the doughnut and pipe in some filling (photograph 3).

7 Coat the doughnuts in sugar when still warm and leave to cool on a cake rack.

TIP » In step 4 you can alternatively divide the dough into 14–16 portions of similar size and then shape these into balls.

Glaze variations: To make **doughnuts with a sugar glaze**, dilute icing (confectioners') sugar with sufficient water to make a spreadable glaze.

To make **doughnuts with a whisky or egg-liqueur glaze**, sift 150 g/5 oz (1⅛ cups) icing (confectioners') sugar, add 3–4 tablespoons whisky or egg liqueur and stir to make a thick glaze. Spread this on the top of each doughnut.

For **doughnuts with pink glaze**, dissolve 2–3 tablespoons red jelly over a bain-marie and spread on the top of the doughnuts.

(continued on p. 176)

1

2

3

ADDITIONAL TIP » You can sprinkle any of the above glazes with chocolate flakes, chopped nuts, flaked almonds, praline or hundreds and thousands, immediately after you have applied the glaze.

Filling variations: To make **doughnuts with a vanilla or egg liqueur filling**, make a custard with 20 g/ ¾ oz (1½ tablespoons) vanilla-flavoured custard powder following the instructions on the packet but using only 250 ml/8 fl oz (1 cup) milk, or with only 200 ml/7 fl oz (⅞ cup) milk and 50 ml/1½ fl oz (3 tablespoons) egg liqueur. Leave the vanilla or egg liqueur filling to cool, stirring regularly, then pipe into the doughnuts.

Eberswalder piped pastries

POPULAR (ABOUT 25 PIECES)

Preparation and baking time: about 90 minutes

For the deep-frier:
deep-frying oil
baking parchment
a little fat

For the choux pastry:
250 ml/8 fl oz (1 cup) water
50 g/2 oz (4 tablespoons) butter or margarine
150 g/5 oz (1½ cups) plain (all purpose) flour
30 g/1 oz (3 tablespoons) cornflour (cornstarch)
25 g/1 oz (2 tablespoons) sugar
1 sachet vanilla sugar
5–6 eggs (medium)
1 level teaspoon baking powder

For the icing:
300 g/10 oz (1½ cups) icing (confectioners') sugar
about 3 tablespoons lemon juice
hot water

1 Put the oil or fat in a chip pan or saucepan and heat to 175 °C/350 °F so that it forms small bubbles when you put the handle of a wooden spoon in it. Cut the baking parchment in squares (about 10 x 10 cm/ 4 x 4 in) and grease them.

2 To make the pastry, bring the water together with the butter or margarine to the boil. Remove the pan from the heat. Mix together the flour and cornflour (cornstarch) and add all at once to the hot liquid. Stir until you obtain a smooth, even ball of dough, then continue cooking for 1 more minute, stirring all the time. Put the dough in a mixing bowl.

3 Stir in the sugar and vanilla sugar with the hand-mixer (kneading hook). Stir the 5 eggs one after the other into the dough with the hand-mixer (kneading-hook) on the highest setting. Beat the last egg and only add enough of the beaten egg to make the dough very shiny and hanging in long strips from the spoon (photograph 1). Only stir in the baking powder when the dough has cooled.

4 Put the pastry in small amounts in a piping bag with a large star-shaped nozzle (about 8 mm/⅓ in) and pipe the pastry in the shape of little crowns (diameter 6–7 cm/ 2½–2¾ in) on the squares of baking parchment you have cut to size (photograph 2). Dip the baking parchment squares carefully into the hot oil and thus slide the crowns of dough into it (photograph 3). Deep-fry until they are light brown on both sides. Take the pastries out of the oil with a skimming ladle, drain thoroughly on kitchen paper and leave to cool on a cake rack.

5 For the glaze, sift the icing (confectioners') sugar, stir in the lemon juice and enough hot water to make a thick but spreadable mixture. Spread this on the pastries.

Per piece: P: 2 g, F: 5 g, C: 19 g, kJ: 539, kcal: 129, CU: 1.5

Almond nuggets

Preparation and baking time:
about 80 minutes

For the deep-frier:
deep-frying oil

For the shortcrust pastry:
325 g/11 oz (3¼ cups) plain (all purpose) flour
1½ level teaspoons baking powder
100 g/3½ oz (½ cup) sugar
1 tablespoon rum
2 eggs (medium), 1 pinch salt
100 g/3½ oz (½ cup) soft butter or margarine

Per piece:
P: 1 g, F: 2 g, C: 6 g,
kJ: 182, kcal: 43, CU: 0.5

1 Heat the oil or fat in a chip pan or saucepan and heat to 175 °C/350 °F so that it forms small bubbles when you put the handle of a wooden spoon in it.

2 To make the shortcrust pastry, mix together the flour and the baking powder in a mixing bowl. Add all the other ingredients and mix using a hand-mixer (with the kneading hook), first briefly on the lowest setting, then on the highest setting until the shortcrust pastry has the right texture. Then shape into a roll with your hands.

3 Roll the dough out on the lightly floured work surface to a thickness of about 1 cm/⅜ in and cut out almond nuggets with the almond-nugget cutter (photograph 1), or shape the almond nuggets with 2 teaspoons.

4 Put the almond nuggets in instalments in the hot oil or fat and fry until golden yellow (photograph 2). Then remove from the oil with a skimming ladle (photograph 3) and drain thoroughly on kitchen paper.

TIP ›› Turn the almond nuggets in sugar while they are still hot.

Rhenish almond nuggets

Preparation and baking time:
about 60 minutes

For the deep-frier:
deep-frying oil

For the pastry:
40 g/1½ oz (⅜ cup) icing (confectioners') sugar
2 eggs (medium)
1 sachet vanilla sugar
250 g/9 oz (2½ cups) plain (all purpose) flour
2 level teaspoons baking powder
2 tablespoons rum

1 Heat the oil or fat in a chip pan or saucepan and heat to 175 °C/350 °F so that it forms small bubbles when you put the handle of a wooden spoon in it.

2 For the pastry, sift the icing (confectioners') sugar and put in a mixing bowl together with the eggs and vanilla sugar and mix using a hand-mixer (with a whisk) on the highest setting for 3 minutes. Mix together the flour and baking powder and whisk with the rum on the lowest setting.

3 Roll out the pastry thinly on the floured work surface and cut into lozenges about 7 cm/2¾ in long with a pastry wheel.

4 Deep-fry the almond nuggets on both sides in the hot oil until golden brown. Remove the almond nuggets from the oil with a skimming ladle and drain thoroughly on kitchen paper.

TIP ›› Sprinkle the warm almond nuggets with 2 tablespoons icing (confectioners') sugar.

Per piece: P: 0.5 g, F: 1 g, C: 3 g, kJ: 86, kcal: 21, CU: 0.5

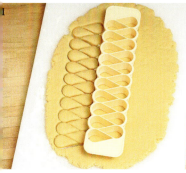

Gelatine information

» Both red and clear gelatine are available as powder and in leaf form.

» 1 sachet of powdered gelatine (9 g) is sufficient for 500 ml/17 fl oz (2¼ cups) liquid and corresponds to 6 leaves of gelatine (10 g).

» Soak the leaf gelatine in plenty of cold water for about 5 minutes. Then squeeze the gelatine leaves lightly, put in a small pan and dissolve over low heat, stirring all the time.

» Put the powdered gelatine in a small pan and stir in about 6 tablespoons of cold water. Leave the gelatine to swell for about 5 minutes. Then dissolve the swollen gelatine in the pan over low heat, stirring all the time.

» You can also dissolve the soaked gelatine leaves or swollen powdered gelatine in hot liquid, depending on the recipe.

» To set whipped cream: first whip the cream almost stiff, then briefly whisk in the sugar. Add the lukewarm dissolved gelatine all at once while still whisking; continue whipping the cream until completely stiff, then proceed following the instructions in the recipe.

» To set fillings for cakes and flans: stir about 4 tablespoons of the filling into the dissolved gelatine to ensure that the temperature of all the ingredients is the same and so prevent lumps from forming. Then stir the gelatine-cream mixture into the rest of the cream with an egg-whisk and continue following the instructions in the recipe.

» Fresh pineapple, kiwis, papaya and figs affect the jellying properties of gelatine because of the particular enzymes they contain. Therefore they must be blanched in hot water before they are used; otherwise use tinned fruit.

» To ensure that preparations containing gelatine set properly, they should be placed in the refrigerator.

Quick cream cheese cake

POPULAR (ABOUT 16 PIECES)

Preparation time: about 30 minutes, excluding cooling time

For the springform mould (diameter 26 cm/10¼ in):
cake doily, cake platter

180 g/6½ oz sponge fingers
120 g/4¼ oz (scant ⅝ cup) butter or margarine

11 g/⅜ oz lemon jelly (Jello) cubes
200 ml/7 fl oz (⅞ cup) water
200 g/7 oz (⅞ cup) full fat cream cheese
125 g/4½ oz (⅝ cup) sugar
1 sachet vanilla sugar
2 tablespoons lemon juice
500 g/18 oz (2¼ cups) chilled whipping cream

1 Put the cake doily on a cake platter and place the closed springform mould ring on top.

2 To make the base, put the sponge fingers in a freezer bag, close the bag and crush with a rolling pin to make fine crumbs. Put 30 g/1 oz aside to garnish the cake later. Melt the butter or margarine in a small pan. Add the crumbs and stir well. Put this mixture inside the springform mould ring directly on the cake doily and press down with the back of a spoon to make an even surface.

3 To make the filling, prepare the jelly with 200 ml/7 fl oz (⅞ cup) water but without sugar, following the instructions on the packet, then leave to cool a little. Stir together the cream cheese, sugar, vanilla sugar and lemon juice with an egg-whisk and stir in the lukewarm jelly. When the mixture begins to thicken, whip the cream stiff and fold into the mixture. Spread this mixture on the sponge biscuit base and smooth the surface even. Put the cheesecake in the refrigerator for about 3 hours.

4 Sprinkle the crumbs you have put aside all round edge of the cake as a garnish. Carefully loosen the springform mould ring with a knife, then remove it. Keep the cake in the refrigerator until you serve it.

Per piece: P: 4 g, F: 21 g, C: 18 g, kJ: 1169, kcal: 279, CU: 1.5

Spicy almond cookie flan

WITH ALCOHOL (ABOUT 16 PIECES)

Preparation time:
about 45 minutes, excluding
cooling time

For the springform mould
(diameter 26 cm/10¼ in):
baking parchment
cake platter

For the base:
200 g/7 oz spicy cookies
100 g/3½ oz (½ cup) butter

For the cream:
6 sheets clear gelatine
200 g/7 oz (⅞ cup) chilled
whipping cream
250 g/9 oz (1 cup) mascarpone
(Italian cream cheese)
500 g/18 oz (2 cups) low-fat
quark
2 tablespoons runny honey
1 sachet vanilla sugar
2 level teaspoons ground
cinnamon
75 g/3 oz (⅓ cup) sugar

For the topping:
2 oranges
2 small pears
60 ml/2 fl oz (4 tablespoons)
orange liqueur
300 ml/10 fl oz (1¼ cups)
orange juice
140 ml/4½ fl oz (⅝ cup) water
2 sachets clear cake glaze
4 tablespoons sugar

For decoration:
25 g/1 oz (scant ⅛ cup) grated
white coating chocolate

1 Place a sheet of baking parchment on a cake platter and put the closed springform mould ring on top.

2 To make the base, put the spicy cookies in a freezer bag. Close the bag and crush the cookies with a rolling pin to make fine crumbs. Melt the butter in a small pan, add the crumbs and stir well. Spread the mixture inside the springform mould ring directly on the baking parchment and press with a moistened tablespoon to make a smooth surface. Put the base in the refrigerator for at least 20 minutes.

3 To make the filling, soak the gelatine following the instructions. Whip the cream stiff. Squeeze the gelatine lightly, put in a small pan and dissolve over low heat, stirring all the time. Mix together the mascarpone, quark, honey, vanilla sugar, cinnamon and sugar. Stir about 4 tablespoons of this mascarpone-quark mixture into the dissolved gelatine, then stir this gelatine mixture into the rest of the mascarpone-quark mixture. Then fold in the cream. Put the filling on the base and smooth the surface even. Put the cheesecake in the refrigerator for about 2 hours.

4 To make the topping, peel the oranges in such a way that you also remove the white pith (photograph 1). Fillet the oranges (photograph 2). Wash the pears, wipe dry, cut into quarters, core, peel and cut into slices. Arrange the fruit decoratively on the filling. Mix together the liqueur, orange juice and water. Mix together the sugar and the glaze in a pan, then gradually add in the liquid, stirring all the time, making sure there are no lumps. Then bring to the boil while still stirring and pour over the fruit. Leave the glaze to set.

5 Loosen the cheesecake off the baking parchment with a cake slice and pull the baking parchment away from under the cake. Carefully loosen the springform mould ring with a knife, then remove completely. Finally garnish the cheesecake with the grated white cooking chocolate.

TIPS » The base can be prepared 1 or 2 days in advance. In that case, cover and keep in the refrigerator. » To make this cheesecake without alcohol replace the liqueur by orange juice.

Per piece: P: 7 g, F: 20 g, C: 29 g, kJ: 1401, kcal: 335, CU: 2.5

Whipped cream cheesecake with nougat

SOPHISTICATED (ABOUT 16 PIECES)

Preparation time:
about 40 minutes, excluding
cooling time

For the springform mould
(diameter 26 cm/10¼ in):
baking parchment
cake platter

For the base:
180 g/6½ oz rusks (Zwieback crackers)
200 g/7 oz nut nougat
20 g/¾ oz (2 tablespoons) butter

For the cheesecake mixture:
6 sheets clear gelatine
750 g/1½ lb (3 cups) low fat quark
100 ml/3½ fl oz (½ cup) milk
50 g/2 oz (¼ cup) sugar
250 g/9 oz (1 cup) chilled whipping cream
100 g/3½ oz nut nougat
1 tablespoon cocoa powder
75 g/3 oz (⅓ cup) sugar

For decoration:
a little cocoa powder

Per piece:
P: 9 g, F: 11 g, C: 30 g,
kJ: 1094, kcal: 261, CU: 2.5

1 Place a sheet of baking parchment on a cake platter and put the closed springform mould ring on top (photograph 1).

2 To make the base, put the rusks in a freezer bag. Close the bag and crush with a rolling pin to make fine crumbs. Melt the nougat with the butter in a small pan in a bain-marie, stirring all the time. Then pour over the crumbled rusks in a bowl and mix well so that all the ingredients are well incorporated. Put this rusk mixture inside the springform mould ring and smooth the surface by pressing it with a tablespoon. Put the base in the refrigerator for at least 20 minutes.

3 To make the cheesecake mixture, soak the gelatine following the instructions on the package. Stir the quark together with the milk and sugar in a bowl. Squeeze the gelatine lightly and dissolve in a small pan over a low heat. First stir about 4 tablespoons of the quark mixture into the dissolved gelatine, then stir this gelatine mixture into the rest of the quark mixture. Whip the cream until stiff and fold into the quark-gelatine mixture.

4 Stir the nougat in a small pan in a bain-marie until soft and leave to

cool. Divide the quark filling into half. Stir the nougat and cocoa powder into one half while stirring the sugar into the other half. Spread the dark filling on the rusk base, then spread the light-coloured filling on top. Draw a fork through the two layers, making a spiral-shaped pattern, thus creating a marble effect on the surface (photograph 2).

5 Tap the springform mould several times on the work surface to settle and smooth the surface again. Put the cheesecake in the refrigerator for about 3 hours.

6 Loosen the cheesecake off the baking parchment with a cake slice, then carefully pull the baking parchment away from under the cheesecake. Then carefully loosen the springform mould ring with a knife (photograph 3) and remove completely.

7 Keep the cheesecake in the refrigerator until you are ready to serve it. Shortly before serving, decorate the cake by sprinkling cocoa powder round the edge.

TIP ›› You can also decorate the cake by drizzling about 100 g/3½ oz nut nougat over the surface.

Lime squares

REFRESHING (ABOUT 16 SLICES)

Preparation time:
about 50 minutes, excluding cooling time

For the baking sheet:
a little fat
baking parchment
square baking frame

For the base:
100 g/3½ oz (½ cup) butter
200 g/7 oz shortbread

For the topping:
1 organic lime (untreated, unwaxed)
8 sheets clear gelatine
750 g/1½ lb (3 cups) full fat quark (40% fat dry weight)
50 g/2 oz (¼ cup) sugar
1 sachet vanilla sugar
150 ml/5 fl oz (⅝ cup) lime syrup
250 g/9 oz (1 cup) chilled whipping cream

For the glaze:
1 sachet clear cake glaze
100 ml/3½ fl oz (½ cup) lime syrup
150 ml/5 fl oz (⅝ cup) water

Per slice:
P: 7 g, F: 18 g, C: 25 g,
kJ: 1242, kcal: 297, CU: 2.0

1 Grease the baking sheet and line with baking parchment, then place a pastry frame measuring about 25 x 25 cm/10 x 10 in on top.

2 To make the base, melt the butter in a pan. Put the petit-beurre biscuits in a freezer bag and close the bag. Crush the biscuits with a rolling pin to make fine crumbs (photograph 1). Stir the crumbs into the melted butter. Put this mixture inside the pastry frame and press down with the back of a spoon to make a smooth, even surface (photograph 2). Put the biscuit base in the refrigerator for at least 20 minutes.

3 For the filling, wash the limes in hot water and wipe dry. Grate the rind finely. Cut the limes into half and squeeze the juice out.

4 Soak the gelatine following the instructions on the packet. Mix together the quark, sugar, vanilla sugar, lime rind and 3 tablespoons lime juice and stir until you obtain a smooth mixture. Squeeze the gelatine lightly and dissolve with the lime syrup in a small pan over low heat, stirring all the time.

5 Stir 4 tablespoons of the quark mixture into the dissolved gelatine mixture, using a whisk. Then stir this back into the rest of the quark mixture.

6 As soon as the quark mixture begins to thicken, whip the cream stiff and fold in carefully. Spoon this whipped cream-quark mixture on the biscuit base and smooth the surface flat. Leave the cake in the refrigerator for at least 2 hours.

7 To make the glaze, prepare a glaze with the glaze powder, lime syrup and water, following the instructions on the package and spoon evenly over the cake (photograph 3). Leave the glaze to set.

8 Carefully loosen the pastry frame from the cake with a knife, then remove completely. Keep the cake in the refrigerator until you are ready to serve it, then cut into portions.

SERVING TIP ›› If you like you can garnish the cake and plate with grated lime rind and segments of lime. To do this, wash 1 organic lime (untreated and not waxed) in hot water, wipe dry and grate the rind with a rind grater. Then garnish each portion with the grated rind.

TIP ›› Lime syrup is available in the supermarket as a base to make limeade or as an ingredient for cocktails.

Kalter Hund
or Cold Dog pudding

EASY (ABOUT 20 SLICES)

Preparation time:
about 60 minutes, excluding
cooling time

For the baking tin
(25 x 11 cm/10 x 4½ in):
1 large freezer bag

For the chocolate cream:
**150 g/5 oz dark coating
chocolate
450 g/1 lb full milk coating
chocolate
200 g/7 oz (⅞ cup) whipping
cream
160 ml/5½ fl oz coconut oil
2 sachets vanilla sugar**

Also:
about 250 g/9 oz shortbread

Per slice:
P: 3 g, F: 23 g, C: 25 g,
kJ: 1360, kcal: 326, CU: 2.0

1 Cut open a freezer bag and line the rectangular tin with it.

2 To make the chocolate filling, chop the two kinds of cooking chocolate into pieces. Heat the cream in a pan. Add the coconut oil and the chopped chocolate and let it melt in the hot cream, stirring all the time. Now stir in the vanilla sugar.

3 Now line the bottom of the baking tin with a layer of petit beurre biscuits; if necessary cut the biscuits with a serrated knife or break them to make them fit. Spoon enough chocolate filling on the biscuits to cover them. Continue in this way, alternating a layer of biscuits and a layer of chocolate filling to fill the tin (7–8 layers, photograph 1).

4 Put the tin in the refrigerator for about 5 hours (overnight is even better) to set the chocolate filling.

5 Very carefully turn put the contents onto a rectangular platter (photograph 2) and gently pull the freezer bag away (photograph 3). Keep the pudding in the refrigerator until you are ready to serve it.

TIPS » Stir 1 teaspoon grated orange zest into the chocolate filling.
» You can also add 2 single-cup sachets (2 g each) of instant espresso coffee.
» To ensure that the freezer bag lining the tin does not slide about, grease the tin lightly before lining the tin with the freezer bag.

Vanilla crescents

POPULAR (ABOUT 90 PIECES/3 BAKING SHEETS)

Preparation time:
about 60 minutes
Baking time: about 10 minutes
per baking sheet
Keeping time: about 3 weeks
in an airtight container

For the baking sheet:
baking parchment

For the shortcrust pastry:
250 g/9 oz (2½ cups) plain
(all purpose) flour
1 pinch baking powder
125 g/4½ oz (⅝ cup) sugar
1 sachet vanilla sugar
3 egg yolks (medium)
200 g/7 oz (1 cup) cold butter
125 g/4½ oz (1¼ cups) ground
almonds

For dusting:
about 50 g/2 oz (scant ½ cup)
icing (confectioners') sugar
1 sachet vanilla sugar

Per piece:
P: 1 g, F: 3 g, C: 4 g,
kJ: 187, kcal: 45, CU: 0.5

1 Line the baking sheet with baking parchment. Preheat the oven:
Top/bottom heat:
about 180 °C/350 °F (Gas mark 4)
Fan oven:
about 160 °C/325 °F (Gas mark 3)

2 For the pastry, mix together the flour and the baking powder in a mixing bowl. Add all the other ingredients and mix using a hand-mixer (with the kneading hook), first briefly on the lowest setting, then on the highest setting until the pastry has the right texture. Then shape into a ball with your hands.

3 Now make pencil-thick rolls and cut into pieces 5–6 cm/2–2½ in long, making the ends slightly thinner (photograph 1). Bend the pieces into crescent shapes and put on the baking sheet. Put this on the middle shelf of the preheated oven. **Bake for about 10 minutes**.

4 Prepare the rest of the vanilla crescents in the same way and put on a piece of baking parchment.

5 Sift the icing (confectioners') sugar and mix together with the vanilla sugar. When the crescents are baked, slide them with the baking parchment onto a cake rack. Sprinkle the warm crescents with the vanilla-flavoured icing (confectioners') sugar. Now slide the crescents you have prepared onto the baking sheet together with the baking parchment and bake. Leave the crescents to cool.

TIPS » If the pastry becomes too soft while you are preparing it, put it in the refrigerator for a while.
» Instead of sprinkling icing (confectioners') sugar on the crescents, gently roll the crescents in sugar while they are still warm.

Ground almond biscuits

TRADITIONAL (ABOUT 50 PIECES/3 BAKING SHEETS)

1 Line the baking sheet and preheat the oven:
Top/bottom heat:
about 130 °C/250 °F (Gas mark ½)
Fan oven:
about 110 °C/225 °F (Gas mark ½)

2 To make the dough, beat the egg whites so that they form stiff peaks. Sift the icing (confectioners') sugar and mix together with the vanilla sugar; then whisk briefly into the egg whites. Next stir in the lemon juice, lemon zest and half the almonds. Now knead enough of the remaining almonds so that the dough is hardly sticky any more.

3 Roll out the dough on a work surface sprinkled with icing sugar to a thickness of about 1 cm/⅜ in. Now cut out crescents with a crescent-shaped cutter and put these on the baking sheet. Put the baking sheet

on the middle shelf in the preheated oven.

4 Then **bake the crescents for about 30 minutes**. Prepare the rest of the crescents as indicated in the recipe and put on a piece of baking parchment.

5 When the crescents are baked, slide them together with the baking parchment onto a cake rack. Then slide the crescents you have prepared together with the baking parchment onto the baking sheet and bake. Leave the crescents to cool on a cake rack.

6 To make the glaze, sift the icing (confectioners') sugar and mix with the lemon juice to make a thick, spreadable glaze. Using a wide-bladed knife, coat the cooled crescents with this glaze. Leave to set.

Preparation time:
about 45 minutes,
excluding cooling time
Baking time: about 30 minutes
per baking sheet
Keeping time: about 2 weeks
in an airtight container

For the baking sheet:
baking parchment

For the pastry:
2 egg whites (medium)
250 g/9 oz (2 cups) icing
(confectioners') sugar
1 sachet vanilla sugar
1 teaspoon lemon juice
1 teaspoon grated lemon zest
about 400 g/14 oz (4 cups)
ground almonds

Also:
a little icing (confectioners')
sugar

For the icing:
150 g/5 oz (1 cup) icing
(confectioners') sugar
2–3 tablespoons lemon juice

Per piece:
P: 2 g, F: 4 g, C: 9 g,
kJ: 336, kcal: 80, CU: 0.5

Oat flakes biscuits

EASY (ABOUT 120 PIECES/4 BAKING SHEETS)

Preparation time:
about 30 minutes, excluding
cooling time
Baking time: about 12 minutes
per baking sheet
Keeping time: about 3 weeks
in an airtight container

For the baking sheet:
baking parchment

For the pastry:
150 g/5 oz (¾ cup) soft butter
or margarine
150 g/5 oz brown sugar
1 tablespoon rum
2 eggs (medium)
200 g/7 oz (2½ cups) soft
oat flakes
150 g/5 oz (1½ cups) ground
almonds
1 level teaspoon baking
powder
1 teaspoon grated lemon zest

Per piece:
P: 1 g, F: 2 g, C: 2 g,
kJ: 121, kcal: 29, CU: 0.1

1 Whisk the margarine or butter in a mixing bowl using a hand-mixer with whisk attachment on the highest setting until soft. Add the brown sugar and flavouring little by little while still whisking. Continue whisking until the mixture has become smooth and even. Whisk in each egg, one after the other, for about ½ minute on the highest setting.

2 Mix together the oat flakes, almonds, baking powder and lemon rind and whisk about two-thirds of this mixture into the butter and brown sugar mixture with the hand-mixer on the medium setting. Using your hands, knead the rest of the oat flakes-almond mixture into the dough on the lightly floured work surface (photograph 1).

3 Shape the dough into 2 rolls each about 30 cm/12 in long. Wrap in clingfilm (plastic film) and store in the refrigerator for a few hours or overnight.

4 Line the baking sheet with baking parchment. Preheat the oven:
Top/bottom heat:
about 180 °C/350 °F (Gas mark 4)
Fan oven:
about 160 °C/325 °F (Gas mark 3)

5 Cut the rolls of dough into slices about 5 mm/³⁄₁₆ in thick (photograph 2) and put on the baking sheet. Put the baking sheet on the middle shelf of the preheated oven.

6 Then **bake the biscuits for about 12 minutes**. Prepare the other biscuits as indicated in the recipe and arrange on a piece of baking parchment.

7 Slide the baked biscuits together with the baking parchment off the baking sheet onto the cake rack. Now slide the prepared biscuits together with the baking parchment onto the baking sheet and bake as indicated in the recipe. Leave the oat flakes biscuits to cool on a cake rack.

TIPS » You can use grated orange instead of grated lemon zest.
» With a fan oven you can bake 2 baking sheets at the same time.
» You can also drizzle some melted cooking chocolate on the oat flakes biscuits (photograph 3).

TIP FOR STORING » After taking the biscuits off the baking sheet, allow them to cool completely on a cake rack. They must only be put away for storing when they are completely cold. Then store them in a cool, dry place.

Cinnamon stars

TRADITIONAL (ABOUT 40 PIECES/2 BAKING SHEETS)

Preparation time:
about 60 minutes
Baking time: about 25 minutes
per baking sheet
Keeping time: about 2 weeks
in an airtight container

For the baking sheet:
baking parchment

For the pastry:
3 egg whites (medium)
250 g/9 oz (2 cups) icing
(confectioners') sugar
1 sachet vanilla sugar
1 level teaspoon ground
cinnamon
about 400 g/14 oz (4 cups)
ground almonds or hazelnuts

Also:
a little icing (confectioners')
sugar

Per piece:
P: 2 g, F: 6 g, C: 7 g,
kJ: 371, kcal: 89, CU: 0.5

1 Line the baking sheet with baking parchment. Preheat the oven:
Top/bottom heat:
about 140 °C/275 °F (Gas mark 1)
Fan oven:
about 120 °C/230 °F (Gas mark ½)

2 To make the dough, whisk the egg whites using a hand-mixer with whisk attachment on the highest setting until they form stiff peaks. Sift the icing (confectioners') sugar and whisk in briefly. Then remove 2 heaped tablespoons of the stiffly beaten egg whites and put to one side for the icing.

3 Carefully whisk the vanilla sugar, cinnamon and about 150 g/5 oz (1½ cups) of the almonds or hazelnuts into the rest of the stiffly beaten egg whites with the hand-mixer on the lowest setting. Using you hands, knead in enough of the remaining almonds or hazelnuts so that the dough is hardly sticky any more.

4 Roll out the dough on a work sur-face, sprinkled with icing (confec-tioners') sugar to a thickness of about 5 mm/³⁄₁₆ in and cut out the stars (photograph 1), put them on the baking sheet and cover with the beaten egg whites you have put aside (photograph 2). The texture of the beaten egg whites must be such that it can be spread on the stars; add a few drops of water if necessary.

5 Put the baking sheet on the lowest shelf in the preheated oven. **Bake the stars for about 25 minutes.** Prepare the rest of the stars as indi-cated in the recipe and put them on baking parchment.

6 Slide the baked cinnamon stars together with the baking parchment off the baking sheet onto a cake rack. The cinnamon stars should still feel a little soft underneath when you take them out of the oven. Now slide the prepared stars to-gether with the baking parchment onto the baking sheet and bake. Leave them to cool on a cake rack.

TIPS » It is easier to cut out the stars if you dip the cutter in the water first every time you use it.
» The cinnamon stars will remain moist if stores in airtight containers.
» To beat egg whites very stiff, the bowl and whisk must be absolutely fat free and there should be no trace of egg yolk in the egg whites.

Recipe variation: To make **cinna-mon balls** (photograph 3), make the dough as indicated in the recipe but with only 300 g/10 oz (3½ cups) ground almonds. Using 2 tea-spoons, make small heaps of the dough on the baking sheet, leaving enough distance between for them to increase in volume. Use a piping bag to add the beaten egg white gar-nish. If you like, decorate each cin-namon ball with a hazelnut and bake as indicated in the recipe.

German Christmas cookies

FOR GUESTS (ABOUT 30 PIECES/3 BAKING SHEETS)

Preparation time:
about 60 minutes,
excluding cooling time
Baking time: about 25 minutes
per baking sheet
Keeping time: about 2 weeks
in an airtight container

For the pastry:
100 g/3½ oz (½ cup) candied
orange peel or lemon peel
(candied peel)
2 eggs (medium)
200 g/7 oz (2 cups) brown
sugar
1 sachet vanilla sugar
1 pinch ground cloves
1 tablespoon rum
a few drops Dr. Oetker
Natural Lemon Extract
125 g/4½ oz (1¼ cups) ground
almonds
1 pinch baking powder
about 100 g/3½ oz (1 cup)
ground hazelnuts

about 30 pieces rice paper
(diameter about 7 cm/2¾ in)

For the light icing:
150 g/5 oz (1 cup) icing
(confectioners') sugar
1–2 tablespoons hot water

For the dark icing:
75 g/3 oz dark chocolate
1 teaspoon cooking oil,
e.g. sunflower oil

Per piece:
P: 2 g, F: 6 g, C: 17 g,
kJ: 533, kcal: 127, CU: 1.5

1 Preheat the oven:
Top/bottom heat:
about 140 °C/275 °F (Gas mark 1)
Fan oven:
about 120 °C/230 °F (Gas mark ½)

2 To make the dough, chop the candied orange peel or lemon peel very finely. Whisk the eggs using a hand-mixer with whisk attachment on the highest setting for 1 minute until foamy. Mix together the sugar and vanilla sugar, sprinkle into the beaten eggs while stirring for 1 minute, then whisk for another 2 minutes and stir in the cloves and flavouring.

3 Mix together the almonds and baking powder and whisk briefly into the egg-mixture on the lowest setting together with the candied orange peel or candied lemon peel and enough of the hazelnuts that the dough is still spreadable.

4 Using a knife dipped in water, put 1 tablespoon of dough on each wafer, then shape it into a dome, covering the whole wafer (photograph 1). Put the wafers on the baking sheet.

5 Put the baking sheet on the middle shelf in the preheated oven. **Bake the wafers for about 25 minutes.**

6 To make the light-coloured icing, sift the icing (confectioners') sugar and add the hot water to make a thick, spreadable glaze (photograph 2). Coat half the cookies with this light-covered glaze as soon as they have come out of the oven (photograph 3) and leave to cool on a cake rack. Prepare the other wafers as shown in the recipe and bake. Leave the cookies without glaze to cool on a cake rack as well.

7 To make the dark chocolate glaze, break the chocolate into pieces and melt with the oil in a bain-marie over low heat. Coat the remaining cooled cookies with this chocolate glaze and leave the glaze to set.

TIPS » If you have a fan oven you can bake 2 or 3 baking sheets at the same time.
» It is best to leave the Christmas cookies well-wrapped for a few days to enable the flavours to develop.

Chocolate hazelnut bars

TRADITIONAL (ABOUT 40 PIECES/2 BAKING SHEETS)

Preparation time:
about 70 minutes, excluding
cooling time
Baking time: about 10 minutes
per baking sheet
Keeping time: about 4 weeks
in an airtight container

For the baking sheet:
a little fat

For the topping:
about 200 g/7 oz (2 cups)
hazelnuts

For the pastry:
50 g/2 oz (4 tablespoons)
butter or margarine
125 g/4½ oz (½ cup) molasses
50 g/2 oz (¼ cup) sugar
1 pinch salt
2 tablespoons milk or water
50 g/2 oz (¼ cup) brown
candy sugar
a few drops Dr. Oetker
Natural Lemon Extract
½ level teaspoon each ground
aniseed, ground cloves and
ground cinnamon
250 g/9 oz (2½ cups) plain
(all purpose) flour
3 level teaspoons baking
powder

For the icing:
250 g/9 oz chocolate
1–2 tablespoons cooking oil,
e.g. sunflower oil

Per piece:
P: 2 g, F: 7 g, C: 13 g,
kJ: 503, kcal: 120, CU: 1.0

1 For the topping, peel the hazelnuts. To do this, place the hazelnuts on a dry, clean baking sheet and roast in the oven preheated with top and bottom heat to about 200 °C/400 °F (Gas mark 6) until the brown skins are easily rubbed off. Put the hot hazelnuts in a clean tea towel and rub off the skin with circular movements of your hands (photograph 1).

2 To make the dough, melt the butter or margarine together with the syrup, sugar, salt in milk or water in a pan, while stirring slowly. Transfer into a bowl and cool in the refrigerator.

3 Whisk the crushed brown candy sugar, flavouring, aniseed, cloves and cinnamon into the almost cold mixture using a hand-mixer with whisk attachment on the highest setting. Mix together the flour and baking powder and whisk two-thirds of it in several instalments into the above mixture with the hand-mixer on the medium setting. Now knead the rest of the flour into the mixture on the work surface to make a smooth dough. Wrap the dough in clingfilm (plastic film) and put in the refrigerator for about 30 minutes.

4 Grease the baking sheet. Preheat the oven:
Top/bottom heat:
about 180 °C/350 °F (Gas mark 4)
Fan oven:
about 160 °C/325 °F (Gas mark 3)

5 Cut the peeled hazelnuts into half. Roll out the dough to a thickness of about 5 mm/³⁄₁₆ in and cut out rectangles of about 7 x 2.5 cm/2¾ x 1 in.

6 Put the rectangles on the baking sheet, then arrange the hazelnuts on the squares of dough. Put the baking sheet on the middle shelf in the preheated oven. **Bake for about 10 minutes.**

7 After baking, take the chocolate hazelnut bars off the baking sheet and leave to cool on a cake rack. Prepare the remaining chocolate hazelnut bars as indicated in the recipe and bake.

8 To make the glaze, break the chocolate into pieces and melt with the oil (photograph 2) in a bain-marie over low heat and coat the cooled bars with this glaze.

TIPS » If you have a fan oven, you can bake 2 baking sheets in the oven at the same time.
» Hazelnut bars should be stored in airtight containers with baking parchment between the layers.
» Leave the hazelnut bars, well wrapped, for a few days to enable the flavours to develop fully.
» The topping of these bars can also be made with other nuts.
» The bars can also be brushed with a little milk and sprinkled with coarse granulated sugar.

INGREDIENT INFORMATION
» Molasses or black treacle is the thick, dark syrupy liquid made from sugar which is often used in Christmas confectioneries.

Almond cookies

TRADITIONAL (ABOUT 140 PIECES/4 BAKING SHEETS)

Preparation time:
about 60 minutes
Baking time: about 12 minutes
per baking sheet
Keeping time: about 3 weeks
in an airtight container

For the baking sheet:
a little fat

For the pastry:
375 g/13 oz (1⅞ cups) soft
butter or margarine
250 g/9 oz (1¼ cups) sugar
2 sachets vanilla sugar
1 pinch salt
500 g/18 oz (5 cups) plain (all
purpose) flour
125 g/4½ oz (1¼ cups) ground
almonds

Per piece:
P: 1 g, F: 3 g, C: 4 g,
kJ: 188, kcal: 45, CU: 0.5

1 Grease the baking sheet. Preheat the oven:

Top/bottom heat:
about 180 °C/350 °F (Gas mark 4)
Fan oven:
about 160 °C/325 °F (Gas mark 3)

2 For the pastry, mix together the butter and margarine in a mixing bowl with the hand-mixer with whisk attachment on the highest setting until soft. Whisk in the sugar, vanilla sugar and salt little by little. Continue whisking until the sugar has completely dissolved and you have obtained a smooth, even mixture. Now whisk in two-thirds of the flour in instalments with a hand-mixer on the medium setting.

3 Knead the rest of the flour and almonds briefly into the dough on the work surface until both are well incorporated. Shape the dough into rolls, put the rolls in a pastry press and squeeze the dough onto the baking sheet (photograph 1). Put the baking sheet on the middle

shelf in the preheated oven. **Bake for about 12 minutes**.

4 Take the biscuits off the baking sheet and put them on a cake rack to cool. Prepare the other biscuits as indicated in the recipe and bake.

TIPS » You can also squeeze the dough through a meat mincing (grinding) machine with a special attachment (photograph 2) and arrange them on a baking sheet, lined with baking parchment, in S-shapes, rings or sticks.
» You can also dip the ends of the cold biscuits in melted chocolate (photograph 3) and sprinkled with chopped pistachio nuts.

Recipe variation: To make chocolate biscuits, knead a mixture of 10 g/⅓ oz (1½ tablespoons) sifted cocoa powder and 10 g/1⅓ oz (1 tablespoon) sugar into one third of the dough and shape into a roll, put in the pastry press and bake as described in the recipe.

Egg yolk cookies

POPULAR (ABOUT 120 PIECES/4 BAKING SHEETS)

Preparation time:
about 60 minutes
Baking time: about 15 minutes
per baking sheet
Keeping time: about 3 weeks
in an airtight container

For the baking sheet:
a little fat
baking parchment

1 Grease the baking sheet and line with baking parchment. Preheat the oven:
Top/bottom heat:
about 180 °C/350 °F (Gas mark 4)
Fan oven:
about 160 °C/325 °F (Gas mark 3)

2 For the pastry, mix the butter and margarine in a bowl with a hand-mixer with whisk attachment on the

highest setting until soft. Whisk in the sugar, vanilla sugar, egg yolk, lemon rind and salt little by little. Continue whisking until the sugar has completely dissolved and you have obtained a smooth, even mixture. Mix the flour and baking powder and whisk two-thirds of it in instalments, alternating with the milk, into the above mixture using the hand-mixer on the medium setting. Knead the rest of the flour into the dough on the work surface.

3 Squeeze the dough through a meat mincing (grinding) machine with a special attachment, cut into pieces of the chosen length and arrange on the baking sheet as sticks and rings.

4 Put the baking sheet on the middle shelf in the preheated oven and **bake the biscuits for about 15 minutes**. Prepare the rest of the biscuits as shown in the recipe and put on baking parchment.

5 Slide the baked biscuits together with the baking parchment off the baking sheet onto a cake rack to cool. Now slide the prepared biscuits with the baking parchment onto the baking sheet and bake as indicated. Leave the biscuits to cool on the cake rack.

TIP » You can make the dough the day before, wrap in clingfilm (plastic film) and keep in the refrigerator.

For the pastry:
250 g/9 oz (1¼ cups) soft butter or margarine
250 g/9 oz (1¼ cups) sugar
2 sachets vanilla sugar
3 egg yolks (medium)
1 pinch salt
1 teaspoon grated lemon zest
500 g/18 oz (5 cups) plain (all purpose) flour
2 level teaspoons baking powder, 1 tablespoon milk

Per piece:
P: 0.5 g, F: 2 g, C: 5 g,
kJ: 170, kcal: 41, CU: 0.5

Spicy glazed biscuits

GOOD TO MAKE AHEAD (ABOUT 50 PIECES/2 BAKING SHEETS)

Preparation time:
65 minutes, excluding
cooling time
Baking time: about 15 minutes
per baking sheet
Keeping time: 2–3 weeks
in an airtight container

For the baking sheet:
baking parchment

For the shortcrust pastry:
250 g/9 oz (2½ cups) plain
(all purpose) flour
1 ½ level teaspoons baking
powder
160 g/5½ oz (⅞ cup) sugar
1 teaspoon grated lemon zest
1 pinch salt
1 egg (medium)
1 pinch each ginger,
cardamom, cloves, allspice,
white pepper (all ground)
3–4 tablespoons milk
25 g/1 oz (¼ cup) ground
almonds
25 g/1 oz (2 tablespoons) finely
chopped candied lemon peel

For the icing:
175 g/6 oz (1 cup) sifted icing
(confectioners') sugar
2 tablespoons hot water

Per piece:
P: 1 g, F: 0.5 g, C: 11 g,
kJ: 216, kcal: 52, CU: 1.0

1 To make the dough, mix together the flour and baking powder in a mixing bowl. Add the sugar, lemon rind, salt, egg, spices, milk, almonds and candied lemon peel. Mix all the ingredients thoroughly using a hand-mixer (kneading hook), at first briefly on a low setting, then on the highest setting.

2 Then knead the dough on the lightly floured surface until very smooth. Divide the dough into two rolls, each about 25 cm/10 in long. Wrap the rolls of dough in cling-film (plastic film) and leave in the refrigerator for a few hours or overnight.

3 Line the baking sheet with baking parchment. Preheat the oven:
Top/bottom heat:
about 180 °C/350 °F (Gas mark 4)
Fan oven:
about 160 °C/325 °F (Gas mark 3)

4 Reshape the rolls if necessary, cut into slices about 1 cm/⅜ in thick and arrange on the baking sheet (while you are cutting the rolls, put them back regularly in the refrigerator so that they are easy to cut).

5 Then put the baking sheet on the middle shelf in the preheated oven and **bake the biscuits for about 15 minutes.** Prepare the rest of the biscuits as indicated in the recipe and put on the baking parchment.

6 Slide the biscuits together with the baking parchment onto a cake rack and slide the prepared biscuits together with the baking parchment onto the baking sheet. Bake as indicated in the recipe. Leave the spicy biscuits to cool on a cake rack.

7 For the glaze, mix together the icing (confectioners') sugar and hot water to make a thick, spreadable glaze. Coat the biscuits with it. Allow the glaze to set completely.

TIPS » You can leave the rolls of dough in the freezer for a little while, then cut with a sharp knife or a slicing machine.
» If you have a fan oven, you can bake 2 baking sheets at the same time.

Gingerbread House Cake

FOR CHILDREN

**Preparation time:
about 60 minutes,
excluding drying time
Baking time: about 15 minutes**

**For the baking sheet
(40 x 30 cm/16 x 12 in):**
a little fat
baking parchment

For the pastry:
240 g/8½ oz (1 cup) honey
120 g/4¼ oz (scant ⅝ cup)
margarine or butter
375 g/13 oz (3¾ cups) plain (all
purpose) flour
4 level teaspoons baking
powder
3 level teaspoons cocoa
powder
3 eggs (medium)
1 tablespoon gingerbread
spices (ground ginger,
cinnamon, nutmeg, cloves and
allspice)
1 teaspoon grated orange zest
150 ml/5 fl oz (⅝ cup) milk

For the icing:
4 sheets clear gelatine
500 g/18 oz (2½ cups) icing
(confectioners') sugar
40 g/1½ oz (5 tablespoons)
cornflour (cornstarch)
5–6 tablespoons water

Also:
sweets (candy) to taste
icing (confectioners') sugar

1 Grease the baking sheet and line with baking parchment. Fold the baking parchment several times where it faces the sloping side of the baking sheet to make an edge. Preheat the oven:
Top/bottom heat:
about 180 °C/350 °F (Gas mark 4)
Fan oven:
about 160 °C/325 °F (Gas mark 3)

2 For the pastry, melt the honey, margarine or butter in a pan and bring to the boil. Put the honey and butter/ margarine mixture in a bowl and allow to cool. Mix together the flour, baking powder and cocoa powder and add to the honey-butter mixture together with the eggs, spices, flavourings and milk and whisk using a hand-mixer with whisk attachment to make a smooth dough.

3 Spread the pastry evenly on a baking sheet and put on the middle shelf of the preheated oven. **Bake for about 15 minutes**, then leave to cool on the baking sheet, placed on a cake rack.

4 Cut out a paper pattern, as shown in the template, and cut the individual parts in the baked pastry (photograph 1). If necessary, leave the cut-out pastry to dry out overnight (photograph 2), so that it becomes firmer.

5 Before assembling the house, soak the gelatine following the instructions on the packet. Sift the icing (confectioners') sugar and cornflour (cornstarch) in a mixing bowl. Squeeze out the gelatine, put in a pan with 5–6 tablespoons water and dissolve over low heat, stirring all the time.

6 Add the dissolved gelatine immediately to the icing sugar-cornflour you have previously mixed together and whisk using a hand-mixer (whisk attachment) until the mixture thickens sufficiently. Put the mixture immediately in a piping bag with a star-shaped nozzle (diameter about 12 mm/½ in) and assemble the gingerbread house on a board or cake platter.

7 First stick the back wall and one half of the roof together, then add all the other parts (photograph 3). Then put in the door with icing (confectioners') sugar mixture and stick the sweets on the house (photograph 4). Allow the gingerbread house to dry completely, then finally sprinkle with icing (confectioners') sugar.

TIPS » If you do not have a piping bag, you can use a freezer bag and cut off one of the corners.
» Cut the left-over pastry into triangles to make a garden fence round the house.

In all (excluding garnish):
P: 60 g, F: 105 g, C: 906 g, kJ: 20341, kcal: 4861, CU: 75.5

Pattern

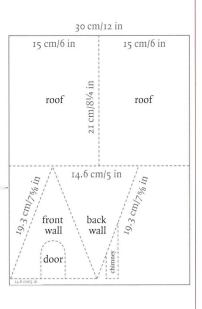

30 cm/12 in

15 cm/6 in | 15 cm/6 in

roof | roof

21 cm/8¼ in

14.6 cm/5 in

19.3 cm/7⅝ in

front wall | back wall

19.3 cm/7⅝ in

door | chimney

14.6 cm/5 in

1

2

3

4

Honey cake

TRADITIONAL (ABOUT 20 SLICES)

Preparation time:
about 30 minutes, excluding
cooling time
Baking time: about 20 minutes
Keeping time: about 10 days in an
airtight container

For the baking sheet
(40 x 30 cm/16 x 12 in):
a little fat

For the dough:
250 g/9 oz (1 cup) honey
125 g/4½ oz (⅝ cup) butter or
margarine
2 eggs (medium)
1 tablespoon gingerbread spices
(ground ginger, cinnamon,
nutmeg, cloves and allspice)
1 teaspoon grated lemon zest
375 g/13 oz (3¾ cups) plain (all
purpose) flour
1 sachet baking powder
2 level teaspoons cocoa powder
100 g/3½ oz (⅝ cup) currants
100 g/3½ oz (1 cup) hazelnuts

For coating and sprinkling:
a little milk
100 g/3½ oz (⅞ cup) slivered
almonds

For the apricot glaze:
5 tablespoons apricot jam

For the icing and for garnishing:
200 g/7 oz dark chocolate
1 tablespoon cooking oil
walnuts, hazelnuts, almonds
chocolate flakes

1 Grease the baking sheet. Preheat the oven:
Top/bottom heat:
about 180 °C/350 °F (Gas mark 4)
Fan oven:
about 160 °C/325 °F (Gas mark 3)

2 For the dough, slowly melt the honey with the butter or margarine in a pan while stirring; pour into a bowl and allow to cool.

3 Now whisk the eggs, gingerbread spices and lemon rind into the almost cold mixture using a hand-mixer (whisk attachment) on the highest setting. Mix together the flour, baking powder and cocoa powder and stir into the mixture in spoonfuls with the hand-mixer on medium setting. Now briefly stir in the currants and hazelnuts.

4 Spread the dough on the baking sheet, drizzle a little milk on top and sprinkle with almonds. Put the baking sheet on the middle shelf of the preheated oven and **bake for about 20 minutes**.

5 To make the apricot glaze, rub the apricot jam through a sieve and brush over the cake as soon as you have taken it out of the oven; then leave the cake, still on the baking sheet, to cool on a cake rack.

6 To make the chocolate glaze, break the chocolate into pieces and melt with the oil in a bain-marie over low heat, then pour over the cooled cake. Garnish the cake with walnuts, almonds or chocolate flakes.

7 When the glaze has set completely, cut the cake into pieces and store in an airtight container.

TIPS » To make the apricot glaze you can puree the apricot jam instead of rubbing it through a sieve.
» It is best to keep the honey cake for a few days, well wrapped, to enable the flavours to develop before enjoying it.

Per slice: P: 6 g, F: 18 g, C: 38 g, kJ: 1422, kcal: 340, CU: 3.0

Christmas stollen

GOOD FOR FREEZING – WITH ALCOHOL (ABOUT 16 SLICES)

Preparation time:
about 35 minutes, excluding
soaking and rising time
Baking time: about 50 minutes

For the baking sheet:
baking parchment

For the yeast dough:
100 ml/3½ fl oz (½ cup) rum
200 g/7 oz (1⅓ cups) raisins
100 g/3½ oz (⅔ cup) currants
375 g/13 oz (3¾ cups) plain
(all purpose) flour
1 sachet (42 g/1½ oz) fresh
yeast
50 g/2 oz (¼ cup) sugar
100 ml/3½ fl oz (½ cup)
lukewarm milk
1 sachet vanilla sugar
1 pinch salt
1 tablespoon stollen spices
(ground cinnamon, cardamon
and nutmeg)
2 eggs (medium)
175 g/6 oz (⅞ cup) soft butter
or margarine
100 g/3½ oz (½ cup) candied
orange peel
100 g/3½ oz (½ cup) candied
lemon peel
100 g/3½ oz (1 cup) ground
almonds

For coating and sprinkling:
75 g/3 oz (⅜ cup) butter
a little icing (confectioners')
sugar

Per slice:
P: 6 g, F: 18 g, C: 44 g,
kJ: 1587, kcal: 379, CU: 3.5

1 For the dough, pour rum over the raisins and currants and leave to soak overnight.

2 The next day, put the flour in a mixing bowl and make a well in the middle. Crumble the yeast inside, add 1 teaspoon sugar and lukewarm milk. Using a fork, stir the three ingredients carefully with a little of the flour and allow the leaven to rise for about 15 minutes at room temperature.

3 Now add the remaining sugar, the vanilla sugar, salt, spices, eggs and butter or margarine and whisk everything together with the hand-mixer (kneading hook attachment), first briefly on the lowest setting, then on the highest setting for about 5 minutes until the dough has become smooth and even.

4 Briefly knead the candied orange peel, candied lemon peel, almonds and soaked raisins and currants into the dough on the lightly floured work surface. Cover the dough, put in a warm place and leave to rise until it has visibly increased in volume.

5 Line the baking sheet with three layers of baking parchment (this will prevent the stollen from getting too dark underneath).

Preheat the oven:
Top/bottom heat:
about 250 °C/480 °F (Gas mark 9)
Fan oven:
about 220 °C/425 °F (Gas mark 7)

6 Shape the dough into the long, round shape of a stollen. To do this, roll out the dough to make a rectangle of about 30 x 25 cm/12 x 10 in. Roll up the dough, starting from the long side, then with the rolling pin make a depression lengthways (photograph 1). Now fold the left side over the right side but slightly offset (photograph 2). Again using your hands, make a bulge lengthways along the middle (photograph 3).

7 Put the stollen on the baking sheet and leave it to rise in a warm place again until it has visibly increased in volume. Put the baking sheet in the bottom third of the preheated oven. **Immediately lower the oven temperature by 90 °C/155 °F for ovens with top/bottom heat to about 160 °C/325 °F (Gas mark 3) and by 80 °C/150 °F for fan ovens to about 140 °C/275 °F. Bake the stollen for about 50 minutes.**

8 Melt the butter and brush over the warm stollen. Leave the stollen to cool on a cake rack, then sprinkle with icing (confectioners') sugar.

Quark stollen

TRADITIONAL – WITH ALCOHOL (ABOUT 20 SLICES)

Preparation time:
about 30 minutes,
excluding soaking time
Baking time: about 55 minutes

For the baking sheet:
baking parchment

For the pastry:
100 ml/3½ fl oz (½ cup) rum
375 g/13 oz (2½ cups) raisins
500 g/18 oz (5 cups) plain (all
purpose) flour
1 sachet baking powder
150 g/5 oz (¾ cup) sugar
1 sachet vanilla sugar
1 pinch salt
a few drops Dr. Oetker
Natural Vanilla Extract
1 pinch each cloves, ginger,
cardamom, nutmeg, cinnamon
(all ground)
1 teaspoon grated orange zest
2 eggs (medium)
200 g/7 oz (1 cup) soft butter
or margarine
250 g/9 oz (1 cup) low fat
quark
250 g/9 oz (2½ cups) ground
almonds
100 g/3½ oz (½ cup) each
candied lemon peel and
candied orange peel

For coating and sprinkling:
100 g/3½ oz (½ cup) butter
50 g/2 oz (¼ cup) icing
(confectioners') sugar

Per slice:
P: 8 g, F: 20 g, C: 49 g,
kJ: 1796, kcal: 429, CU: 4.0

1 For the dough, pour rum over the raisins and leave to soak overnight.

2 Line the baking sheet with three layers of baking parchment (this will prevent the stollen from getting too dark underneath). Preheat the oven:
Top/bottom heat:
about 250 °C/480 °F (Gas mark 9)
Fan oven:
about 220 °C/425 °F (Gas mark 7)

3 For the dough, mix the flour and baking powder together in a mixing bowl. Add the other ingredients for the dough (except for the almonds, candied lemon peel and candied orange peel) and knead everything briefly using a hand-mixer (with kneading hook attachment) on the lowest setting, then on the highest setting until the dough is smooth and even. Then knead the almonds, candied lemon peel, candied orange peel and soaked raisins into the dough on the lightly floured work surface until all the ingredients are well incorporated.

4 Roll out the dough to make a square about 30 x 30 cm/12 x 12 in. Roll up the dough, starting from the long side, then with the rolling pin make a depression lengthways. Now fold the left side over the right side but slightly offset. Again using your hands, make a bulge lengthways along the middle.

5 Place the stollen on the baking sheet and put this in the bottom third of the preheated oven. **Immediately lower the oven temperature by 90 °C/155 °F for ovens with top/ bottom heat to about 160 °C/325 °F (Gas mark 3) and by 80 °C/150 °F for fan ovens to about 140 °C/275 °F. Bake the quark stollen for about 55 minutes.**

6 Melt the butter in a small pan. Brush the stollen with half the melted butter immediately after you have taken it out of the oven and sprinkle half the icing (confectioners') sugar on top. Put the stollen on a cake rack to cool a little. Then repeat the operation with the remaining butter and icing sugar.

Recipe variation: For quark stollen with marzipan, knead 200 g/7 oz raw marzipan until soft. Then roll out the softened marzipan on icing (confectioners') sugar to make a rectangle of about 28 x 20 cm/11 x 8 in and place it on top of the rolled-out square of dough. Then continue as described in step 4 and bake.

TIP » When the stollen has cooled down completely on the cake rack, wrap it first in aluminium foil, then a plastic bag, for instance, a freezer bag. If stored in a cool and dry place, the stollen will remain fresh for up to 4 weeks and the aromas of the fruit and spices will develop fully.

Red wine and plum chocolates

SOMETHING SPECIAL (ABOUT 30 PIECES) BOTTOM OF PHOTO

Preparation time:
about 40 minutes,
excluding soaking time
Keeping time:
about 5 days in a cool place

For the pralines:
15 stoned, dried prunes
75 ml/3 fl oz (⅜ cup) red wine
150 g/5 oz marzipan
50 g/2 oz (scant ½ cup) sifted
icing (confectioners') sugar
150 g/5 oz bitter chocolate
(about 70 % cocoa content)
1 teaspoon cooking oil

Per piece:
P: 1 g, F: 4 g, C: 8 g,
kJ: 311, kcal: 74, CU: 0.5

1 Cut the prunes in half lengthways. Bring the red wine to the boil in a small pan, add the plums and simmer over low heat for about 3 minutes. Put the plums in the red wine in the refrigerator for about 1 hour for the flavours to develop.

2 Knead the icing (confectioners') sugar into the marzipan on a work surface, lightly sprinkled with icing sugar. Roll out to make a square of about 30 x 30 cm/12 x 12 in. Cut this into 30 rectangles of about 5 x 6 cm/ 2 x 2½ in each (photograph 1). For each marzipan rectangle, place 1 plum half in the middle. Fold up the sides and enclose the plums in the marzipan (photograph 2).

3 Break the chocolate into pieces and melt with the cooking oil in a small pan in a bain-marie over low heat. Stick the marzipan rolls on a fork and dip into the melted chocolate, then leave to drain on baking parchment (photograph 3). If necessary, warm up the chocolate again. Allow the chocolate to set.

TIPS » Drizzle the rest of the melted chocolate, warmed up again, on the chocolate-coated pralines when they have set.
» Alternatively roll the pralines in cocoa powder after coating them with the melted chocolate.
» Serve the pralines in small paper praline cases.

Chocolate oat biscuits

A GREAT GIFT (25–35 PIECES) TOP OF PHOTOGRAPH

Preparation time:
about 20 minutes, excluding
cooling time
Keeping time:
about 10 days in a cool place

**cake platter, baking
parchment**

For the chocolates:
100 g/3½ oz (⅔ cup) dried
apricots
100 g/3½ oz (⅜ cup) oat flakes
200 g/7 oz dark chocolate
1 teaspoon cooking oil

1 Line the cake platter with baking parchment and, if necessary, stick to the platter with a few drops of melted chocolate. Chop the apricots into very small cubes and stir into the oat flakes in a bowl.

2 Break the chocolate into small pieces and melt with the cooking oil in a small pan in a bain-marie over low heat. Stir the apricot-oat flakes mixture into the melted chocolate and put on the baking parchment.

3 Flatten the mixture on the baking parchment with a large wide blade knife and make a circle with a diameter of about 30 cm/12 in. Put in the refrigerator for about 1 hour until the chocolate has solidified.

4 Remove the slab of chocolate and oats off the baking parchment and break into small pieces.

TIP » Instead of plain chocolate you can use blocks of cooking chocolate.

Per piece: P: 1 g, F: 3 g, C: 7 g, kJ: 233, kcal: 55, CU: 0.5

Sunflower seed rolls

POPULAR (12–14 ROLLS)

Preparation time:
about 30 minutes,
excluding rising time
Baking time: about 25 minutes

For the baking sheet:
a little fat

100 g/3½ oz (1 cup) sunflower
seeds

For the dough:
300 g/10 oz (3 cups)
wholemeal wheat flour
200 g/7 oz (2 cups) wholemeal
rye flour
1 sachet dried yeast
1 level teaspoon sugar
1 heaped teaspoon salt
about 375 ml/13 fl oz (1⅝ cups)
hot water
1 sachet (15 g) sourdough
extract

Per roll:
P: 6 g, F: 5 g, C: 26 g,
kJ: 749, kcal: 179, CU: 2.0

1 Roast the sunflower seeds in a pan without fat, stirring occasionally, then leave on a plate to cool. Put aside 1–2 tablespoons of these roasted sunflower seeds for the garnish.

2 For the dough, put the wholemeal wheat and rye flour in a mixing bowl and carefully stir in the dried yeast. Add all the other ingredients and mix using a hand-mixer (with the kneading hook), first briefly on the lowest setting, then on the highest setting for about 5 minutes until the dough is smooth and even.

3 Just before you have finished kneading with the hand-mixer, knead in the sunflower seeds. Cover the dough and put in a warm place to rise until it has visibly increased in volume.

4 Grease the baking sheet. Preheat the oven:
Top/bottom heat:
about 200 °C/400 °F (Gas mark 6)
Fan oven:
about 180 °C/350 °F (Gas mark 4)

5 Sprinkle a little flour on the dough and knead again thoroughly on the lightly floured work surface. Shape the dough into a roll. Cut the roll into 12–14 pieces of similar size and shape each into a ball.

6 Put the rolls on the baking sheet and brush with a little water. Sprinkle the sunflower seeds you put aside earlier on the rolls and press them lightly into the dough. Put the rolls in a warm place to rise until they have visibly increased in size.

7 Put the baking sheet on the middle shelf in the preheated oven and **bake the sunflower seed rolls for about 25 minutes**.

8 Put the rolls on a cake rack to cool.

TIP ›› Serve the rolls with herb quark.

Sweet poppy and sesame seed croissants

FOR CHILDREN (12 PIECES)

Preparation time: about 30 minutes
Baking time: about 20 minutes

For the baking sheet:
baking parchment

For the quark & oil dough:
300 g/10 oz (3 cups) soft wheat flour
1 sachet baking powder
150 g/5 oz (⅔ cup) low-fat quark
100 ml/3½ fl oz (½ cup) milk
100 ml/3½ fl oz (½ cup) cooking oil, e.g. sunflower oil
80 g/3 oz (⅜ cup) sugar
1 pinch salt

For coating and sprinkling:
1 egg yolk (medium)
1 tablespoon milk
1–2 tablespoons poppy seeds
1–2 tablespoons sesame seed

Per piece:
P: 5 g, F: 11 g, C: 26 g,
kJ: 956, kcal: 228, CU: 2.0

1 Line the baking sheet with baking parchment. Preheat the oven:
Top/bottom heat:
about 200 °C/400 °F (Gas mark 6)
Fan oven:
about 180 °C/350 °F (Gas mark 4)

2 For the dough, mix together the flour and the baking powder in a mixing bowl. Add all the other ingredients for the dough and mix using a hand-mixer (with the kneading hook) briefly on the lowest setting to make a smooth dough (do not knead too long or the dough may become sticky). Then shape into a roll on the lightly-floured work surface.

3 Cut the roll into 12 pieces and shape each piece into rolls 18 cm/7 in long while making the ends slightly thinner.

4 Beat the egg yolk and milk together. Brush the top of the rolls of dough with this milk and egg yolk mixture. Sprinkle half the rolls with poppy seeds and the other half with sesame seeds. Put the rolls on the baking sheet and shape them into crescents as you do so. Put the baking sheet on the middle shelf of the preheated oven. **Bake for about 20 minutes.**

5 Take the baked croissants off the baking parchment and put on a cake rack to cool.

TIP ›› Croissants taste best when eaten fresh but they can also be frozen. If so, crisp up the defrosted croissants in the oven preheated top/bottom heat to about 200 °C/ 400 °F (Gas mark 6).

Recipe variation: To make **poppy and sesame seed rolls**, make the dough as indicated in the recipe. Then cut the quark & oil dough roll into 12 pieces and shape these into balls. Make a cross-shaped incision with a sharp knife on the top of each roll. Brush the top of each roll with milk and egg yolk, sprinkle with sesame and poppy seeds and bake the rolls as indicated in the recipe.

Rye bread with pumpkin seeds

SUITABLE FOR FREEZING

Preparation time:
about 30 minutes,
excluding rising time
Baking time: about 40 minutes

For the baking sheet:
baking parchment

For the yeast dough:
**250 g/9 oz (2½ cups)
wholemeal rye flour
250 g/9 oz (2½ cups) hard
wheat flour
1 sachet dried yeast
1 level teaspoon sugar
1 level teaspoon salt
375 ml/13 fl oz (1⅝ cups)
warm water
150 g/5 oz (1 cup) pumpkin
seeds**

For coating and sprinkling:
**a little water
a little plain
(all purpose) flour**

In all:
P: 92 g, F: 75 g, C: 367 g,
kJ: 10581, kcal: 2526, CU: 30.5

1 For the dough, mix together the wholemeal rye and the flour in a mixing bowl, then carefully stir in the dried yeast. Add all the other ingredients for the dough (except the pumpkin seeds) and mix using a hand-mixer (with the kneading hook), first briefly on the lowest setting, then on the highest setting for about 5 minutes until the dough is smooth and even.

2 Just before you finish kneading, add the pumpkin seeds and knead them in briefly. Cover the dough, put in a warm place and leave to rise until it has visibly increased in volume.

3 Line the baking sheet with baking parchment. Preheat the oven:
Top/bottom heat:
about 200 °C/400 °F (Gas mark 6)
Fan oven:
about 180 °C/350 °F (Gas mark 4)

4 Sprinkle the dough with a little flour, take out the bowl and knead briskly on the work surface. Shape the dough into a loaf and put on the baking sheet. Put the baking sheet in a warm place and leave to rise until the dough has visibly increased in volume.

5 Brush a little water over the loaf and sprinkle a little flour on top. Put the baking sheet in the bottom third of the preheated oven. **Bake the bread for about 40 minutes.**

6 Put the loaf on a cake rack and leave to cool.

Variation: You can knead sunflower seeds into the dough instead of pumpkin seeds.

BREADMAKING INFORMATION
» A firm dough must be kneaded again by hand afterwards so that the texture does not become too dense during baking.
» Place a heat-resistant bowl filled with water in the oven; this will keep the texture moist and the crust firm.
» The crust will be even crispier if you brush the bread with a little water just before the end of the baking time.

Plaited spelt loaf with pumpkin seed

FOR GUESTS

Preparation time:
about 40 minutes,
excluding rising time
Baking time: about 30 minutes

For the baking sheet:
a little fat if neccessary
baking parchment

For the yeast dough:
70 g/2½ oz (⅝ cup) pumpkin
seeds
500 g/18 oz (5 cups)
wholemeal spelt flour
1 sachet dried yeast
2 level teaspoons salt
300 ml/10 fl oz (1¼ cups)
warm water
2 tablespoons cooking oil,
e.g. sunflower oil

For dusting:
a little wholemeal spelt flour

For coating and sprinkling:
a little water
1–2 tablespoons pumpkin
seeds

In all:
P: 100 g, F: 73 g, C: 354 g,
kJ: 10368, kcal: 2477, CU: 29.5

1 For the dough, coarsely chop the pumpkin seeds. Put the wholemeal spelt and dried yeast in a mixing bowl and mix carefully. Add the salt, chopped pumpkin seeds, water and cooking oil. Add the other ingredients and knead using a hand-mixer (with kneading hook), at first briefly on the lowest setting, then on the highest setting for about 5 minutes to make a smooth dough.

2 Sprinkle the dough with flour, cover and put in a warm place until it has visibly increased in volume (about 40 minutes).

3 Grease the baking sheet and line with baking parchment. Preheat the oven:
Top/bottom heat:
about 250 °C/480 °F (Gas mark 9)
Fan oven:
about 220 °C/425 °F (Gas mark 7)

4 Sprinkle a little flour on the dough, knead it again briefly on a lightly floured surface and shape it into a roll. Cut the roll of dough into three portions of equal size. Shape each portion of dough into a roll about 30 cm/12 in long (photograph 1).

5 Place the rolls of dough next to each other on the work surface and weave into a plait (photograph 2). Press the ends tightly together and turn under the plait. Put the plaited dough on the baking sheet, brush a little water on top and sprinkle with pumpkin seeds (photograph 3).

6 Cover the plaited dough and put in a warm place to rise until it has visibly increased in size (about 20 minutes). Put the baking sheet in the bottom third of the preheated oven. **Bake for about 5 minutes. Then lower the oven temperature by 50 °C/80 °F to about 200 °C/400 °F (Gas mark 6) for top/bottom heat ovens or to 180 °C/350 °F (Gas mark 4) for fan ovens and bake the plaited loaf for another 25 minutes.**

7 Take the spelt loaf off the baking parchment and leave to cool on a cake rack.

BREAD INFORMATION » You can check whether the bread is done by tapping the top and bottom of the bread. It will sound hollow when it is done.

1

2

3

White bread

EASY

Preparation time:
about 20 minutes,
excluding rising time
Baking time: about 45 minutes

For the bread tin
(30 x 11 cm/12 x 4½ in):
a little fat
plain (all purpose) flour

For the yeast dough:
125 ml/4 fl oz (½ cup) milk
500 g/18 oz (5 cups) soft wheat
flour
1 sachet dried yeast
1 level teaspoon sugar
1 scant heaped teaspoon salt
2 eggs (medium)
1 container (150 g/5 oz)
crème fraîche

In all:
P: 76 g, F: 71 g, C: 380 g,
kJ: 10414, kcal: 2496, CU: 31.5

1 For the dough, heat up the milk. Put the flour in a mixing bowl and stir in the dried yeast. Add the other ingredients for the dough and the warm milk and knead all the ingredients using a hand-mixer (with kneading hook attachment) briefly on the lowest setting, then on the highest setting for about 5 minutes to make a smooth dough (photograph 1).

2 Cover the dough and put in a warm place to rise until it has visibly increased in size.

3 Grease and flour the mould. Preheat the oven:
Top/bottom heat:
about 180 °C/350 °F (Gas mark 4)
Fan oven:
about 160 °C/325 °F (Gas mark 3)

4 Knead the dough again briskly and shape into a roll about 28 cm/ 11 in long. Put this roll in the tin (photograph 2) and put in a warm place to rise again until it has visibly increased in size.

5 Using a sharp knife make a lengthways incision 1 cm/⅜ in deep (photograph 3) but do not press down. Brush with water and put the tin on a shelf in the bottom third of the preheated oven. **Bake the bread for about 45 minutes**.

6 Take the bread out of the tin and leave to cool on a cake rack.

Recipe variation: You can make white bread with raisins simply by kneading 150 g/5 oz (1 cup) raisins into the dough.

1

2

3

Carrot bread

FOR CHILDREN

Preparation time:
about 45 minutes,
excluding rising time
Baking time: about 35 minutes

For the bread tin
(30 x 11 cm/12 x 4½ in):
a little fat

For the preparation:
200 g/7 oz carrots
100 g/3½ oz (1 cup) shelled
walnut halves
100 g/3½ oz (⅔ cup) hazelnuts

For the yeast dough:
100 g/3½ oz (1 cup) wholemeal
rye flour
400 g/14 oz (4 cups)
wholemeal spelt flour
1 sachet dried yeast
2 level teaspoons salt
250 ml/8 fl oz (1 cup) warm
water

For dusting:
a little rye flour

In all:
P: 99 g, F: 139 g, C: 381 g,
kJ: 13253, kcal: 3166, CU: 32.0

1 Top and tail the carrots, then wash them. Peel, rinse and wipe them dry, then grate them. Coarsely chop the walnuts and hazelnuts.

2 For the dough, carefully mix together the two kinds of flour with the dried yeast in a mixing bowl. Add the salt, water, grated carrots, hazelnuts and walnuts and mix using a hand-mixer (with the kneading hook), first briefly on the lowest setting, then on the highest setting for about 5 minutes until you obtain a smooth dough.

3 Sprinkle the dough with flour, cover and put in a warm place until it has visibly increased in size (about 60 minutes).

4 Grease the mould. Preheat the oven:
Top/bottom heat:
about 250 °C/480 °F (Gas mark 9)
Fan oven:
about 220 °C/425 °F (Gas mark 7)

5 Sprinkle the dough with a little flour and knead again briefly on a floured work surface. Shape into a roll about 28 cm/11 in long and put it in the tin. Sprinkle with flour, cover and put in a warm place to rise again until it has increased visibly in volume (about 40 minutes).

6 Using a sharp knife, cut the top of the loaf, making incisions about 1 cm/⅜ in deep, so as to create a criss-cross pattern. Put the tin in the bottom third of the preheated oven. **Bake the bread for about 10 minutes. Then lower the oven temperature by 50 °C/80 °F to about 200 °C/400 °F (Gas mark 6) for top/bottom heat ovens or to 180 °C/350 °F (Gas mark 4) for fan ovens. Continue baking the bread for about another 25 minutes.**

7 Turn the bread out onto a cake rack, turn it the right side up and leave to cool.

BREAD INFORMATION » It is the consistency of the dough which determines the shape of the loaf. A soft dough must be baked in a tin. A firm dough can be baked without a tin, just on the baking sheet.

Ovens, kitchen utensils and baking utensils

Ovens and baking temperatures

Just as important as the correct preparation of the dough is the temperature of the oven. Today ovens can be electric or gas and usually have top and bottom heat, heated air circulation by a fan and a grill, with the ability to select various combinations of these.

The temperatures indicated in this book refer to electric ovens and gas ovens. The temperature settings in gas ovens vary depending on the manufacturer so that it is very important to check the manufacturer's instructions so as to determine the correct temperature setting matching the temperature indicated in the recipe.
It is also helpful to have an oven thermometer so that you can check the oven temperature while the cake is baking.
When baking in a fan oven you can bake on several shelves at the same time. But make sure that the temperature is about 20 °C/25 °F below that used when baking with top and bottom heat.
For all cakes, the oven must be pre-heated and have reached the temperature indicated in the recipe before you put the cake in. Depending on the oven, the baking time indicated in the recipe may be slightly increased or decreased. It is therefore important to follow the manufacturer's instructions. It is also why you should check the cake towards the end of the baking time.

The height of the shelves

Any dough which is baked in a tin or mould must always be placed on a grid shelf and never on a baking sheet or directly on the bottom of the oven.
Tins or moulds with high sides or semi-high sides are usually put on the bottom shelf while shallower tins or moulds are usually baked in the middle of the oven. Flat cakes, small pastries, biscuits, cream puffs and meringues are also baked on the middle shelf in the oven. The indications in the recipe and the instructions of the oven manufacturer should also be taken into account.

Kitchen utensils and baking utensils

Following a recipe will be much easier if you have the necessary kitchen and baking utensils, as follows.

Utensils for weighing, mixing and kneading – photograph 1

The **hand-mixer** mixes, stirs and kneads. With the whisk and kneading hook attachments you can make dough, pastry, sauces, and cream-based mixtures. A stick mixer is also very useful.

A **stand mixer** will make it easier to mix dough, whip cream and knead heavy bread dough. Because a stand mixer is more powerful, any type of dough will be mixed much more quickly. For this reason it is important that you should always follow the manufacturer's instructions. In our recipes we recommend the use of a hand-mixer.

A **timer** is invaluable for timing the mixing and baking times.

for rubbing jam through. A **large sieve** is useful for draining fruit.

Pastry cutters for biscuits, cookies and other small pastries must have sharp, clean edges so that they make clean cuts in the dough or pastry.

Pastry brushes are used for greasing tins and moulds, for spreading dough and pastry and for applying glazes.

A **pastry frame** is used when making tall-sided cakes and for square cakes and tarts. It can be adjusted to different sizes.

A **pastry press** is used to make cookie-press biscuits and pastries.

Stirring spoons are used to stir all kinds of ingredients.

A **whisk** is recommended for whisking eggs or sauces and to fold in light, delicate mixtures.

Weighing scales are indispensable in every kitchen. They are available with analogue or digital indication. It is particularly useful if they also have a tare function, which enables the weight to be reset to zero after the container is placed on the balance.

Measuring jugs are used to measure liquids accurately and should be clearly graduated.

You need **bowls and mixing bowls** in several sizes. To mix dough or

pastry, whip cream or egg whites, it is best to mixing jugs and bowls made of strong plastic with a rubber ring built into the underside. These are stable and will not slip. Stainless steel bowls are very good for melting chocolate in a bain-marie.

A **fine sieve** is used for dusting cocoa powder or icing (confectioners') sugar over cakes and also

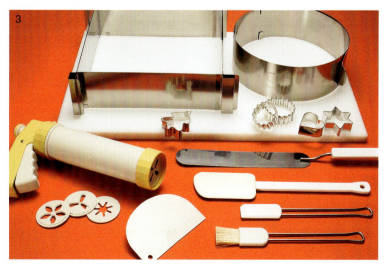

A **pallet knife** is made of metal and looks like a wide bladed knife with a rounded end but without a cutting edge. It is used to release dough if it sticks to the work surface while it is being rolled out. It is also used for spreading cream or glaze on dough, flans and cakes and to turn out small pastries and cakes.

A **tart ring** can be used on its own and is also ideal for filling tarts.

A **pastry scraper** made from a flexible plastic material is used to divide the dough, scrape bits of dough from the sides of the bowl and for cleaning the work surface. It is also ideal for smoothing pastry and making creamy fillings flat, as well as for decorating the sides of cakes.

A **dough scraper** with a steel blade is useful for transferring dough and for spreading it out in baking tins.

Utensils for rolling out, cooling and garnishing – photograph

With a **cooking roller** you can roll out the edges of the dough more thinly on the baking sheet.

A **cake rack** is a metal grill on which you put the pastry cool. Unlike a normal cake platter, the grid structure prevents the pastry or cake sweating underneath and becoming soggy. Cake racks have feet so that the air can get to the pastry on all sides.

Kitchen scissors are used to cut dough and baking parchment to the size required.

A **grater** can be used to grate lemon rind and chocolate.

Piping bags with star-shaped or plain nozzles are available in several sizes and are used to decorate cakes and pipe pastry.

A **pastry wheel** cuts rolled-out pastry, at the same time giving it a serrated or wavy edge.

A **cake divider** is very useful for cut the top of a cake into slices of similar size.

A **cake decorating comb** is the ideal tool for creating beautiful designs on glazed or iced cakes and for

garnishing flans. It can also be used to transfer a flan onto a cake plate or to move layers of cake onto a plate or another cake layer.

A **rolling pin** may be made of wood, stainless steel, plastic or glass. It is used for rolling out dough and for crushing solid ingredients, such as praline, biscuits and sponge biscuits.

Garnishing and decorating

Garnishing with a paper piping bag

A home-made piping bag (see the diagram) is perfect for making fine filigree decorations because you can determine the size of the hole of the piping bag yourself – the smaller the hole, the finer the lines of icing or melted chocolate.

To make a paper piping bag, cut a square piece of baking parchment (about 24 x 24 cm/9½ x 9½ in) and fold diagonally to make two triangles (a). Now take the triangle and hold the middle of the long side with your left hand, then with your right hand foldi the upper tip inwards onto the right-angled tip to make a cornet (b). With your left hand (which is now free), turn the bottom tip towards the two tips already placed on top of each other, take hold of them and pull the three tips together so that they are on top of each other and the cornet has a pointed end at the bottom (c). Now fold the three tips inwards, press down firmly (d, e) – and you're ready!

Now fill the cornet almost half full with the icing or glaze, close it by folding down the opening several times and press firmly to secure. Fold the resulting corners towards the back. Now cut off a small piece of the point of the cornet (f). You can now pipe the icing or glaze through the opening you have just made and decorate the cake or flan. Instead of making the piping bag with baking parchment, you can use a small freezer bag. Twist the opening of the freezer bag to close it and cut off a small corner through which you pipe the icing or glaze.

Icing

Sift the icing (confectioners') sugar and stir in enough water, tea, liqueur or juice, a little at a time, to make a thickish glaze. You can also stir some cocoa powder or instant coffee into the sifted icing sugar before stirring it into the liquid. You can colour the icing the colour of your choice by adding a few drops of food colouring to the finished icing. If the icing is made with hot liquid the icing will become very shiny and hold better. It is important to apply the icing immediately after you have made it because it begins to set very quickly and is then very difficult to apply.

Chocolate and couverture chocolate icing

When you are using chocolate or couverture chocolate, it is important that the chocolate should not come into contact with the water as it is melted in a bain-marie over low heat. This is because even a few drops will prevent the chocolate from setting and a larger amount of water will make the melted chocolate grainy as well as not setting.

Melting the chocolate or couverture chocolate

To ensure that the melted chocolate or couverture chocolate is beautifully shiny and that it remains easy to cut even when the chocolate coating has cooled and set, it must be melted very slowly. To do this, break or chop the chocolate into small pieces and melt two-thirds of it in a pan or bowl in a bain-marie over low heat, stirring all the time. Then take the container out of the bain-marie and stir in the rest of the chopped or broken up chocolate; then continue stirring until all the pieces have melted. If the chopped chocolate added after removing the container does not melt properly, put it back in the bain-marie for about 3 seconds. Then remove it again and stir until all the pieces have melted.

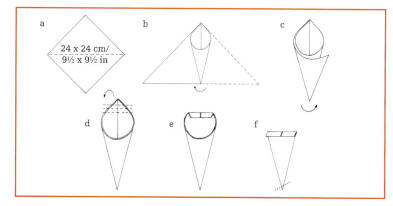

The right temperature?
To check whether the melted chocolate will be easy to work with, there is an easy test: dip a corner of a pastry scraper into the melted chocolate, tap it a little and leave the chocolate to dry. Or put a few drops of melted chocolate on a piece of baking parchment, spread it a little and leave to set for 3–5 minutes. Do not stir at this moment, so as not to change the temperature. If the mixture does not set, it means that it is too hot; in this case put the pan briefly in cold water and give it a good stir.

If you can see a grey film, the chocolate mixture is too cold; in this case put it back in the warm bain-marie for a few seconds and stir well.

To make chocolate curls and shavings
Melt the chocolate as described above and then pour it on a plate or cake decorating plate (photograph 1). Now "tap" the plate on the table (photograph 2) so that the chocolate spreads. Then leave it to cool until it is almost set (but do not refrigerate).

You can make beautiful, large chocolate curls by holding a spatula at a very low angle to the plate and then scrape the chocolate with light, regular movements (photograph 3). Important: the chocolate must not have set too hard or the curls will break and become crumbly.

You can also make chocolate shavings by scraping a bar of

chocolate with a potato peeler (photograph 4). Again, make sure that the chocolate is not too cold or you will only get grated chocolate instead of chocolate shavings.

To make sure that the chocolate curls and shavings do not melt or break, do not use your fingers to move or position them: use a spatula or a wide knife.

To make chocolate glaze
To coat cakes and pastries with a chocolate glaze, coarsely chop the chocolate. Melt the pieces with a little cooking oil in a pan in a bain-marie over low heat, stirring all the time. You will get a beautifully shiny glaze which is easy to work with by

adding about 1 teaspoon cooking oil per 100 g/3½ oz chocolate or about 25 g/1 oz coconut fat per 100 g/3½ oz couverture chocolate.

Baking ingredients

Types of flour, fat, sugar and eggs
It is always best to use high quality ingredients which are fresh. If the ingredients are too old or of lower quality they may spoil your baked goods.

Which kind of flour for which kind of pastry?

The following are German types of flour, for which you will find the corresponding types of British and American flour on page 233.

Spelt flour

Wholemeal spelt flour

Type 1800 coarsely ground rye flour

Wholemeal rye flour

Type 1150 rye flour

Type 405 wheat flour
This fine, very white flour is the preferred flour for general use and is also used for flans, cakes, biscuits etc. If the type of flour is not specifically mentioned in the recipe, you should always use type 405 when baking.

Type 550 wheat flour
This flour is very good for making yeast dough in general and rolls and white loaves in particular. But you can also make cakes and pastries with it.

Type 1050 wheat flour
This dark-coloured flour which is rich in minerals is very good to make bread and many other tasty pastries and confectionery goods.

Wholemeal wheat flour
The wholemeal wheat flour is made from whole grains of wheat including the husk and the ground wheat germ; it has a very full, rich taste. It is mainly used for bread and rolls.

Spelt flour and wholemeal spelt flour
Spelt is closely related to wheat and, like it, has similar good baking qualities.

Type 1150 rye flour
This dark flour is mainly used for making bread and rolls.

Type 1800 coarsely ground rye flour and wholemeal rye flour
Both are made from ground whole grains, finely or coarsely ground depending on the size of the grains. It is used for making bread, for instance.

Wholemeal flour
Wholemeal flours are not suited for all purposes and therefore cannot simply replace white flour in the recipe. Wholemeal flour needs more liquid, its baking qualities are less good for many purposes and

Type 405 wheat flour

Type 550 wheat flour

Type 1050 wheat flour

Wholemeal wheat flour

simply replacing the white flour with wholemeal flour will make the pastry drier and harder.

Butter, margarine or cooking oil?

Using the right fat is not only important for consistency and texture but it also ensures that the pastry remains moist and that the various flavours stand out. Margarine and butter are most frequently used in recipes, while cooking oil on the other hand is only used occasionally.

In most recipes in this book you can use butter or margarine, depending on your preference. But the recommended kind of fat is always the one mentioned first in the recipe. You can also use a mixture of butter and margarine.

Because butter becomes hard when cold, unlike spreadable margarine, it should be taken out of the refrigerator in good time so that it is easy to work with.

On the other hand, cooking oil is very good for making quark & oil dough and all-in-one sponge. It must have a neutral taste, for instance, sunflower oil or corn oil, so that the taste of the pastry is not affected and dominated by the taste of the oil.

1 sachet of vanilla sugar or Bourbon vanilla sugar corresponds to 2 level teaspoons.

One sugar for everything?

Sugar is available in forms and kinds:
» White caster (superfine) sugar is the type of sugar most frequently used in the kitchen. It is fine-grained, very versatile and can be used for pastries and puddings.
» Decorating or pearl sugar is very coarse-grained white sugar which is used for instance to decorate cakes and pastries.
» Icing (confectioners') sugar is very finely ground white sugar which must be sifted before use to remove lumps.
» Brown sugar is a collective term to describe brown-coloured sugar. It includes brown candy sugar which is used for making gingerbread and gingerbread cake and cane sugar which is produced from sugar cane.
» Coarse brown sugar is coarse candy sugar. It is highly aromatic and is the preferred sugar for gingerbread, gingerbread cake and nut biscuits.

Eggs: they must be fresh

In Britain, eggs come in various sizes. In this book all recipes use medium-sized eggs. It is important that the date of laying or the sell-by date of the eggs should be clearly marked.
If you are not sure of the freshness of an egg, put it in a glass of water. A fresh egg will remain at the bottom. An egg which is about 7 days old will rise slightly since the air chamber inside it becomes larger as the egg gets older. An egg 2–3 weeks old will start to float.

Beat each egg separately in a cup so that you can throw it away if it is bad and also so that you can remove any small fragments of egg shell which may have fallen in when breaking it.

Brown sugar

Demerara sugar

Candy sugar

White caster sugar

Pearl sugar

Icing (confectioners') sugar

Baking terms

What do they mean?

Coating – photograph 1
Coating a pastry base or cake with liquids such as fruit juice, a sugar solution or alcohol.

Crisping up
Putting in the oven and re-baking for a short time. It is done to revive cakes and pastries which been frozen and defrosted or have lost some of their freshness while being stored, such as bread and rolls. Cakes and pastries with icing or glaze cannot be crisped up.

Dusting
Dusting cakes and pastries with icing (confectioners') sugar or cocoa powder by shaking through a sieve or flour dredger.

Folding in – photograph 2
The careful incorporation of whipped cream, beaten egg whites, almonds, etc. into another mixture, pastry or dough. It is done with a spatula, cooking spoon or whisk.

Garnishing
Giving food a pleasing appearance. This includes piping whipped cream or icing on cakes and pastries, and applying other decorations.

Kneading
Working several ingredients to make a smooth, even dough. A hand-mixer with a kneading hook attachment can be used to knead the dough or you can knead the dough with your hands.

Stirring in – photograph 3
The slow, careful stirring in and mixing of fine substances such as flour or liquids into a dough with a spatula, cooking spoon or whisk.

Flour types

German flour type	UK equivalent	US equivalent
Type 405 wheat flour	none	Pastry flour
Type 550 wheat flour	Plain flour	All-purpose flour
Type 1050 wheat flour	Strong flour	"First clear" flour
Wholemeal wheat flour	Wholemeal flour	Wholewheat flour
Spelt flour and wholemeal spelt flour	Spelt flour and wholemeal spelt flour	Spelt flour and whole grain spelt flour
type 1150 rye flour	Light rye flour	Medium rye flour
Type 1800 coarsely ground rye and wholemeal rye flour	100% wholemeal rye flour	Coarsely ground rye flour and whole grain rye flour (pumpernickel flour)

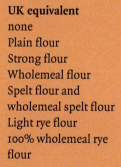

CONTENTS

CONTENTS

CONTENTS

ALPHABETICAL INDEX

If you have any questions, suggestions or comments, please contact the Consumer Service of the Dr. Oetker Test Kitchen
Telephone: + 49 8 00 71 72 73 74 Mon–Fri 8 am–6 pm, Sat 9 am–3 pm or the staff of Dr. Oetker Verlag
Telephone +49 521 520651 Mon–Fri, available hours: 9 am–3 pm. Or you can write to us: Dr. Oetker Verlag KG, Am Bach 11, 33602 Bielefeld (Germany) or visit us on the Internet at: www.oetker-verlag.de oder www.oetker.de.

Environmental notice	This book and its cover were printed on chlorine-free bleached paper. The shrinkwrapping to protect it from getting dirty is made from environmentally-friendly recyclable polyethylene plastic.
Copyright	© 2010 by Dr. Oetker Verlag KG, Bielefeld
Editorial	Andrea Gloß, Carola Reich no:vum, Susanne Noll, Leinfelden-Echterdingen
Editorial consultancy	Dr. Judith Borgwart, Frankfurt
Cover photograph **Photographs in the book**	Thomas Diercks (Fotostudio Diercks), Hamburg Christiane Krüger (Fotostudio Diercks), Hamburg
Food styling	Eike Upmeier-Lorenz, Hamburg
Recipe development and advice	Dr. Oetker Versuchsküche, Bielefeld
Translation	Rosetta Translations SARL, France
Nutrition calculations	Nutri Service, Hennef
Graphic concept and design **Cover design**	BCW Gesellschaft für Kommunikation mbH, Hamburg kontur:design, Bielefeld
Reproduction **Typesetting** **Printing and binding**	Repro Ludwig, Zell am See, Austria JUNFERMANN Druck & Service, Paderborn Firmengruppe APPL, aprinta druck, Wemding
With thanks for their generous assistance	Leifheit AG, Nassau/Lahn Peter Kölln, Elmshorn

ISBN: 978-3-7670-0934-9